MW00812628

THE SYNTHETIC UNIVERSITY

The Synthetic University

How Higher Education Can Benefit from Shared Solutions and Save Itself

James L. Shulman

PRINCETON UNIVERSITY PRESS

PRINCETON AND OXFORD

Published by Princeton University Press
41 William Street, Princeton, New Jersey 08540
99 Banbury Road, Oxford OX2 6JX

press.princeton.edu

Library of Congress Cataloging-in-Publication Data

Names: Shulman, James Lawrence, 1965– author.
Title: The synthetic university : how higher education can benefit from
    shared solutions and save itself / James L. Shulman.
Description: Princeton : Princeton University Press, [2023] |
    Includes bibliographical references and index.
Identifiers: LCCN 2022058351 (print) | LCCN 2022058352 (ebook) |
    ISBN 9780691190990 (hardback) | ISBN 9780691237626 (ebook)
Subjects: LCSH: Universities and colleges—Economic aspects. |
    Infrastructure (Economics) | Education, Higher—Aims and objectives.
Classification: LCC LC67.6 .S38 2023 (print) | LCC LC67.6
    (ebook) | DDC 378.1/06—dc23/eng/20230310
LC record available at https://lccn.loc.gov/2022058351
LC ebook record available at https://lccn.loc.gov/2022058352

British Library Cataloging-in-Publication Data is available

Editorial: Peter Dougherty, Matt Rohal, and Alena Chekanov
Production Editorial: Natalie Baan
Jacket Design: Hunter Finch
Production: Erin Suydam
Publicity: Alyssa Sanford and Kathryn Stevens
Copyeditor: Anne Sanow

Jacket image: Ryan Herron / iStock

This book has been composed in Adobe Text and Gotham

Printed on acid-free paper. ∞

Printed in the United States of America

10 9 8 7 6 5 4 3 2 1

to Katie, Kai, Camilla, and Emma

CONTENTS

How Higher Education Can Benefit from Shared Solutions and Save Itself

The United States has more than 3,500 colleges and universities. The individuals who make decisions within these institutions all live with—indeed, have insisted upon—a paradox: while they value their freedom to set their own course above all else, they end up carrying out almost exactly the same set of activities in the same way as other institutions. While the committees may have different names at each campus, their institutions all admit students in similar ways as their peers within the sector, teach many of the same classes, offer mostly the same majors and programs, reward the same faculty and staff behaviors, and provide more or less the same services to their students and alumni. Thousands of institutions are made up of millions of faculty members and staff who have confidence that they are the only ones who can design and provide the right solution for their campus. And yet they are unconsciously drawn into *iso-morphism*, the tendency for institutions to become more and more similar within their peer group. This happens because, as individuals and as institutions, they understand local needs and are drawn to harmonize in how they are responsive to the shared markets in which they compete for almost everything.

In pursuit of everything from increasing the number of student applications to winning the good will of legislators, they chase both specific shared metrics of success and commonly held dreams. The result is that a college sports team's uniforms might be blue or they might be red, but the underlying functions of their colleges or universities tend to be very similar. And just as each member of each athletic team wearing either a blue or a red jersey feels that the outcome of each game is laden with profound significance, the faculty, administrators, and staff at each campus have a sense that they too are living their lives on a symbolic plane. They defend their autonomy by separately but redundantly pursuing what they see as their highly individualized and sacrosanct mission.

In some situations, this redundancy of behaviors across the landscape of isolated institutions constitutes a productive activity; a hundred different biologists studying the same cell creates new knowledge. But more than a century of physical isolation of campuses has fostered an instinct for self-reliance in most aspects of how institutions approach their sprawling set of goals and functions. Dedicated people with deep knowledge of local institutional particularities tend to see their campus as a unique and complete world unto itself. They are anything but villains in this story; without their care, campuses would fail as enterprises and as communities. But to protect the institutional autonomy that we value, we need to enhance our capacity for collective action.

The Synthetic University describes a particular model for cost-effective change in higher education within the context of this broad constellation of isolated acts of passionate autonomous action. In this book, I describe a type of organization that lives outside of any one college and provides realistic and mission-aligned solutions to collective institutional challenges. These *synthetic service providers* are one part of an underdeveloped interinstitutional infrastructure that colleges and universities need for the cross-pollination of good ideas and for the evolution of transinstitutional norms. While as a sector we do not engage in enough collective sharing of new approaches and adjustments to long-standing norms, we struggle the most with synthetically designing, financing, accepting, and integrating shared services.

What do I mean by "synthetic" enhancements to the practices of colleges and universities? Technically, a synthetic material combines elements to create something new. When we eschew fur, we might wear synthetic fur made from compressed acrylic polymers; hospital burn units have used varieties of artificial skin (constructed from collagen) to help patients regenerate their own skin, and robotics firms are now creating synthetic skin consisting of live cells that can be attached to robot "fingers."[1] In some contexts, the word "synthetic" is considered synonymous with "fake," with its negative connotations—a sweater made of rayon may be seen as less desirable than one made of wool or cotton. But rayon can be used in ways that wool or cotton can't, and it lasts longer and costs less. So even though something synthetic is by definition "artificial," and even though it may be looked at askance by some people for being so, it may be of significant value; it may provide an answer to an otherwise unmeetable need. Accepting a synthetic solution no doubt requires some trade-offs, some compromise. In philosophy, Hegel proposed that human knowledge advances as a thesis is countered by an antithesis that can then produce a new result: a synthesis. In the field of synthetic biology, innovators introduce human engineering to the complexity of nature; for example, rice can be infused with DNA blocks of beta carotene to provide undernourished people with Vitamin A via a food staple that might otherwise be filling but nutritionally insufficient.

Synthetic biology offers a relevant model for the kind of systemic change that higher education needs: deliberately designing solutions that alter the practices and outputs of a complex system. Pragmatists value this sort of tinkering because it can address significant needs in cost-effective ways. But conversely, and depending on the problem being addressed, the approach being taken, and the viewpoint of the critic, such interventions might also be rejected as presumptuous, corrupting, or morally compromised. When individuals resent outside agents intervening in what they see as the natural order of how a system *should* work, rejection of synthesized solutions is often based on principle.[2] And of course, there are times when such suspicion can be justified; consider the ways in which some engineering goes too far toward risking the destabilization of a natural order (as in the case of some genetically modified foods). But within institutions that are constructed by people, there is no *natural order*. The people leading colleges and universities—department chairs, deans, presidents—meet with a great deal of resistance when they try to bring about change in their institutions. But the institutional structures, policies, and practices of colleges and universities are not forces of nature; they are not tornados or the tides. They have been created by people and reinforced through the actions of people over time.

In the real world of institutional life, where individuals have competing versions of what constitutes the optimal direction for a mission-driven institution, the grafting of new and old is rarely painless. The diverse landscape of US higher education constitutes a complex system; left to itself, change within individual institutions (let alone across the fragmented landscape of colleges and universities) comes about slowly because components of the institutional structure have evolved to resist change effectively. As a society, we need these institutions to adapt. We need ways to ensure that colleges and universities control the growth of their costs, and we need to strengthen a severely underdeveloped interinstitutional infrastructure that supports collective solutions. Because we have few answers about how to enact change within or across these change-resistant institutions, every college and university is left to address every challenge on its own—and struggles under the weight of doing so. Meanwhile, students, families, and society are growing ever more dissatisfied with this almost imperceptible rate of change.

This book describes an alternative to the existing dominant model of institutional behavior. At the other extreme from this instinctive reliance on local problem solving, the free market offers an alternative but sometimes problematic model: the idea of disruptive change, which often takes the form of interventions created by and implemented by profit-maximizing vendors. These firms might be able to accelerate change, but they do so from the outside, without any necessary regard for the well-being of the host institutions.

Instead of either of these two existing models for change within US higher education, *The Synthetic University* proposes that effective synthesis begins with an outside organization—institutional entrepreneurs—who understand and respect the myths that undergird the daily behavior of those who work on college campuses. Like those who work on a campus, these entrepreneurs are mission-driven, but they must also bring solutions that are pragmatically compelling enough to pass a market test. The decision-makers on a campus have to be convinced that they can trust an external solution and getting their buy-in is never easy. But getting that buy-in proves the validity of the externally provided approach.

While many Americans have grown increasingly skeptical of many institutions, some of us continue to believe that institutions of higher education are needed more than ever: for the basic and applied research that they conduct; for their role as anchors for industry and their local communities; for providing equitable access to opportunities for those who have not had such access, including Black, Latino/a, and Indigenous people, as well as first-generation college goers; and for college's capacity to prepare students to be thinking and feeling people and citizens. At their best, nonprofit institutions steward and promote work, values, and ideas that the market may not be concerned with in the short term. However, when they are not at their best, colleges and universities (and the people who populate them) can sacrifice some of these higher goals for more institutionally self-serving aims. When financial pressures grow, colleges swerve to accommodate donors who may not be aligned with their values, or they create new graduate programs that seduce students into paying tuition for degrees that in some cases do little good in advancing their careers. And as a standard practice, colleges and universities have no choice but to compensate for their ever-rising costs and decreasing federal and state subsidies by extracting ever-increasing tuition and fees from the students and families who come to them with dreams about what college can be. A synthetic approach requires both acknowledging the truth about where college costs are going and understanding that we do have the ability to take action against their otherwise inevitable rate of increase.

This fate—of college costs rising forever at higher rates than other goods and services—doesn't hurt only students and families; it also hurts the values and the work of the institutions themselves. In the 1960s, William G. Bowen first identified the "disease" in which the costs of college activities tend to rise faster than costs in the larger society because of higher education's dependence on the hard-to-improve productivity of people rather than machinery. In his argument, Bowen also described ways that institutions can cover these costs through increased fundraising and more sophisticated endowment management (for those fortunate enough to have endowments). But he also predicted that those strategies would eventually reach their limits: "Over the longer run, it takes no Cassandra to offer an even grimmer prognosis. Institutional morale is a delicate thing. . . . Nor is it clear, thinking purely in financial terms, that the rates of increase in tuition income and in private gifts and grants incorporated in our projections could be achieved indefinitely."[3] The outcome that Bill Bowen predicted in 1968 has come to pass, and yet many of us who care about colleges and universities seem to be reconciled to what he saw as the "even grimmer prognosis." Outside the gates, however, society is losing patience.

For a very long time, tension between autonomy and collective action has defined debates about whether or how colleges and universities should act to address shared challenges.

> At nearly every institution progress has been made along certain lines, but generally it has been a "lone fight"; one institution doing one thing and another doing another without any of the mutual help and cooperation which is given in the business world. Indeed, it is not going beyond the facts to say that in the colleges there is less *real cooperation* than one finds in those industries where competition is the most intense. [emphasis added]
>
> —MORRIS LLEWELLYN COOKE, *ACADEMIC AND INDUSTRIAL EFFICIENCY* (1910)[4]

Cooke's 1910 book, which was sponsored by the Carnegie Foundation for the Advancement of Teaching (CFAT), began as an investigation of the practices of physics departments. The author came from outside of the academy; he was an engineer and a colleague of the famous Frederick Winslow Taylor (an efficiency expert considered the creator of management consulting). Cooke had been hired by Henry Pritchett, whom Andrew Carnegie had hired in 1903 to lead CFAT with the specific charge to create a shared pension plan for university professors, a foundation goal that eventually led to the creation of TIAA-CREF. From the beginning, the foundation's goal of promoting transinstitutional efficiencies such as a shared pension plan for faculty met strong resistance. For example, Syracuse University's chancellor, James R. Day, lashed out against what he saw as the foundation's "fatal mildew of such unwise and impracticable standardizing." He wrote to Pritchett, "The use of the pension fund has been perverted into impertinent meddling with the work of the lawfully constituted education departments of the States and the chartered autonomy of the institutions which are in no way responsible to you."[5] Today, TIAA survives and thrives, and for over a century colleges and universities have outsourced the work of designing and managing faculty retirement accounts to it (and more recently to other firms as well). Given TIAA-CREF's evident success in serving a collective, widespread need, are those who, like Chancellor Day, resist collective action in the name of local autonomy simply recalcitrant, selfish, or foolish? The answer is not simple.

The United States' sprawling and diverse landscape of 3,500 largely autonomous institutions with mostly autonomous departments populated by essentially autonomous faculty and staff has served as the foundation of the country's competitive and innovative success; US colleges and universities are remarkably creative and productive in their scholarship, in their fostering of individual and institutional innovations, and in launching the careers and lives of their graduates. The accomplishments of US colleges and universities both in research and in their model of undergraduate education, which many see as "the secret sauce" of the country's innovative workforce, have long been the envy of the world.[6] Is it possible to bring about some collective action—the "real cooperation" that Morris Llewellyn Cooke suggested was missing—among thousands of colleges while avoiding the "fatal mildew of impracticable standardizing?" The answer is a cautious Yes. *The Synthetic University* traces a narrow path in which market-tested solutions can be reconciled with mission-driven values to address shared institutional needs. Doing so can help amplify the benefits of the creative solutions that the fragmented landscape of competitive autonomous institutions generates. The system has grown dramatically over the century since Cooke published *Academic and Industrial Efficiency* in 1910, and so have the stakes of how institutions balance autonomy and collective action. In 1910, college tuition cost about $140 a year (only $4,364 in 2022 dollars). Even then, both Cooke and the foundation saw the endless stream of individual colleges' isolated solutions as problematic, but at that time, only 4 percent of the US population attended college; today over 65 percent does. Today, the ever-increasing cost of college affects a significantly wider swath of the population and a much more financially diverse set of students and families than was the case in 1910. The tensions in the system that generate these costs have always been in plain sight, but the urgency of finding a better balance between unbridled institutional autonomy and collective action has increased as the tuition-paying population has expanded dramatically.

This book is about the behavior of complex people and institutions. Parts of the book rely on sociology and organizational theory; parts lean on storytelling since narratives about institutional life are central to understanding these institutions. **Chapter 1** explains why some intermediary firms have been successful in bringing about synthetic change and why others have struggled. How do these efforts balance the methods of the market and the methods of serving a mission? **Chapter 2** recounts the successes and failures of Artstor, an organization that my colleagues and I developed and that I was responsible for leading for its first fifteen years. What we learned at Artstor provides an evidence base for much of what I argue in the rest of the book. Those readers who are interested in institutional sociology and theories of change will see familiar vocabularies in **chapters 3 and 4**; these two chapters argue that repeatable systems change (as opposed to lucky strikes) requires a twofold theory that accounts for how colleges and universities resist change so successfully and for how a particular strategy of institutional entrepreneurship has the capacity to overcome that resistance. **Chapter 5** lays out the financial strategies that can help to bring these entrepreneurial organizations into being and help them to thrive. Methods sometimes categorized as "venture philanthropy" or "impact investing" provide parts of the answer. **Chapter 6** explores why it would be difficult, but perhaps not impossible, to use these approaches to reduce the growth of college costs in even the most central and sacred practices of higher education: classroom teaching.

———

In 1993, I finished my dissertation about how individual characters in Renaissance epic poems made decisions in situations that forced them to reconcile their personal impulses with the pressures they felt to complete a mission that was defined for them by forces larger than themselves. As much as I loved the ideas that I studied in the humanities, I decided that I wanted to work on the decisions that shape colleges and universities rather than reading and writing about the decision-making of literary heroes. After I spent some time working as a management consultant, my friend Kevin Guthrie introduced me to the aforementioned William G. Bowen, then the president of the Andrew W. Mellon Foundation. Becoming Bill's student, colleague, coauthor, and friend shaped my career and life. You will see his intellectual fingerprints all over this book, and I am grateful for all that he taught me and for the trust that he placed in me. While I worked with Bill on research projects, I also worked with Mellon's chief investment officer, Dennis Sullivan. From Dennis and another Mellon colleague, Lauren Meserve, I learned about investing—at least enough to inform the sections of this book that consider the business models of the organizations I write about. During the years I worked at Mellon (in the 1990s and from 2016 to 2018), I made friends and had teachers who have shaped (and improved) this book: Bro Adams, Rachel Bellow, Armando Bengochea, Kevin Guthrie, Mike McPherson, Pat McPherson, Jo Ellen Parker, Gene Tobin, Michele Warman, Don Waters, and Harriet Zuckerman. In 2001, Bill (and the Mellon trustees) gave me the opportunity to try to do something about the problem of redundant efforts and rising costs in higher education by entrusting me with pulling together various Mellon Foundation activities focused on digitizing art images for educational use and asking me to create and lead a new organization that we called Artstor. That story begins in chapter 1.

At Artstor, I benefitted greatly from the guidance of a board of trustees who engaged with one another and with the endless puzzles of mixing the modes of mission-based and market-based thinking. Their diverse viewpoints helped our new organization thrive amid the quixotic challenge of trying to overcome the do-it-yourself impulses of colleges and universities. From the cultural leaders who served on the board—Anthony Appiah, Paul Courant, Jim Cuno, Anne d'Harnoncourt, Dan Greenstein, Carol Mandel, Michelle Myers, Jock Reynolds, Mariet Westermann, and especially our chair, Neil Rudenstine—I learned much of what this book tries to convey about the wants and needs of the passionate people who form the core of mission-driven institutions. From the business-minded Artstor trustees, Greg Avis, Lewis Bernard, Robert Kasdin, George McCulloch, Donald Opatrny, and Peter Wendell, I learned (either by following their counsel or by failing to do so) every lesson in this book about operating and capitalizing a growing firm. All of these Artstor trustees were so helpful because they all valued both modes of our work, regardless of their experience base. I'm grateful for the support of Earl Lewis, Mariët Westermann, and Danielle Allen, who welcomed me back to Mellon as a senior fellow after my time with Artstor. That fellowship gave me time to figure out what was worth sharing about the experience of an organization as unusual as Artstor.

Dan Weiss and Alex Welcome gave me writing advice when I was stuck on the starting blocks. I'm grateful for the time and insights of those whom I interviewed for this book, including Wayne Anderson, Dan Boehmer, Tony Broh, Alice Handy, Don Hossler, Thomas Kalaris, Bruce Miller, Kenny Morrell, Daniel Reid, Jennifer Reynolds, John Tormondsen, Mara Zapada, and Lynzi Ziegenhagen. I benefited also from formative conversations with Matt Bannick, Paul Brest, Paul DiMaggio, Steve Mintz, Richard Reeves, and Burt Weisbrod. Josh Lerner generously pointed me toward some very helpful sources. Friends and colleagues who read and commented on the manuscript include Ed Balleisen, Peter Bearman, Peter Brooks, Paul Courant, Susan Engel, Cappy Hill, Tom Kane, John Katzman, Nancy Malkiel, Larry Manley, Mike McPherson, Jo Ellen Parker, Mark Shulman, Gretchen Wagner, and Bob Weisbuch. Checking one's thinking is always important but perhaps even more so when one's evidence base derives partially from lived experience. The critiques of three anonymous readers for Princeton University Press made this a better book.

The American Council of Learned Societies (ACLS) has provided a perfect laboratory for working through these ideas. Situated in the middle of the flow of information from various strata of higher education, ACLS has enabled me to work with talented colleagues in the organization and across the sector who are devoted to advancing the humanities and interpretive social sciences in healthy and productive ways. The board (led by Bill Kirby) has cheered me on, and I am particularly grateful to ACLS president Joy Connolly, who encouraged connections between my work on intermediary organizations and our ACLS work together on institutional change. She has been a creative, supportive, and inspiring colleague in every way.

I'm grateful to Steve Rigolosi, who helped me figure out which nine words to use when I was inclined to use eleven, to the team at Princeton University Press, especially Natalie Baan, who displayed heroic dedication to the production of the book, and to my editor, Peter Dougherty, who has been a true thought partner throughout the process; if not for his encouragement, I would never have written this book. My beloved father and stepmother, Stephanie Spangler, brother Mark and his husband Diego have been endlessly supportive. My daughters, Emma, Camilla, and Kai, and my wife, Katie Winter, have each sharpened my focus in their own ways and have shaped both me and this book, at every turn in the path. I'm grateful for their patience and their love, most of all.

1

The Synthetic Service Provider

"What's in it for us?"

Kenny Morrell, professor of classics at Rhodes College, read this one-line email from the new dean a couple of times. No salutation; no closing. The question at hand was Morrell's just-approved application to the Andrew W. Mellon Foundation for a second round of funding for Sunoikisis, the interinstitutional virtual classics department that Morrell had created with faculty colleagues at fifteen liberal arts colleges reaching from Texas to Virginia. It was 2001—long before internet bandwidth made Zoom video conferences possible. Thirty-two classics professors at these colleges linked together via the Associated Colleges of the South (ACS) had overcome many barriers and were beginning to function as one large and coordinated interinstitutional department. Bill Troutt, the Rhodes College president, had just called Morrell to congratulate him and his colleagues on receiving the grant and to express his appreciation for their efforts. Then the note from the new dean arrived.

Sunoikisis was a promising effort to strengthen all of the colleges through coordinated faculty collaboration. Plenty of challenges remained, however. On all of the campuses, the time and effort that faculty members were putting into the project did not count toward their evaluation for promotion and tenure, and the professors who were donating their time to the effort might at any point lose momentum. They had been stretching their days to coordinate synchronized course schedules, plan the logistics for collaborative summer institutes, set up a means of accounting for whether a given department had a net inflow or net outflow of students, and reconcile the requirements and needs of the different departments and colleges. Faculty members at participating campuses with larger departments were reluctant to participate fully in the collaboration because they had a more secure place in their own college. Students were unwilling to take a class offered by a member of the consortium if they couldn't register for it seamlessly through their school's course registration software, just one of many technological barriers associated with reconciling local campus needs and the possibilities of an intercampus network of course offerings.

In reading the dean's note, Morrell remembered the constant tug of war involved in creating and maintaining Sunoikisis. Students wanted more classes available to them, but they also wanted college to cost less. College presidents recognized the devastating long-term problems associated with schools competing endlessly to outdo one another in every aspect of their academic and nonacademic programs, but they often made decisions that were inevitably aligned instead with the reality that they were hired and rewarded on their ability to distinguish their institution from their peers'. Morrell had an enthusiastic partner in Wayne Anderson, who served as executive director of the Associated Colleges of the South, but Anderson and ACS had few resources of their own and were subject to the wishes and priorities of the participating presidents and the Mellon Foundation.

The previous dean, who had been supportive of Morrell's and Rhodes' entrepreneurial leadership of the innovative consortium as a way of strengthening the college, had retired, and the pendulum swung in the opposite direction. The new dean, who wanted the faculty to return to more traditional roles, saw Morrell's request for additional external support as a waste of the college's limited bites at Mellon's funding apple.

A few earlier years earlier, as the experimental virtual classics department gained traction, Morrell and his colleagues had wanted to signal the deep collaboration that enabled the faculty to plan and work together. For that reason, they had renamed the project Sunoikisis after a group of fifth-century BCE Greek city-states that had banded together to resist the dominance of Athens. At moments like this, Morrell remembered that Athens had methodically laid siege to the leaders of the rebellion and overwhelmed the coalition. In Thucydides's telling of the story, the episode is best known not for the success of the coalition, which was ultimately defeated by mighty Athens, but for the debate in the Athenian senate over whether to execute all of the men in the conquered cities or only a thousand from each city to teach the inhabitants a lesson.

"We might be just ever so slightly ahead of the curve," Morrell thought as he read the dean's note, "but if we don't do this, if we don't succeed, someone else will. It's just a matter of time."[1]

———

Was Kenny Morrell right? Will colleges and universities eventually figure out how to work together to reduce costs while remaining educationally effective? Because the institutional barriers to cost-efficient change are remarkably strong and resilient, it is not clear that they will. Meanwhile, the costs associated with running a college continue to rise. State funding, which once heavily subsidized public higher education, is being systematically withdrawn; the number of private and public colleges with endowments that provide enough financial aid can be numbered in the dozens, not in the hundreds or thousands. The federal government will not come riding in to subsidize colleges beyond the current (and mostly static) levels of scientific research funding and $6,000 Pell grants for the neediest students. As the cost of college increases and public subsidy falls, the financial burden increasingly falls on students and their families.

The results of this steady upward cost escalation include significant student debt and ever-increasing pressure on graduates to reap immediate financial returns when they navigate the job market. On campuses, the gulf between faculty and administration widens, and so does the divide between faculty who have made it onto the life-boat of tenure-track jobs and the ever-larger pool of contingent and job-insecure faculty. The water in the pot heats up around frogs who tell themselves that at least it isn't boiling.

It isn't as if the ever-increasing challenge of rising institutional costs lurks as an undiscovered issue. But as Harvard president Larry Bacow has noted, "It is difficult to control costs in a university setting precisely because there is no natural constituency for cost control on a university campus."[2] Bacow recognizes the trap that most institutions face when noneconomic priorities are kept separate from economic priorities: while students and their families fervently desire lower tuition prices, they also are aligned with faculty who prefer costly practices such as smaller classes and more course offerings, and they are lured to individual campuses by expensive, attractive dorm rooms and dazzling flower gardens. Simultaneously, individual colleges and universities continue to shy away from the deep collaborative strategies that could slow their rush toward deeper financial struggles. One ambitious advocate for change, Franklin Patterson, has noted the urgency of the need for practical answers:

> No amount of sunny sentiments about cooperation, no viewing with alarm, no cynicism about the slight accomplishments of consortia, and certainly no plethora of preaching at institutional presidents will do the job. What is needed is some substantial, positive action by those outside the consortia movement with enough resources to cause it to turn around.[3]

Patterson wrote that in 1966. Little has changed.

So was Sunoikisis simply ahead of the curve, as Morrell optimistically surmised? The slope of the curve doesn't indicate an arc of progress with respect to the challenge that Patterson, Morrell, Bacow, and many others have identified. The many valuable contributions to scholarship, teaching, and technological innovation that US colleges and universities generate comes with a corresponding challenge: the effective rejection of possible cost efficiencies that could be achieved through deep and effective interinstitutional collaboration. There doesn't seem to be a curve for Sunoikisis to be ahead of.

It is difficult to deny the many daily and ongoing successes of US higher education. Classes are taught, basketballs are dunked, and students continue to study and figure out who they are by working and playing together. Teachers teach and experiments are conducted in labs. The United States continues to be a net exporter of research and a net importer of students from around the world, and 25 US universities are ranked in the top 50 of all world universities.[4] But the fragmented and uncooperative nonsystem of US higher education also experiences strain due to the cost of running the enterprise. Ever-increasing costs contribute to colleges losing some of society's good will. As sociologist Robert K. Merton argued, "When net balance of the aggregate of consequences of an existing social structure is clearly dysfunctional, there develops a strong and insistent pressure for change."[5] Pressure for change in these institutions may be rising, but they seem to resist change very effectively. Government subsidies for higher education could cover over some of the results of this change-resistance, but those subsidies show no signs of materializing.

Colleges and universities shouldn't wait until society has reached the limits of its tolerance for the cost disease of higher education. But is there any reason to believe that these fiercely autonomous institutions can derive collective solutions to address their shared challenges? Will mighty Athens—a metaphor for the apparently insurmountable institutional barriers to change—always win, or is there reason to believe that colleges can prevent the primacy of autonomy from defeating their embrace of some shared solutions? We will turn later to how and when Sunoikisis ran into limits, but for now it is worth noting that some intermediary organizations, including the National Student Clearinghouse, have been able to play synthetically engineered roles that have found acceptance in the loose network of colleges and universities.

The National Student Clearinghouse

In the early 1990s, Sallie Mae, the enormous company created in the 1970s by the federal government to serve as the primary issuer of government-funded student loans, set out to solve an ongoing logistical headache. Sallie Mae vice president Dan Boehmer was tasked with working with college and university registrars across the country to track whether students with loans were still enrolled at any college or whether they had stopped attending college.[6] If they were no longer enrolled in college, then they had to begin paying off their loans. At the time, no one knew if a student who had left the University of Michigan was now enrolled at the University of Florida. No federated system existed for determining a student's college enrollment status, and yet schools that didn't report students' status correctly faced significant penalties. The paperwork and lack of coordination created a nightmare for all concerned: governments, registrars, financial aid offices, admissions offices, and students.

Coming up with a solution for such a far-reaching and complicated problem wasn't simple. But by the mid 1990s, Boehmer and his colleagues had made significant progress in building partnerships with almost every US college and university. The new National Student Clearinghouse gradually expanded the data that it compiled, and it was able to provide trend data concerning enrollments by self-identified gender and race. After it solved the original problem (determining whether a student is enrolled *somewhere* and hence can defer loan repayment), it recognized that its interinstitutional data-sharing network could provide other services to students, to colleges and universities, and to the greater world. Its second service, DegreeVerify, was launched in the late 1990s. It uses the Clearinghouse's platform to provide degree verification for employers, search firms, and individuals. By some estimates, DegreeVerify provides the Clearinghouse with $50 million a year in revenue.

As the technological infrastructure advanced through improved bandwidth and dramatic increases in processing power, the Clearinghouse is on its way to becoming even more useful. In 2018, the Lumina Foundation and the Bill and Melinda Gates Foundation announced a new data resource, the Postsecondary Data Partnership (PDP). Recognizing the potential in the infrastructure that the Clearinghouse had established, Lumina and Gates provided the working capital to expand the Clearinghouse's infrastructure to accommodate the aggregation of students' full transcript records. Today, as the PDP program is being implemented in stages, the network of registrars with the Clearinghouse in the middle enables the collection and collective analysis of detailed individual student transcripts from an increasing number of public and private institutions—every student, every course, and every grade.

PDP was created in part because the foundations that fund it were eager to find efficient and effective ways to gauge the effectiveness of programs such as Achieving the Dream and Complete College America, which work to help students complete their college degrees. One of the challenges that funders encountered in assessing the effectiveness of such programs is that most students don't follow "traditional" paths: they alternate between attending and not attending college, and they transfer credits as they move or seek to fit classes around work and family responsibilities. Before the development of PDP, these organizations had to chase students wherever they might go or canvass every institution to see if the student had ended up there. For the programs that it is tracking (and perhaps eventually for all institutions and all students), PDP makes it possible to find every student and trace the particular details of courses that they enrolled in on their path no matter which of the 3,500 US colleges and universities they might attend at different points in time.

The National Student Clearinghouse and PDP are astounding systemic efforts in a higher education landscape that might be defined by its lack of system-wide efforts. By any imaginable measure, the National Student Clearinghouse has succeeded. It is a model of synthesis between outside agencies and the internal practices of colleges; this synthetic approach shows how the independence of individual colleges and universities can be compatible with a degree of standardization and that centrally determined goals can be reconciled with autonomous local needs.

If one simply looks at the Clearinghouse as a business, it might be considered a successful entrepreneurial platform that filled a gap in a two-sided market. A paper by leading venture capital firm Sequoia describes how a company that bridges a two-sided market by matching suppliers and demanders can become a thriving business:

> The two sides of demand and supply need to be incentivized to use the platform to create strong network effects. As an example, a two-sided cleaning service marketplace that connects a cleaner to a home will work the first time. But over a period of time, once the cleaner has made enough connections, they are unlikely to use the platform. The platform needs to create unique and recurring value to both parties to retain them on the system.[7]

The Clearinghouse created unique and recurring value, and like other successful mega-businesses of our time, such as Amazon or Uber, it then expanded its content and services to efficiently serve both sides of its market. But the marketplace of underlying organizations and the terms of exchange were very different from Amazon's.

Dan Boehmer had visited campuses in the mid-1990s to convince the assembled staff that the Clearinghouse would make their lives easier because they would no longer have to check hundreds of pages of printouts against their student records system every semester. However, he quickly learned that someone from the corporate world of student loans was not instantly welcomed as a friend. How on earth, the staff asked, will we be able to provide you with information about our students, given the provisions of FERPA (the Federal Educational Rights and Privacy Act)? In some early meetings he was chased out of the room, with words like "sacrosanct" hurled at him as he left.

What accounts for the tension around introducing efficient externally provided services in higher education? Economist Gordon Winston noted that colleges and universities are deeply conflicted institutions. On the one hand, they are commercial enterprises that process inputs and sell services; on the other, they offer a leap-of-faith contract with their customers. That contract essentially says, "It's hard to measure whether you will get what you are seeking from this transaction, so trust us and become emotionally attached to us so that you will continue to sing our praises and freely choose to give us money for the rest of your life." In the service of the noncommercial mode, they engage in economically irrational activities. They subsidize fields and research that people aren't asking for, and they subsidize students' education, even those paying full price. In a bid to win currency in reputation markets, they undertake all kinds of strategies in pursuit of prestige (measured in rankings and reputation) that may or may not have financial returns. They do all kinds of things to attract customers who will enhance the reputation of the institution and perhaps make the product better (via positive peer effects and higher rankings). In these noncommercial modes, they function as *donative firms*, meaning that they seek voluntary support rather than earned income. They are, as Winston noted, a mix of two completely different approaches:

> The donative-commercial firm is essentially part church and part car dealer—devoted partly to charity and partly to commerce, to "ideology" and "rationality." The result is a tension between doing good and doing well. It plagues administrators trying to decide which behaviors—those of the charity or those of the firm—are appropriate to a college or university.[8]

The question is how to reconcile these modes. When should staff and faculty act as if they are working on behalf of a church-like entity? When should they act in a commercial-minded way? There are no clear guidelines, which is one of the reasons that institutional change is so difficult.

For Boehmer, promoting the idea of the Clearinghouse into this conflicted environment required trust-building that went far beyond the normal sales cycle that he knew from his career in underwriting commercial loans. C. Anthony (Tony) Broh was the registrar at Princeton at the time. Looking back, he recalls his mixed feelings about the creation of the Clearinghouse:

> Sure, I remember when Sallie Mae came up with the idea of the "Clearinghouse." I didn't particularly like it. We had one staff person who was dedicated to the certification process—every month or so, we would get a seven-page printout from Citibank or whomever and that person would check it. I didn't want to lose

that person and frankly I didn't want to lose control. We had just gotten to the point in the establishment of the registrar's office where the analysis that we were doing of students—where they came from, where they went, what they did—was being valued by the university. So, when we were approached by the Clearinghouse, I started raising issues of confidentiality. These were valid; we did care about these things. But the idea of sending our data off to someone else—and I can see this now, 25 years later—also felt like a threat to my internal position. The FERPA issues and the tangible effects on our staff and our place in the Princeton universe blurred. Eventually, the Clearinghouse became inescapable and incredibly valuable when enough places joined; but when it started, I wasn't a fan.[9]

To garner the support he needed, Boehmer assembled a team of "insider" relationship builders led by the former registrar of Brigham Young University, Jeff Tanner, who also had served as president of the American Association of College Registrars and Admissions Officers (AACRAO). People like Tanner were known and respected by people like Broh, and they were needed to convince conflicted participants—users who had a big stake in the topic who couldn't be counted on to make efficient decisions. The Clearinghouse had the resources of Sallie Mae behind it, so it could pay out of pocket for the customized programming needed to connect campus databases to the Clearinghouse's. Because it had sufficient working capital, it could make the investments that could ease the hard-to-move wheels of change.

None of what the Clearinghouse did in 2018 in launching the new service (PDP) that gathers individual student transcripts would have been possible if an organization had not been created in 1993, *de novo*, to elbow—and charm—its way into the crowded and fragmented institutional landscape of colleges and universities. All of the institutions that the Clearinghouse needed to buy into its effort were populated with serious, dedicated individuals (such as Tony Broh), eager to do their work in ways that both upheld longstanding institutional values and reinforced their own job security and advancement. Serving as a stable and trusted connective node in the midst of isolated and individualistic institutional data managers enabled the Clearinghouse to grow beyond its original mission and eventually create DegreeVerify, which might otherwise have been perceived by campus constituencies as too much car dealership and too little church. In gaining the trust of registrars around the country, the Clearinghouse overcame the social part of a massive sociotechnical problem in which issues of trust and responsibility for a symbolic mission are tangled up in the mixed-up market of colleges and universities.

The Problem with Relying Only on the Market

How does the half-church and half-car-dealer nature of the higher education market support or not support the most widely used market-driven mechanism for cost-reduction—outsourcing? Isn't the most obvious solution to rising costs simply to rent services or solutions from customer-focused for-profit firms? Most firms in any sector reduce costs by delegating parts of their production to external firms, which may or may not include offshoring work to other labor markets. Outsourcing allows the organization to focus on core areas of expertise or on coordinating activities, and it may spare the organization from making capital investments that require support and eventually replacement. (Think of the widespread practice of leasing copy machines rather than owning them.)

In many ways, entering the difficult selling environment that Dan Boehmer faced was just another entrepreneurial decision to build a service and offer it to a market of institutional buyers. To be sure, selling a solution in an environment where decision-makers can rely on church-like dogma to justify inefficiency might be harder than selling to a car dealer (or a firm with more of a car-dealer ethos). But the possible rewards of doing so are significant because the higher education market is very large. Aramark, which provides dining hall and other services to colleges, is thriving, and on many campuses Barnes and Noble has replaced what used to be independent college bookstores. Oracle and Workday have created enterprise software systems to serve higher education because even the most do-it-yourself inclined university rarely believes that it can create its own human resources or payroll systems. Public universities, which educate the vast majority of students, are experiencing dramatic decreases in state funding and believe that partnerships with private firms are their best hope for doing all that they need to do. Ashish Vaidya, president of North Kentucky University, has argued that the COVID-19 pandemic made the need for partnerships even more apparent: "For regional public colleges, partnerships may even be the key to survival. As grim as so much of this crisis has been, it has also provided clarity on the need to embrace new solutions to the goals that we all share—including educational, economic, and social prosperity for learners of every kind, at every stage of their lives."[10]

Firms that seek such partnerships have used insider knowledge of higher education to build new products and have hired notable academic and community leaders to establish bona fides, much as the Clearinghouse hired the Brigham Young registrar to serve as its chief proselytizer. Academic Analytics, a for-profit firm that provides data analytics concerning faculty research productivity and allows institutions to compare their own departments' results to those of their peers, hired Peter Lange, the well-respected former provost at Duke, and Robert Berdahl, former president of the University of Texas at Austin, to serve as academic advisors. Coursera, which along with edX spurred the enthusiasm around massive open online courses (MOOCs) in 2011, hired former Yale president Richard Levin as its president (and later senior advisor). And although both of these enterprises have encountered their share of faculty criticism, they are successful companies that provide services to colleges and universities at a scale that individual institutions cannot take on.[11] When COVID-19 made it impossible for many high school seniors to sit for the SAT and ACT, selective colleges faced the prospect of making admissions decisions with fewer data than they had before, and plenty of firms stepped in to offer new products to admissions offices. In an *Inside Higher Ed* article about the suspension of standardized testing as an admissions criterion, Catherine

McDonald Davenport, Dickinson College's vice president for enrollment and dean of admissions, noted that there was no shortage of
firms offering products to the higher education market: "Everybody
seems to have an idea and a solution for my unnamed problem. It's
somewhat comical."[12]

Purveyors of public/private ventures gather at the annual P3.edu
meeting, where both cautious and convinced academic administrators come together with real estate developers and other sophisticated market-driven firms that are used to navigating the policy and
lender requirements associated with capital-intensive functions like
building dormitories. There is no doubt, as Goldie Blumenstyk wrote
in the *Chronicle of Higher Education*, that these partnerships are moving from more ancillary areas into areas closer to the educational mission of institutions, offering "a range of other services that colleges
increasingly eye as ripe for partnership with outside parties. Among
them: managing online programs, predictive-analytics systems, skills
training and boot camps, and even career counseling."[13] The idea of
a partnership seems fairly uncontroversial, as colleges coinvest with
sophisticated real estate developers to negotiate with local munici-
palities and carry out multimillion-dollar construction projects. But
the contours of partnership arouse more frustration—and resistance—as outside providers move closer to the mission-driven core
of the enterprise. Bridget Burns, executive director of the University
Innovation Alliance (a coalition of very large universities collaborating to increase graduation rates), noted that a partnership with higher
education needs to truly be a two-way street:

> We appreciate all of the great apps and software solutions that
> you're creating for Higher Education, but please know that when
> we talk about "partnering," we don't really mean that you let us
> test your app for you and help you make it better. For us, partner-
> ing is about your spending time listening to how our users need
> to work, helping our already-busy faculty figure out how your
> solution supports their work in the real world, and then providing
> the project management and onboarding to help make this hap-
> pen. For some of you this really doesn't work with your business

model because it is too labor-intensive. But from the university's point of view, that is what separates a partner from a vendor.[14]

Burns was speaking at ASU-GSV, the annual major conference of educational technology hosted by a public-private partnership between Arizona State University and Global Silicon Valley. The conference features presentations and pitches from hundreds of firms working on everything from career services to remote grading to online learning platforms across K-12, corporate, and higher education. These firms are backed by over a billion dollars of annual investment in the K-12 and higher education markets.[15] But are these well-funded, entrepreneurial for-profit firms the right solution for the problem of escalating costs for colleges as they come to recognize that they can't and shouldn't build everything themselves?

To answer the question of whether relying on motivated market players will help with the escalating costs of college, we first have to think about how institutional buyers of solutions act and are treated in the open market. As mission-driven nonprofit organizations, colleges and universities might have every reason to have different rules than normal market buyers and sellers. But a telling episode in how these institutions conduct themselves commercially arose with the notorious 1992 Department of Justice (DOJ) case that charged MIT, the Ivy League universities, and other schools that worked together to jointly set financial aid offers for students who applied to overlapping institutions with illegal price fixing. The case was legally complicated. It was originally brought by the DOJ against Brown University, which decided (along with the other Ivy League institutions) that it would be too costly to fight the case. MIT chose to appeal the case and eventually won, but by then the die had been cast. The institutions acknowledged that their practices were collusive and stopped sharing information about aid offers. Their decision has been interpreted to cover a wide range of practices that might be considered collusive. This is the crux of the matter: what the DOJ and the courts saw as illegal market behavior—collusion—was, as a subsequent *New York Times* editorial noted, "surely a charitable activity." Institutions agreeing how to allocate aid so as to serve their collective missions seemed to be substantially different from "price fixing by commercial enterprises that exploit customers."[16]

Today we see the far-reaching implications of the decision and the model that it sanctioned. Competition among colleges is now considered an unadulterated good, accompanied by a societal and governmental faith that the market will work things out to the benefit of consumers. Competing without limits for students who are in any way desirable is sanctioned because that competition is supposedly good for the consumer. With unbridled competition blessed in this way, merit aid—the enrollment strategy of discounting tuition for the sake of achieving an institutional objective, such as attracting students who can boost a school's rankings because they carry high test scores—thrived in the 1990s and into the 2000s. This method of using financial aid (which, before the DOJ case, had been allocated largely on the basis of a shared conclusion about a student's financial need) leads schools to compete for students in entirely self-serving ways that end up serving particular students well at the expense of the amount of financial aid available in the system. For example, it is now widespread practice for schools to use tuition discounts as a strategy for attracting students who are entirely capable of paying a school's full tuition but who can be lured to the school by the offer of a $10,000 or $15,000 discount in the form of a merit scholarship.[17] Individual interests (of those particular students and that particular college) are served while the collective mission of the sector is not. As Winston lamented, "Without coordination, parental haggling and individual schools' positional bidding for student quality [will] divert . . . resources from low-income students who [are] willing but unable to pay the full price to high-income students who [are] able but unwilling to pay."[18] The ruling in the DOJ case was one step in uncorking colleges' inclination to compete endlessly. As a result, the presidents whose faculty members were interested in collaborating to build a shared classics department lived in a world where they were charged with *avoiding* collaboration. In short, colleges' impulses to compete have been thoroughly blessed, even legislated. And compete they do.

These thousands of institutional buyers of all sorts of services from athletic equipment to library databases to magnetic resonance spectrometers make decisions that constitute a market estimated at $300 billion, and they can look like fish in a barrel to businesses seeking growth opportunities. And where there's competition among buyers, the market is very good at incentivizing profit-minded firms to provide profit-maximizing solutions.

Consider EAB, a higher education data analytics company that provides data services consulting to a thousand colleges. While it also consults on enrollment recruiting strategies, its main line of business is providing integrated planning and advising services that help colleges and universities help their students to graduate.[19] With over $300 million in annual revenue, EAB is thriving, and a private equity firm purchased the firm for $1.55 billion in 2018. It's fair to note that the work of EAB and similar firms is not simple. That work requires the mapping, integration, analysis, and utilization of various campus data sources that are idiosyncratically stored on each campus. But the firms' skills and tools are reapplied in each engagement. They can apply the lessons learned to their core business offering, using their experiences with other colleges when they begin working with the next one. The colleges themselves don't financially benefit from working with firms that have the economies of scale of having worked with many different but similar institutions. For example, in 2018 Laramie County (WY) Community College (LCCC), with an enrollment of 3,174 full-time students, published the results of its student success vendor search. It chose EAB, at an annual estimated cost that began at $138,000 per year. LCCC felt that it had to pursue the arrangement for both church and car-dealership reasons: "While student success technology is expensive and is not easy to implement, we have an obligation to our students and community to provide excellence in education and service."[20]

The for-profit firms that provide complex services to colleges and universities can essentially name their price. In his investigation for the *Huffington Post*, titled "The Creeping Capitalist Takeover of Higher Education," Kevin Carey describes how graduate programs expanded online via locked-in revenue-sharing deals with companies such as 2U. When USC dean of social work Marilyn Flynn signed up with 2U to produce online master's degrees that cost students the same amount as in-person degrees ($107,000), it didn't matter that 2U locked in 60 percent of all revenue from such courses on an ongoing basis, because the revenue that remained after USC paid 2U was all additive to USC's existing tuition revenue. Carey writes:

> The company [2U] assumed all of the financial risk. College deans could use their cut to lure star research professors by promising them large salaries and small or nonexistent teaching loads, pushing programs up the rankings. The online courses would be staffed by adjuncts, most working far from the campus and much cheaper to employ. "This is a cash cow," Flynn says bluntly. "Universities are struggling to find a business plan that works. And I was very aware that we would have a dramatic increase in revenue from this."[21]

Interestingly, by the end of his time at 2U, founder John Katzman criticized the model in which online program managers such as 2U lock in deals with universities to fill and profit from scalable online master's degree programs: "There are CEOs who believe they have a fiduciary duty to their stockholders to just market the most expensive programs and encourage schools to jack up tuition," Katzman said. "I am horrified. That was not the goal."[22]

When colleges recognize that they can't keep up with the technology involved in ambitious new programs and directions, they become captive to vendors. There's no shortage of experts who can scale their own profits by replicating their work as they pass from college town to college town. As colleges and universities buy these wares, their costs rise and the consumers—students and their families—end up paying more.

What are the alternatives?

The expansion of National Student Clearinghouse into the Post-secondary Data Partnership could put the Clearinghouse in a position to provide analytics services similar to EAB's to its member institutions. As the PDP project gathers more and more institution-wide troves of student transcripts, the Clearinghouse will have—in one structured and standardized format—more and more capacity to mine student data. Instead of watching colleges and universities pay market rates for predictive analytics about student success to firms such as EAB, ReUp Education, or Civitas, the Clearinghouse could add these services to the analytics that it already provides, including (as promoted on its website), "Powerful multivariable filtering tools to analyze deep, disaggregated data, characteristics, such as age, race, gender, cohort term, and first-generation-student status."[23] In short, the Clearinghouse could expand its role as a trusted intermediary—an enterprise that synthetically supports institutions' missions while connecting isolated colleges and universities. Doing so would generate scalable value and services, under the watchful eyes of a Board of Trustees that represents the community rather than financial investors and shareholders.

Artstor: One Shared Solution

The passionate people who work at colleges and universities are inclined to solve their own problems.[24] Sometimes they should, and sometimes they shouldn't. When they do engage an external provider, they would be better off if that the provider will care about the school's mission as if that mission were truly its own. At the same time, external mission-driven providers need to recognize college and universities' deep commitment to autonomy, they need to endure long enough to develop trust, and they need to develop a business model that supports their capacity to be responsive enough to the needs of individual campuses to sustain that trust and sense of value.

The Mellon Foundation's creation of Artstor provides an illustrative example of a mission-aligned synthetic service provider. Before 1.4 trillion digital photos were taken each year and before lecture notes were routinely posted to learning management systems, students studied art and architectural history by sitting in darkened classrooms wherein professors supported their lectures by use of images that they projected onto a wall by shining very bright light bulbs through 35-millimeter film slides. To study for exams, students gathered in a room or a hallway in the art history department that was designated as the "photo study" area. There they would study (and sometimes sketch) the photographs that were thumbtacked to a wall; these photos roughly corresponded to the slides that they had seen in class. By 1999, innovative art history departments, librarians, and academic technologists had begun to believe that digitizing those teaching slides and sharing them with their students on campus via the internet would be a vast improvement over existing practices.

In fact, dozens of colleges came up with the same idea: asking the Andrew W. Mellon Foundation for funds to digitize the art history slide collection. Don Waters, who led Mellon's program in libraries and scholarly communication, started receiving inquiry after inquiry, grant application after grant application. Provosts wrote to ask for $800,000 or $1 million to digitize their teaching slides. Each proposed to scan their 35mm slide of the *Mona Lisa* and tens of thousands of other artworks that had mostly been photographed from printed pictures in published books. The goal of their grant applications was to create a database that allowed the institution to attach searchable words and phrases, such as "Leonardo da Vinci," "da Vinci," "Italian painting," or "Portraits," to the digital image files. To support the use of these digital files, they also sought funds to build or buy software to manage the images and data and to ensure that access to the image was restricted to use on the campus, so that the museum, the textbook publisher from which they got the image, or the photographer who had taken the photograph wouldn't sue them. The final result on each campus would be a digital library of tens of thousands of images that students could consult as they prepared for exams and faculty could use in their research.

Don, along with Mellon president Bill Bowen and a few others, began to look at the individual institutional proposals. I had been working with Bill on research projects about issues that affected the whole college sector, such as the role of race in college admissions and the appropriate balance between college sports and educational values. Bill knew that I had gotten my PhD in the humanities, and we shared very similar ideas about working on system-wide challenges in scalable ways. From Mellon's transinstitutional perspective, all of these pleas for funds looked fairly similar. It didn't take us long to figure out that we would run through a billion dollars if we gave a million dollars to a thousand different campuses. Even worse, that billion dollars would have created a thousand digital image databases that were largely redundant and isolated in institutional silos that were reinforced by software incompatibility and protective rights-management policies. The need for digital images that allowed students to study for exams via the web was a real one, but the solution—using a billion dollars to digitize the country's thousand un-networked and locally isolated pools of analog content—was clearly not the right one.

So in the townhouses that house the Mellon Foundation on a quiet side street in Manhattan, a complicated puzzle was starting to take shape. On the one hand, campuses were ready, willing, and able to solve their own problem—but each needed a million dollars to do so. On the other hand, the Mellon Foundation was proposing a very different solution: the creation of a new organization, called Artstor, to build and provide a large and growing digital image library to colleges and universities for use in teaching and research. If we could figure out how to share digital images over the web while respecting intellectual property rights, the cost savings across the US college and university system would be enormous.

But Artstor would have to be developed within a complicated reality. The do-it-yourself approach on each separate campus was representative of the kind of complicated interdepartmental undertaking that staff at nonprofit institutions instinctively feel only they can and should do. Staff and faculty deeply believe that one size does not fit all, and that anyone who offers a shortcut around the local relationships, reporting lines, and sources of institutional anxiety and territoriality must either be naïve or nefarious.

The fit between individual art history departmental image collections and the Mellon Foundation was apparent to staff on campuses and to administrators looking for external funding. Mellon had been the country's most significant supporter of humanistic scholarship since its founding in 1970. It also had a deep interest in the visual arts, dating back to Andrew Mellon's gift of the National Gallery of Art to the nation and to his son Paul's passion for art. (Paul Mellon was the foundation's founder.) Beyond bringing together art and scholarship, the foundation had under the leadership of Bill Bowen shown an active interest in using technology to serve teachers and scholars. Based on research that he had been conducting about the future of libraries, Bowen had started to be convinced that technology might offer a solution to the dilemmas associated with an ever more costly enterprise. In the 1990s, Bowen and Kevin Guthrie had created JSTOR, the digitized archive of scholarly journals that stands out as an extraordinary success in bringing technology into the service of scholarship across the arts and sciences. To Bowen, the idea of providing digital images of art to campuses made very good sense. But the approach that we came up with was different from the one that that the individual schools had sought in their grant requests.

The next chapter tells Artstor' s stories—its ups, its downs, and the lessons that we learned from building a collective solution rather than funding endless and isolated local solutions. Before moving on to that chapter, we can reflect on a key but perhaps subtle point that I will make throughout this book: that while relying only on redundant local solutions to shared needs isn't the right answer, neither is relying solely on external profit-maximizing vendors. As the Mellon Foundation worked with colleges and universities, we noticed that wherever we went to build out Artstor as a shared solution, for-profit vendors followed in our wake. Software providers wanted to sell tools to each campus for building up local efforts in ways that aligned with the Artstor tools; proprietary image vendors wanted to sell their content on a campus-by-campus basis through our platform. We didn't want to interfere with their businesses, but we also didn't want to facilitate what we saw as extractive rather than compatible solutions. We worked to convince some of the world's most important holders of photographs (including one-of-a-kind collections held by for-profit image distributors such as Italy's Scala and highly desirable nonprofit collections such as the Museum of Modern Art's) that Artstor's shared approach—which sought primarily to cover its costs rather than to maximize profits—was a good and fair way to reach the educational audience. If Artstor hadn't been invented with the mission-aligned ethos that we created, these owners of valued and valuable content would surely have found ways to license images to each place, one by one, thus increasing their own surpluses. That's their job. But doing so would have been to the detriment of the institutions that constitute the system and the collective support of teaching cultural history.

Forging synthetic solutions isn't easy. This book argues for a particular approach to the cost problem, an approach that is not based on deus ex machina revenue sources or magical thinking about institutions choosing to collaborate when all of their impulses pull them to compete. In the following chapters, I propose that colleges and universities need a set of mission-driven and market-supported organizations that live and thrive in the middle of the institutional forest of thousands of individual distinctive institutions. Passionate and brilliant faculty and staff on campuses remain devoted to the craft of teaching, scholarship, and service. Collective solutions should not be forged without their deep involvement and their discerning eye. We need to understand the forces that shape their options and decisions, understand the skills and the ecosystem that can create and foster new interinstitutional organizations, and reconcile mission and market in ways that can save higher education.

2

Scanning Mona Lisa

A Conversation with a Professor

Sitting across from James Beck in September 2004, I realized that it was time for me to sit quietly and listen for a while. The author of thirteen books and a professor at Columbia University, Beck (1930–2007) was one of the world's most renowned scholars of Italian Renaissance art. He had crossed over into the realm of public fame when, in 1987, he castigated the Vatican for its ambitious restoration of the Michelangelo frescoes that adorn the ceiling of the Sistine Chapel. In an interview with *People* magazine, he hadn't minced words as he recalled going up on the scaffolding in the early days of the restoration project: "I just said, 'Oh God, this is a disaster.' It looked as if the soul of the fresco had been stripped away."[1] Later, Beck pushed back on a 1991 Italian conservation project of a Jacopo della Quercia sculpture. When he wrote that it looked like it had been "scrubbed with Spic and Span and polished with Johnson's Wax,"[2] he provoked a lawsuit for aggravated slander from the Italian conservator in charge. Like many scholars, Beck had worked tirelessly for decades, believed deeply in his work, and was not timid about standing up for what he believed in.

A few years had passed since Mellon had been besieged with grant requests to digitize the slide libraries of various individual colleges, and in the meantime I had become Artstor's first executive director. Artstor's key goal was to build one shared reservoir of content, and in doing so to help US colleges and universities avoid the enormous costs of building and indexing their own libraries of 50,000 to 100,000 (or more) digitized images. The process was fairly complicated; in 2000, images were hard to come by on the web, and so colleges were intent on scanning the 35mm slides that they had created, cared for, and projected in the classroom for more than fifty years. To find and use its digitized slides, each college would also need to create electronic cataloging records for each slide. The use and sharing of content from copyrighted sources meant that each school would require its general counsel or outside attorneys to determine whether the school was even allowed legally to do all of this. As a result, the staff would need to buy or build software to control access to the digitized content so as to diminish any legal risk associated with the creation and use of these newly digitized images. As noted in chapter 1, this is exactly the kind of problem-solving of complicated challenges that staff at nonprofit institutions often feel they can best do themselves.

When I went to see Jim Beck, Artstor had been live as a subscription service since the spring of that year and was in the very earliest stages of being introduced at more than a hundred campuses. A few weeks earlier I'd met with the Mellon Foundation Board of Trustees about our progress—about the various collections we had been building, our progress in identifying and overcoming technical challenges, and our headway vis-à-vis our projections in terms of signing up institutional subscribers. It was always fun to present information about Artstor because we could show beautiful pictures and tell great stories. In 2003, big, dazzling high-resolution images of art weren't widely available, so when we showed highlights of collections and then zoomed in on details of a painting or a vase, our audiences swooned. We also told gripping detective stories of working out agreements with the stewards of quirky image collections that my colleague, Max Marmor, had found in attics on Bleecker Street or estates in Switzerland and which we were using Mellon funding to scan. Some of these collections lived in museums, but others had been built in ways that could never be recreated. For example, John and Susan Huntington, professors at Ohio State, had spent over thirty years trekking through Southeast and Central Asia photographing objects and sites of Buddhist art. They sometimes hiked through jungles to reshoot a site that they had already documented because they realized years later that they wanted the same shot at a different time of day. Like many other collections that we were aggregating, their collection had been built on the strength of their passion for their field. For years such collections had been accessible only when someone created a physical copy of a photograph or a slide and sent it to the requester through the mail. Now these collections could be shared with teachers and scholars at thousands of colleges, universities, and other schools via the web.

Fortunately, it wasn't too difficult to explain to the Mellon trustees why creating a new entity—Artstor—was worth the cost and effort. In our presentations, we showed the Huntingtons' photographs of the 70-foot sculpture of Buddhas at Bamiyan in Afghanistan that the Taliban had blown up and which would never be photographed again. It wasn't hard to make the case that these images, and many others, would be valuable to teachers and students everywhere. While it certainly wasn't going to be easy to get faculty and staff to change their behavior—to use a shared image collection rather than a locally created set of images—irreplaceable collections like the Huntingtons' made a vivid case that the transition would not only be cost efficient but would also democratize access to the world's cultural heritage. With Artstor, every college, community college, and high school in the country could have access to the same image collection as Princeton or Harvard.

Making the case for the value proposition to a roomful of foundation trustees who were reviewing hundreds of grants to colleges, museums, dance companies, research organizations, and botanical gardens also meant making a case for why Artstor was worth the investment of limited philanthropic funds. Increasingly, foundations (including Mellon) were thinking of grants as "investments."

The language of "strategic philanthropy," omnipresent today, was certainly entering the vocabulary of Mellon staff and trustees as we were attempting to get Artstor off the ground. Since its creation in 1970, Mellon had heavily relied on a strategy of delivering funding to well-established institutions and maintaining a hands-off approach to how the institutions' leaders deployed those funds. Mellon had been known for "institution-building," meaning that it was inclined to support what it saw as centrally important functions of strong institutions: functions, such as art conservation and the cataloging of manuscripts, that were important for scholarship over the long term and for which it was difficult for the institution to raise money from other sources. Focusing its support on well-known institutions also enabled Mellon to remain small in terms of staff, in that Mellon's traditional philanthropy had delegated the decision-making and support of these core functions to the institutions. Bill Bowen, the president of Mellon at the time, often noted that the "cost of search" was high: finding a great project or team at a lesser-known college or museum was certainly possible, but relying on the selection mechanisms that the most famous institutions used to select faculty and staff made the foundation's efforts to choose recipients of funds more efficient.

But other Mellon initiatives in the late 1990s began to lead the foundation in a different direction. Under Bowen's leadership, the foundation had fostered an in-house research capacity that evolved into a research and development function. When Bowen and his research collaborators identified problems in the sectors in which the foundation had a longstanding interest, he and the foundation's board moved toward a different kind of philanthropic action, Mellon's version of "venture philanthropy."

Bill Bowen hadn't set out to be a venture philanthropist, though he did enjoy being involved in big deals. Throughout his presidency at Mellon, he not only served as a director of American Express and Merck but also chaired the Rockefeller family investment trust that owned and in 1995 sold Rockefeller Center. As the president of Mellon, he embraced the fundamental idea that creating knowledge—in the form of rigorous, applied policy research—was both a good use of Mellon's financial assets and a way of building cultural capital to support the work of nonprofit institutions.

In the late 1980s and early 1990s, Bowen (along with his colleagues Anthony Cummings, Richard Ekman, and Richard Quandt) had been writing about the issues facing libraries, including the capital costs associated with housing miles of back issues of printed journals. When he and others at Mellon saw work on optical character recognition that was being done at the University of Michigan, he shifted out of the foundation's generally hands-off approach to grant-making and stepped in to accelerate work that would quickly become the basis of JSTOR (short for Journal Storage), the now-ubiquitous essential resource for scholars, teachers, and students around the world. Starting JSTOR—determining its governance model, who should pay for and own the technology, and how to get it into use—pushed Mellon to begin acting as an investor in its nonprofit start-up rather than a hands-off grant maker. The foundation (and JSTOR as it spun out as an independent organization) began figuring out how to manage the intellectual property of hundreds of thousands of authors and publishers, how to make the technology work when only a fraction of the academic world was even using email regularly, and how to set up a business model that worked for libraries that would not instantly be able to capture the cost savings associated with saving shelf space

The presence of business CEOs on the Mellon board, including Goldman Sachs chairman John Whitehead, NCR chief executive officer Charles Exley, and Fiduciary Trust CEO Anne Tatlock, and the enthusiasm for the success of Mellon Foundation endowment investments in venture firms such as Kleiner Perkins, Matrix, Sierra, and Benchmark Capital, surely contributed to Mellon's version of a venture philanthropy mindset when it came to the creation of entities like JSTOR. It was clear to the economist in Bill Bowen that philanthropic funds could generate outsized mission "returns" if those funds were put to work in support of networked approaches to the issues that the foundation cared about. Philanthropy, once a sleepy old-boy network that supported cherished old institutions, was venturing into territory where a new and exciting possibility was imaginable: scale.

As part of this new mode of hands-on philanthropy, Artstor's board chair Neil Rudenstine and I presented periodically to the Mellon Board of Trustees. Aware of the scope of the challenges, Mellon had invested heavily in Artstor, and the board sought, as investors, periodic reports regarding this high-risk, high-reward venture. The foundation carefully tracked our progress toward goals articulated in our business plan, including how many subscribing institutions Artstor had signed up and how many images we were processing and launching each year. Following the model of venture capital firms, the Mellon board also had a presence on the Artstor board (Lewis Bernard, formerly chief operating officer of Morgan Stanley, sat on both the Mellon and the Artstor boards). At the September 2004 board meeting, five months after Artstor had gone live as a fee-charging service, we shared the progress toward our business goals. Largely due to riding the coattails of JSTOR's success and Mellon's reputation, we had already signed up more than a hundred fee-paying institutions, although usage of the new content and tools was taking time to build. We shared some images of new collections that we had recently funded, including photos of hard-to-reach mosques and hard-to-access textiles from the personal collections of professors Walter Denny, Jonathan Bloom, and Sheila Blair. The board was dazzled by the high-resolution images that we showed.

Toward the end of the presentation, Mellon trustee Larry Ricciardi spoke up. "I was talking to a Columbia professor last week," he noted, in a warm but determined tone, "and he hates Artstor." The rest of the board knew that Larry, who had been the general counsel at IBM, enjoyed playing the role of the skunk at the garden party. But nothing grabs the attention of a board with fiduciary responsibility for billions of dollars more than the possibility that they are being shown data (or, in this case, beautiful high-resolution images) that might misrepresent the reality of how successfully the funds that they steward are being used. "Well, I'm sure that's true," was all I could say. "Everyone hates change. I'd be happy to talk to him. I generally learn a lot from conversations like that." Having it announced that Artstor was hated, even by just one person, slightly diminished the excitement of our presentation to the board. Larry had been a friendly skeptic of Artstor all along. He loved art (he would go on to serve as the chair of the board of the Morgan Library), but whenever we reported to the Mellon board, he always predicted that Artstor was not going to be financially successful. So his announcement that we had a vocal critic in James Beck wasn't a complete surprise. And off to Columbia I went a few weeks later.

I had a sense of what I would encounter in my meeting with Beck. In the three-year process of transforming Artstor from a sensible idea to a service that delivered digital content and tools over the internet into a diverse variety of library and learning environments, my colleagues and I had engaged in many conversations with passionate people, including faculty who were passionate about their teaching and library and visual resources staff who were passionate about supporting their users. Few of these people began these conversations with an instinctive enthusiasm for what an outside entity could do for them. It's very common for people to resist change unless it is immediately obvious that change will help them rather than hurt them. Among academics, resistance to change is particularly high because they are not just trying to "get through the day." They're passionate about their chosen field, and they generally do not welcome changes, particularly changes that might seem to be the work of efficiency experts.

The early days of Artstor sales and implementation had taught us valuable lessons about the quirks of trying to sell a service whose success depended on changing the behavior of faculty members who prize their autonomy. At the same time, the economic motivations of the stakeholders involved in the decision to buy or use any new service were either mixed or mixed up. Faculty members, including Jim Beck, were unaware of the costs of the materials that they used. We therefore needed to "sell" opinion-leading faculty members like Beck on the value of Artstor, but we had to do so without talking about its economic benefits for the institution, for reasons I explain below. We also had to be very careful to avoid suggesting that Artstor was a cost-cutting machine aimed at dismantling the cherished departmental slide library. We were competing with the hand-tailored service that the slide library provided, a system in which a professor put yellow sticky notes on a set of images in books and had a set of slides miraculously appear a day later. To fit into this world, we positioned Artstor as a complementary service, a digital supplement to what the department already had, not a replacement. Within the slide library, we were understandably viewed as a threat to the jobs of people who provided local, handcrafted service. To that community of visual resources curators who could either promote or denigrate Artstor to the faculty, we highlighted Artstor's ability to add to their capacity rather than threaten it.

To have any chance at getting the faculty to even try Artstor, we needed the visual resources people on our side. So as part of the diplomacy needed to explain what we were doing and how it would help faculty and staff, most Artstor staff attended and took an active part in the annual meeting of the Visual Resources Association (VRA). We volunteered to serve on working groups, and we shared the lessons we had learned. But the VRA was not the economic decision-maker in the chain. There were more ducks to align.

Based on our experiences with JSTOR, we had decided from the beginning that Artstor would sell subscriptions only to the main library of a college or university, not to art libraries and not to art history departments. This policy was particularly relevant because we were offering a service that could have been viewed as narrowly tailored to one small and impecunious department. We sold Artstor to the main library for reasons that were both practical and important for institutional change. Libraries could afford a significant license fee—art libraries and departments could not. But we also genuinely believed that Artstor's content did not and should not belong to one department; work on college campuses was becoming increasingly interdisciplinary, and many other fields were eager to use images like the Huntingtons' and Walter Denny's in their teaching and research. So long as the doors to existing slide libraries were guarded to ensure that faculty members from other departments (and students) were kept out or watched carefully, the department was not the right place to house a campus-wide database. But this plan faced a significant obstacle: the library bought books and journals. It did not pay for images.

The library, which was being asked to pay, had a different problem than the professors and the visual resources staff when it came to accepting the value of Artstor. Paying for Artstor required writing a new check that it hadn't written before. And no matter how that financial investment might work out for the institution—that is, if the university might save money on the costs of building its own collection within the art history department—any such savings were unlikely to accrue to the library. Nor would the library benefit from savings that might be gained down the line. Over time, converting images from slides to digital format could mean that the physical slide library might be able to go away, and space (usually a valuable commodity on campus) could be reclaimed. The campus would benefit, but the library wouldn't get anything. Even if the campus made the difficult decision not to replace a visual resources curator who retired, resulting in a nontrivial savings for the campus or the department, the library wouldn't benefit. We learned pretty quickly that the ideas of *an institution* and *institutional savings* were much too broad and had little meaning on the ground. At the operating level, a college isn't one institution; instead, it is composed of hundreds or thousands of loosely coordinated autonomous units for whom the greater good of the institution is basically irrelevant to their decision-making processes.

Ultimately, as libraries underwent the identity redefinition associated with acquiring access to content rather than physical objects such as books and journals, the idea of a digital image service increasingly appealed to them. They began to see their opportunity to strengthen their role as the gateway to all content, and that role aligned with their interest in moving closer to the action of classroom teaching and course reserves. Some libraries looked to the future and realized that the content, particularly digital content, used in the classroom and in other types of student support could end up being "owned" by instructional technology or academic computing staff—offices that sometimes were part of the library but often were not. For some libraries, this was an area to grow into, and Artstor might help them do so.

Because this territory was new to them, we knew we would have to bear the costs of onboarding and oversupporting them to establish our value. At the same time, the only way to appeal to faculty was to assure them that Artstor only added to what they already had and were accustomed to. The only way to appeal to the visual resource staff, whom we needed to introduce Artstor to faculty, students, and staff, was to go above and beyond to assure them that they shouldn't see themselves as conflicted buyers. That is, we had to make the case that they were needed in the ecosystem alongside Artstor and that they would benefit from joining the forward movement of progress.

Upton Sinclair famously noted the essential economic motivation that drives many decisions at the office: "It is difficult to get a man to understand something, when his salary depends on his not understanding it."[3] Sinclair's insight is particularly relevant when economic motivations are reinforced by the nonprofit currency of the realm: passion for one's particular area of focus. One lesson that we learned over and over again as we tried to diagnose the needs of the fragmented and powerful constituencies on campus was that doing whatever we could to help ease the wheels of change into motion required that we take the time to really listen to what they wanted, and to over- rather than underserve them so as to earn their trust. Listening to influential and opinionated people became our highest priority. Even if a Mellon trustee had not raised the issue, I would have enthusiastically welcomed the chance to sit with James Beck in his office.

"Sometimes when I look at the Artstor images," Beck began, "it looks like someone has vomited on my screen." Larry Ricciardi had been right; Jim Beck did, in fact, hate Artstor. But at least he cared enough to hate what we were doing. At some level, I felt, he wanted us to do what we were doing, but just do it better. In our efforts to build an image library in a short period of time to serve the teaching and research needs of thousands of scholars who worked on all aspects of cultural history across cultures, time periods, and media, we'd needed to make compromises. We knew that negotiations with skeptical and anxious museums, archives, and those who represented the commercial interests of artists and their heirs would take time. So rather than waiting to launch Artstor until we had acquired perfect images from tens of thousands of museums, photographers, scholars, publishers, churches, and private collectors, we leaned on the imperfect 35mm slides that teachers had been so eager for Mellon to digitize in the first place. But in some cases, image quality was, as Beck pointed out with zeal, a genuine concern. In our attempt to launch a service that institutions would value enough to license, we had digitized an enormous library of teaching images because customers wanted a set of images that would more or less cover the mainstream art history courses. Knowing that Artstor needed to include these images, we had scanned almost 200,000 slides from UC–San Diego. Those slides were, well, slides. Some were of high quality, but others were old and tired and miscolored.

We had chosen the UCSD collection for a number of reasons. First, because UCSD was created relatively recently as a university (in 1960) and had added art history classes during a time of rapid growth in the 1970s, it had already landed on the approach that we would later emphasize: the images should belong to the campus, not to one department. Thus UCSD had located its slide library in the university's main library rather than in the art department, and consequently each image was catalogued like a book, electronically, often with subject key words, as is common practice with books. For example, key words such as "Impressionism" and "silver" were added to individual records of slides, along with other cataloguing data that followed the Library of Congress's standardized taxonomy for books' subject matter. We knew these data would be very useful when the images were indexed in a database rather than physically sitting in a drawer filled with slides.

Although we knew that the cataloguing would be extremely useful, we also knew that the quality of the images would vary greatly. The main sources of these images were printed books and journals. Someone in the department—a faculty member, a graduate student, the departmental administrative assistant—was charged with using a copy stand that held a camera steady over the picture to take a slide photograph. The slides were thus pictures of pictures, and their quality varied with the size, quality, and level of detail of the underlying printed image that was another step removed from the underlying work. Moreover, the slide film changed over time, with hues changing as the film aged. We knew that the inconsistent quality of the digitized images would be a challenge, but we had been working under the assumption that professors had settled for these second-generation images in the past and would continue to do so in the Artstor library. We neglected to think through what we had heard in the original requests for funds to digitize individual schools' slide libraries: faculty would be happy with the pink slide that they knew and held dear from the local drawer, but it turned out that they would curse the pink slide from someone else's slide drawer. And as Professor Beck made clear, that is exactly what they did.

"And the cataloging?" Beck continued. "How can I possibly let my students loose on these records? They're just kids. They don't know that an attribution is just wrong. This is crazy." He paused: "You have no idea what you're doing." I waited for him to finish, and we sat quietly for a moment, facing each other across a grand wooden table in his book-lined office. "Thanks so much for making the time to talk about what we're doing, and also for your candor—" I began, only to be cut off by another complaint: Why weren't we allowing users to download the largest possible image?

At that point, I had been working on the project for four years; I knew about all of these issues. The cataloging was "wrong"? The cataloging data (the year a painting was painted, for example) had been typed into the UCSD computer by the person looking at the book that had served as the source of the image. That book, like any academic work, was the product of one person's argument—exactly the kind of information that Jim Beck, like all scholars, made a career of arguing with. When a local slide department created a slide, it could choose its own "facts." In other words, the local service to which they were accustomed enabled scholars like Beck to see teaching (and the material that one teaches from) as an autonomous realm governed by a particular idea of what constituted academic freedom. With Artstor, their students had unmediated access to someone else's version of the facts. Removing experts' ability to control the information that they present to students is not likely to make those experts happy. In this way, faculty members' autonomous impulses insinuate themselves what might—to outside observers—seem like straightforward institutional purchasing processes. The purchase of an off-the-rack solution like Artstor must have struck scholars like Beck as more than just a corporate or neoliberal gesture when it forced him to expose Columbia students to some academic rival's judgment about who painted a work or when. This wasn't simply a difference of opinion; to Beck, it was a major incursion against the most sacrosanct of academic values. And to be fair, this kind of change, which from afar might seem trivial, matters a great deal. As a society, we want and need experts to be experts and to care deeply about their work.

I was eventually able to get in a word or two. We knew about the issues Beck was raising, and efforts were underway to remedy them in steps over time. All teachers know something that all salespeople know: you can say the same thing for a second, third, twenty-fifth, or five hundredth time and still say it in a sincere and meaningful way. Using the same joke or phrase the second time can feel strange, even insincere. But storytelling to advance a cause or an idea is central to institutional change, and one needs to tell stories in the buyer's language. I told Beck that we were in negotiations with Jutta Gernsheim, an eighty-six-year-old woman in Switzerland, who had been photographing old master drawings in European museums since 1936. Beck admitted that it would be interesting to have access to her 179,000 photographs. His teaching assistant, who was sitting next to him during our interview, tried to shoot down the idea that Gernsheim's photos would be helpful, claiming that all of the drawings had already been published. I responded, "There are 80,000 drawings from the Uffizi alone in the Gernsheim collection; do you think that those are all published?" Beck helped on this one and said that probably only about a thousand had been published. Even though we were a long way from being able to get and share access to the Gernsheim photographs, he began to see that what we were trying to do was worth doing—and that perhaps we did have some idea of what we were doing.

Artstor needed champions, and the best way to get them was to demonstrate responsive changes to people like Professor Beck. Within a year of my meeting with Beck, we had reached an agreement with Scala, the great Italian publisher that served as the de facto in-house photographers for museums and churches across Italy, to acquire two thousand high-quality photographs of canonical artworks. I wrote Beck to share this news. "Fantastic," he responded. We had made a convert. His junior colleague, who had attended our meeting, also wrote to me: "Well, now I think of all the times I've been so mean to you, but I write to tell you that I am thrilled to see all of those high-quality images on the website. You did as you promised and now I am ready to be an enthusiastic convert. So, thank you! In addition, I am now able to think in a positive and constructive way viz Artstor as a resource."[4]

By 2009, five years after my meeting with Beck, Artstor's image library had taken hold at 1,400 institutions. It contained 1.4 million images from over 200 sources. It would have cost colleges and universities at least $10 to digitize and catalog each local slide, in addition to the costs of managing that image and addressing the rights issues; licensing an image from Scala would have cost much more. Assuming that staff or faculty at a typical institution would create 5,000 images a year (a low estimate given historic efforts), we estimated that each institution that called upon Artstor's then 1.4 million images avoided spending $10 \times 5,000$, or $50,000 per year at a minimum. If we multiply that cost savings by the number of subscribers (1,400), the annual community-wide savings were roughly $65 million more than the $6 million that they were paying for Artstor. This calculation is intentionally conservative, because Artstor provided not only the content but also rights management software that allowed faculty to download an image group directly into PowerPoint and a mobile "flashcard" app for their students, thereby saving institutions the cost of building or purchasing software to find and manage content.

With the support of venture philanthropy—start-up capital provided by the foundation to support an ambitious project—we were able to respond not only to opinion leaders like Beck but also to anxious content providers. Start-up capital allowed us to make special efforts to make the experience of change reasonably comfortable for change-resistant people and institutions. In the years before Artstor built up a base of paying customers, this investment capital allowed us to attract and retain talent, including not only programmers to create software that balanced the interests of rights-concerned content contributors and users who needed ever more flexibility but also user-facing staff to support librarians and respond to end-users' concerns and complaints about content. And we needed to communicate continually and effectively how our institutional narrative meshed with individual and institutional narratives. We were able to be responsive to our users for two main reasons. First, our market-driven focus allowed us to prioritize our users' needs and then devise and provide solutions. Second, we had the resources (in working capital provided by Mellon) to carry out this work. By year six (2010), we had reached our initial goal of $6 million in recurring revenue, and while there were still critics aplenty, faculty and staff had begun to see us as a useful partner who could help them figure out how to use digital images in teaching and research in art history and many other fields across campus.

Many good lessons can be drawn from the success of Artstor: success stories about how the problem was analyzed; how the solution was designed, financed, redesigned, and modeled; how partnerships were formed; and how the solution was executed. I summarize some of these lessons at the end of this chapter. Unfortunately, the success story also contains the seeds of future failure. Artstor's second chapter didn't go quite as well.

Artstor's Second Product: Shared Shelf

As soon as I walked into conference room 2E in the Northwestern University library and saw the scribblings on the whiteboard, I should have realized that Shared Shelf—Artstor's second major product line—was doomed.

Eight years after my visit with Jim Beck at Columbia, I had a meeting at the Center for Scholarly Communication and Digital Curation, housed in the library at Northwestern University. I was feeling pretty optimistic about our new product: cloud-based software that would allow campuses to catalog, manage, and use their own image and video collections according to the constraints associated with each campus collection's requirements. The need for such software seemed obvious. On every campus that we visited, staff worked with many different software platforms, sometimes dozens of them, to manage their rapidly developing image and video collections. Everyone on campus saw the waste associated with managing all these systems. They also knew that the content in these systems—from images of churches' stained-glassed windows taken by art historians to video clips taken by anthropologists to image collections of plant specimens housed in the ecology department—couldn't be easily shared on or off campus, couldn't easily be mixed with Artstor images or other licensed content, and sometimes couldn't even be reused if the content had been hard-coded into a one-off website built for a particular project.

These incompatible databases didn't make sense programmatically or financially. Moreover, significant additional amounts of institutional money were being spent to manage other growing collections of image files, such as photos of the college president for the communications office and photos of the schools' athletes in action for the sports information office. Colleges and universities were managing their digital media assets in hundreds of inconsistent and incompatible ways, and we knew that our experience in developing Artstor along with our increasingly trusted relationships with the institutions might position us to play a positive partnering role as colleges sought to rationalize their approaches. My colleagues at Artstor knew all about the workflow issues involved in managing image files and the data that make them usable, we knew how users wanted to make use of images, and we knew that collection builders needed to manage rights and access issues. We regaled ourselves with the early evolution of Amazon.com: in the process of selling books and CDs, Amazon had become very good at related activities, including data storage and the logistics of order fulfillment, and it became able to monetize what it had learned along the way. Our new product, Shared Shelf, was going to help campuses manage their different collections in the ways that worked for them. Some of the collections would have very simple data, perhaps just a file name, with each image; others would include the rich, complex data necessary to organize and find the images. Some image collections would be made available alongside Artstor content, others would be sent to the open web for the world to use, and still others would be locked down while the individual scholars who built the collection kept their evidence private until they published their article or book.

Telling the story of what happened with Shared Shelf is instructive of larger trends. This book isn't about the colorful history of how to manage digital images in higher education. It's about how certain types of organizations—the trusted intermediaries that can forge synthetic solutions that are compatible with institutional missions—can, under the right conditions, provide efficient and effective solutions to problems shared by many institutions. Shared Shelf aimed to provide such a solution. Artstor had been created to help colleges and universities solve the "scan my slide of the *Mona Lisa*" problem—a content-sharing problem that we had helped to alleviate. Why did we decide to expand our scope and move into the ambitious realm of building and selling an enterprise software solution? And what can we learn from our attempt to do so?

Convinced that Artstor was only the first step in solving a larger content-sharing problem, we had consulted with our board about what we thought of as "the LexisNexis model" of expanding our reach. LexisNexis had for decades built a strong reputation as a provider of legal documents to law firms. In the 1990s, it had grown from selling a useful aggregation of content (which end-users accessed through their institutional buyer) to providing a set of services that facilitated the use of that content. In the case of LexisNexis, that meant buying or building out the capacity to integrate legal case documents with every other tool that attorneys used, from their time management software to their citation management tools.[5]

In working with campuses to deploy the Artstor image library, we had found that the various locally created content projects were locked in databases and scattered around campuses. Shared Shelf would help campuses create, manage, and share that content depending on the rules governing the collection. To prepare to move from selling a content project to selling a software solution, we had brought in management consultants to determine how to ensure that we were set up for such a big undertaking. And of course, we identified the capital that we needed to build and launch the new product.

Our path of moving from a content service to a new software-as-a service (SaaS) product had deep roots in one of the central elements that helped us win people over to the Artstor image library: a high level of responsiveness to end-users' concerns that helped open their minds to changing long-established local dependencies. For the faculty and the visual resources staff who supported their classroom teaching, nothing mattered more than having access to *any and all* of the images that they wanted to use. I remember running into Jonathan Bloom, scholar of Islamic architecture, at the College Art Association (CAA) meeting in 2005. We had recently reached an agreement to scan his (and Sheila Blair's) photography of Islamic architecture to distribute via Artstor. So while there were plenty of Jim Becks running around the CAA conference, I was happy to see Jonathan, whom I saw as a friend of the endeavor. I asked him how he thought Artstor was doing, and he replied, "Not great."

He went on to ask me to do an Artstor search on my laptop for Hagia Sophia, the famous mosque (and former Byzantine church) in the middle of Istanbul. I did so and proudly showed him the 248 images that the search engine returned: details of mosaics, floor plans, and some very high-quality images. "Don't you see?" Jonathan said, irritably. He paused for a full ten seconds. "You don't have a single image of the mosque looking back from Topkapi Palace at dusk!" I was silent for a few seconds. My first thought was that although I'd worked with him for a few years and had always liked him very much, he was demonstrating the worst stereotypical traits of a demanding, uncompromising, and self-absorbed professor. After all, Artstor had a lot of images even if it didn't have the particular image that he wanted. But as his critique sank in, I realized that he was telling me something fundamentally important, not only to Artstor but also to any organization trying to win over change-resistant users: if we didn't have or couldn't do what our users wanted, we weren't going to succeed. So either we had to add every image that he and everyone else wanted—which we couldn't do—or we had to give them the capacity to do so on their own. Otherwise, we would always fall short in the comparison to their handcrafted local service.

Having some sense of this need, in the early days of building Artstor we had begun a pilot program for hosting institutional collections. Six blocks away from the Mellon Foundation, at Hunter College, the visual resources curator, Steve Kowalcik, was more than happy to work with us to provide images that the college had scanned and that we would include in the Artstor database, which would in turn be provided back to the Hunter faculty. Every month or so, Steve would walk to our offices with a hard drive containing one thousand new images that he had scanned for his faculty, and our database wizard, Riadh Amari, would stay up all night and match the images and the cataloging data in the Oracle database that served as the repository for Artstor. As a result, Hunter faculty had their own images right next to Artstor images from the Art Institute of Chicago and hundreds of other collections. From the beta testing period on, Hunter College was one of Artstor's biggest users.

In addition to providing a "both/and" service to our new faculty users, this pilot program of hosting local image collections had the added advantage of building the goodwill of the support staff, who otherwise might have viewed Artstor as a runaway bulldozer aimed straight at their jobs. The hosting element of Artstor demonstrated that part of the work needed to be local, and it allowed staff to see themselves as part of a collective solution. The hosting dramatically facilitated the take-up of the Artstor images. By 2007 (three years after Artstor went live), nineteen of the twenty leading institutional users of Artstor were taking part in the hosting pilot. Their local collections, ranging from digital image collections scanned by art history departments to personal collections of individual faculty members, incentivized busy teachers to "discover" Artstor content by providing them with the images that they knew (or at least thought) that they wanted alongside images that they didn't know that they wanted. We mixed local images with remote images, and we reconciled local labor with remote labor. In doing so we established that the remote (and networked) service was valuable. All of these supposed oppositions were, in fact, compatible. There was something in it for everyone.

Moreover, Artstor offered the promise of something even more powerful: access to a network. Hunter College is part of the City University of New York, which consists of twenty-six campuses. Because these institutions share a licensing office and had a collaborative intellectual property agreement, we could—with the flip of a switch—allow Brooklyn College or the CUNY Graduate Center to access the 30,000 images that had been scanned and cataloged by Hunter College. Even today, anxiety about the intellectual property issues associated with scanning and using images remains high; such an undertaking in 2008 was both technologically and legally difficult. Doing it via the Artstor hosting program provided value for users, allowed the contributing institutions to be good citizens within the CUNY system, and enabled the CUNY campuses to achieve some of their goals of working together. Everywhere we turned in our hosting pilot, the value seemed high.

Meanwhile, the Artstor staff was required to supply a high level of local-like support. Building these hosted collections required back-end database work, and while our database staff didn't care about sleeping during conventional hours, the queues were starting to build as institutions started to sign on for the hosting pilot. We were using the free pilot to sell subscriptions to Artstor, and while it was working in the sense of easing faculty and staff into believing in a shared approach, we knew that we needed some way to support this work financially.

The story of how we sought to convert this free hosting service into a second product—an enterprise-wide digital asset workflow and management service—throws light on the challenges of funding, creating, and implementing cost-effective infrastructure solutions for colleges and universities. While the Artstor story, including the winning over of faculty members like Jim Beck, shows us how the right alignment of interests and solutions can make a shared solution work, these alignments are hard to build and maintain. Not all opportunities are right for a synthetic service provider to tackle, even if (as in this case) the "opportunity" seems compelling. Psychologist Daniel

Kahneman has written about the optimism that is both essential to attempting new things and also potentially blinding: "One of the benefits of an optimistic temperament is that it encourages persistence in the face of obstacles. . . . Most of us view the world as more benign than it really is, our own attributes as more favorable than they truly are, and the goals we adopt as more achievable than they are likely to be."[6] Kahneman's words go a long way toward explaining my optimism about Shared Shelf's prospects as I walked into the conference room at Northwestern in January 2012.

The day before, I had visited the University of Illinois, Chicago (UIC), where I had met with the visual resources curator, who saw how Shared Shelf could help her expand the reach of her work from art history to other fields with image collections to manage. I had also spoken with other library administrators, who were intrigued by how Shared Shelf might help the library serve UIC's rapidly expanding health sciences programs by managing teaching and research image collections in the biological sciences. A visual resources staff member gave me a tour before the meeting, pointing out UIC's major conversion of the first floor of the 1960s brutalist library into spaces that the students loved with soft sofas, "smart" classrooms, a café, and spaces for social interaction and performances within the shell of a classic but cold building. The UIC staff and I spoke about how Shared Shelf would be hosting a collection of images portraying innovative library and classroom renovations (in support of the Flex Space project created by the SUNY and Cal State systems to share design ideas across campuses). They were intrigued by the idea of showing off their successful reconception and reinhabiting of their own workspace to other libraries via this shared collection. After a positive reception from the UIC team, whom I had never met before, I was feeling pretty good about the prospects of introducing Shared Shelf to old friends at Northwestern.

The scribbles on the whiteboard in Northwestern's Center for Scholarly Communication and Digital Curation had a few of the usual symbols that almost anyone can draw: databases (a square with an oval on top), lines with arrows passing to and through clouds and back to databases, and a few boxy computer monitors representing end-users. The acronyms and labels floating around or on top of the sketches were very familiar to me: ULAN, LCSH, CONA, DOI, IIIF, Kaltura, Hydra, Mirador. Other scribbles, such as "Google Images," would have been familiar to most people. Overall, like most whiteboard scribbles, the whole picture would have been indecipherable to anyone who hadn't been in the room when it was drawn. But as I walked into a room of familiar and friendly faces—Claire Stewart, Harlan Wallach, and Bill Parod—I recognized that what they had scribbled on their whiteboard was remarkably similar to the drawings on the whiteboards and large sheets of easel paper stuck to the walls of our own conference rooms at Artstor's offices in New York. It wasn't going to be a meeting like I'd had with Jim Beck, I thought. We were going to be on the same page.

Before I go any further, I should mention why these members of the Northwestern staff were not only friendly but also friends. Before there was an Artstor, there was the idea of an Artstor, and the Mellon Foundation had undertaken a significant exploration of what the digitization of art would mean—what it would cost, what it would require, how it would work legally—both in the United States and around the world. In 1998, the foundation had been working on digitization, but "working on" meant providing grants to institutions of higher education, art, and culture to solve problems; the foundation itself had no capacity to carry out the operations associated with digitizing art. At that point, Mellon had already seeded the project that quickly grew into JSTOR, which was thriving as an independent entity. But in 1998, president Bill Bowen visited his former Princeton colleague Henry Beinen, president of Northwestern, and while on the Evanston campus, he saw a demo of high-resolution photography that Professor Sarah Frazier, of Northwestern's art history department, had overseen of ninth-century CE wall paintings made by Buddhist monks in Dunhuang, in the middle of the Gobi Desert in China. Bill was entranced by the power of the high-resolution photography, the international scope of the work, and his belief that China was going to be the central node of global growth in the coming years. Over the next five years, the Mellon Foundation committed more than $10 million to create new super-high-resolution photographs of forty of the caves and many of the manuscripts and silk wall hangings that English and French explorers had taken from Dunhuang at the beginning of the twentieth century.

That project was extremely ambitious. The eighteen-foot-high wall paintings in the caves had to be photographed with a minimum of lighting to avoid damage; the interpretation (and hence cataloging) of the images required a deep knowledge of medieval Chinese Buddhist thought. Working with the Chinese, the curators of the British Library, the Bibliothèque Nationale, and the Musée Guimet in Paris (which held the manuscripts and silk wall hangings) required highly polished diplomatic skills to address a hundred years of international tension over the Western nations' having whisked away artworks from Dunhuang in the early 1900s.

As a probe to determine how hard it would be to launch the next Mellon project after JSTOR and to build Artstor, the Dunhuang work provided many insights. We learned about the high cost of doing very-high-quality original photography, and we developed an understanding of the complexities of reconciling the interests of those who cared for objects and sites and those who wanted to use images of that content, along with a million other lessons. For the teams deploying the $10 million in Mellon funding, the investment of time and energy—and the concomitant learning—was immense. Northwestern's Harlan Wallach spent months in China leading teams of photographers who assembled a track (like those used in making movies) to systematically capture every two inches of the walls while carefully navigating around giant sculptures. Bill Parod assembled the massive image files and coordinated them with the cataloging data. And from 1998 to 2002, $4 million of grant funds supporting the Dunhuang work enabled the Northwestern team to accumulate trailblazing experience in the digital imaging world and turned their passion for the project into expertise. By the time I visited the Northwestern library years after the completion of the Dunhuang project, the team had built on their record of digital library accomplishment and created the Center for Scholarly Communication and Digital Curation to tackle similar exciting digital adventures.

While the Northwestern meeting was, indeed, friendly, it became clear over the coming year that Northwestern was not going to sign up for Shared Shelf. At Artstor, we were accustomed to a slow sales cycle given the coalition building required to support library acquisitions. But as 2012 progressed, we heard that Northwestern was becoming a founding partner in a network of library-based software developers who were writing, sharing, and adapting open-source code for a project then called Hydra, later renamed Samvera. In 2013, Tom Cramer, chief technology strategist for the Stanford University Libraries and one of the project's founders, described the effort and why it was able to attract participants:

> The pattern of collaboration is baked into Hydra's DNA; from the very beginning, the software has been a shared development effort. . . . I think the biggest draw to aggressive collaboration is the quality of the technical work on Hydra. Developers like working with good developers. . . . We have a lot of coordination, a lot of consensus building, and very little central planning. In short, there aren't "rules" so much as a community process, and people get out what they put in.[7]

Interinstitutional collaboration through projects such as Hydra give talented staff a way to grow, to learn from others across the network, and to build solutions. Few people argue ideologically against bottom-up communities built around collaboration, and the promise of free software code also usually resonates with nonprofit communities, especially when open-source software is juxtaposed to closed and proprietary products. Joining Stanford, Cornell, the University of Virginia, and other community-leading libraries as a partner in Hydra gave Northwestern staff what they saw as an exciting opportunity for growth and for solving local problems in a way that felt networked and global.

In the early 2000s, Harlan Wallach and his colleagues had invested enormous amounts of time, energy, and creativity in the Dunhuang effort; their "return" on that investment came as they were asked to present their work around the world at illustrious venues, such as the Getty Conservation Institute and the Aga Khan Development

Network. Their work was also featured in *National Geographic*.[8] University staff members' desire to use their creative energies on projects that also grow their reputation and their rewards highlights a significant challenge that we faced in selling Shared Shelf and that many such synthetic service providers face: in many parts of the mission-driven nonprofit world, traditional business measures of success, such as revenue growth, don't apply. The coins of the realm are intellectual leadership, professional development, and the prestige associated with creating compelling solutions. By the time my colleagues and I showed up on the Northwestern campus with a cloud-based digital media solution, the talented staff had already expanded the expertise that the Dunhuang project had fostered. Specifically, Northwestern's Advanced Media Production Studio had been formed as a professional production team within Northwestern University Information Technology (NUIT)'s Academic and Research Technologies. From their Dunhuang experience, they had grown to support all multimedia applications in teaching and research. Moreover, the Library's Center for Scholarly Communication and Digital Curation had established itself as a valued place where local experts supported "Northwestern scholars through active exploration of new models for disseminating research results" and developed "programs to support long-term retention and reuse of the scholarly output of the University."[9]

Larry Bacow's insight into why universities can't save money ("There is no natural constituency for cost control on a university campus") comes to mind when one reads an FAQ response from Northwestern's representative to the Samvera (formerly Hydra) community which Northwestern joined as a programming partner instead of subscribing to Shared Shelf:

Q: How do you describe the Return on Investment of community work for your local resources when it comes to Samvera?

A: It is hard to quantify the return on investment and I think does a disservice to what we gain when working with many people across multiple institutions. I tend to look

> at pull requests and contributors on github repositories
> if I need some data. I ask the developers and metadata
> folks to share stories with me of what they have gained
> personally/professionally.[10]

In other words, the satisfaction (and career-advancement rewards) that accrue to successful innovators within mission-driven organizations can be a priority in decision-making, irrespective of what the principles of fiscal efficiency of the larger institution might be. As I discuss more fully in chapter 5, any particular unit may have its own narrative about the mission of the institution: the college's lacrosse coach believes passionately that a new AstroTurf practice field is the best way for the institution to fulfill its mission, while a particle physicist feels the same way about an upgrade to the linear accelerator. If the library or academic computing department believes that investing in building and continually maintaining open-source software fulfills the institution's mission and if the staff who do so are celebrated as innovative entrepreneurs, then an outside provider of efficient and effective solutions might be sitting in a conference room with a heavily conflicted buyer. The accomplished team at Northwestern was doing exactly what they were rewarded for, and the interest in paying us to do very similar work wasn't going to be aligned with their personal or professional reward structures.

When I first saw the familiar scribbles in the conference room at Northwestern, I should have realized that in this case, being among kindred spirits was *not* promising for Artstor's significant bet on Shared Shelf. Although great minds may think alike, they rarely want to write a check to pay for what their own great minds are ready, willing, and perhaps able to do on their own. With the Artstor image library, we had found a way for various local constituencies to work with us as collaborators in building a collective solution because we could provide some content that they simply couldn't get on their own. In contrast, Shared Shelf came across as a significant challenge to the local do-it-yourself solutions. And as 2012 and 2013 progressed, we ran into other difficulties that we hadn't expected.

In 2007–2008, before embarking on the development of what would become Shared Shelf, we had held a series of meetings with opinion-leading librarians. They told us that a cloud-based asset management service that centralizes the management of images in the library would give them the opportunity to supplement their current role of external collection building (i.e., buying books and journals) with a new role of internal collection building on the campus.

For some of the libraries that we met with, relying on an external partner fit perfectly with their plans. For example, at Harvard the prospect of relying on Shared Shelf worked because the library was eager to replace a locally built image management system that had been functioning as an infrastructure for image management for twenty-one different Harvard departments. That system had been implemented in the 1990s and was now distinctly outdated and difficult to maintain. Yale was in the process of creating a new administrative organization, the Office of Digital Assets and Infrastructure (ODAI), to support the digital work of its libraries, museums, and academic departments.[11] Other leading libraries also saw how the new service could support their own imperatives. As Anne Kenney, the dean of the libraries at Cornell, explained, "The art history department and the School of Architecture are 500 feet apart physically. And the only sharing that they have ever done of images is through the collections that they host in Artstor." Carol Mandel, dean of the libraries at NYU, reminded us that the Shared Shelf project was valuable even without interinstitutional sharing of collections. "If we can even share content on our own campus," she noted, "we would save a lot of money and do a lot of good. Sharing beyond that would be a bonus."

Our excitement was building around the idea of this new product. But as the financial implications of the Great Recession of 2008–2009 played out on campuses, we discussed whether this was really the time to launch a new product. Given that enthusiasm still seemed high among these campus partners even in the face of the newly tightened campus budgets, we convinced ourselves that financial constraints on campuses would motivate colleges to eliminate the inefficiencies that Shared Shelf could replace. As part of our process of demonstrating to the Mellon Foundation that Artstor merited continued investment, we had promised to seek coinvestment from potential Shared Shelf institutions. We had planned on raising $25,000 commitments from ten willing partners, or a total of $250,000, but we did so much better than that. Recognizing how important an enterprise-wide system like Shared Shelf would be, Harvard and Yale each committed $300,000 to the creation of the service, while nine other colleges and universities pledged another $600,000. As we announced the partnership in July 2009, knowing that budgets were going to be under stress because of the crash of endowments and the Great Recession, these institutional commitments persuaded us that we had the right product for the times.

Times Change

Artstor had begun as an idea in 2000, became legally independent from the Mellon Foundation in 2003, and launched as a live service in 2004. Between the initial Artstor product launch and the announcement of Shared Shelf in July 2009, other changes beyond the Great Recession took place. In 2006, Mellon's longtime president, Bill Bowen, who had worked with the Mellon board to provide many millions of dollars in grant funds for the project, turned seventy-three and was required by Mellon bylaws to retire. The new president of the foundation, former University of Chicago president Don Randel, began his service in March 2007. During the transition, we knew that we might have to prove ourselves. But we didn't know that we wouldn't be awarded any further working capital from the Mellon Foundation until 2015.

In 2007 we began to work on the idea of Shared Shelf, and I had thought our shared DNA with the Mellon Foundation, combined with our meeting the goals that we had jointly developed, would lead to Mellon's continued support. Mellon continued to provide us with free office space in their complex, and we reported to the Mellon board regularly. We understood that a new president had every right to decide whether to continue funding for Artstor or any other project, and we were encouraged by Don Randel's deep commitment to the humanities and his early comments in support of digitization as a method of decreasing the costs of physical slide libraries. We had many conversations with our former colleague, program officer Don Waters, about what Shared Shelf might be and how it might advance the goals that we all had started Artstor to carry out. But given the new president's unfamiliarity with the project, the foundation suggested commissioning an external review to help the foundation understand how well Artstor was actually progressing. In an email from December 2007, Don Waters noted that the study would "help Mellon evaluate Artstor from several key perspectives—organizational, financial, governance, and service— and would make recommendations with the aim of making Artstor a permanent fixture in the community." He added that the review would be available to Artstor and Mellon to help with "planning and decision-making on both sides."[12]

The foundation suggested that Donald Opatrny conduct the external review. Opatrny was a Goldman Sachs partner whom Randel knew from his time as provost at Cornell, where Opatrny had served on the board. Opatrny worked with a subcommittee of trustees and Artstor senior leaders during the first half of 2008, and we subsequently presented the results first to Mellon program staff, then to the Mellon officers, and finally to the Mellon board in December 2008. As part of the Opatrny review, we presented a plan for instituting regular subscription-fee increases, using some of our reserves, and building out Shared Shelf sales. At the end of the process, Opatrny accepted an invitation to join the Artstor board. But despite the external review being positively received, we were not able to raise any additional funding from Mellon for Shared Shelf. In chapter 5, I'll return to the complexities of depending on philanthropic funding for growth equity.

In the eight years that we sought Mellon funding for Shared Shelf, we tried a lot of different ways to fund ourselves. Along the way, we had some evident successes. For example, in 2009, while Mellon was still considering support for Shared Shelf, it made a grant to the Society of Architectural Historians (SAH), a leading academic society with three thousand members, to host the collections of its scholar-photographer members on Shared Shelf. That collection would live on the platform in the same way that Harvard's would, and the $900,000 that would come to us via the grant to SAH was a good sign of Mellon's enthusiasm for the larger Shared Shelf project. In the fall of 2010, the Institute of Museum and Library Services (IMLS), the major federal funding agency for libraries, awarded us (in partnership with Columbia University) one of only two National Leadership Awards to build a project on the Shared Shelf platform. Between the $750,000 IMLS grant, the $900,000 from SAH, and the $1.2 million raised from our eleven college and university partners, we were excited by our success at bootstrapping, and we were confident in our ability to raise the larger investment that we needed from Mellon. We knew that we needed that investment because building a scalable cloud-based digital asset management system was a big job. As people were creating more and bigger digital files, they were starting to turn to services like Dropbox, which were setting high bars for performance but still were not integrated into the academic environment in the way that we were.

At first, Mellon was troubled by a mistake in a financial report that our outsourced finance office (shared with JSTOR's parent organization, ITHAKA) had filed. After that problem was cleared up, the foundation told us that before we sought any new funds, we should spend down the amount remaining in a content sponsorship grant that we had received in 2006. I probably didn't help matters by conveying subtly or not so subtly to Don Waters, our program officer with whom I had worked to create Artstor, my sense that I felt that Artstor was entitled to more support. After all, it had accomplished what the foundation had created it to accomplish, and the external review had been very successful. By the time I visited Northwestern in January 2012, we had 48 colleges and universities signed up as subscribers for Shared Shelf. We had come pretty far, but we also had a long way to go. In 2012, as we struggled to gain momentum on sales, we also found ourselves up to our ears in difficult-to-fulfill promises and evolving expectations.

In 2009, we had been excited to announce the partnership that helped us launch Shared Shelf. We had testimony—and very real cash commitments—from an outstanding set of campuses. We all were pulling our oars in the same direction. By 2012, things had begun to change. Our partnership with Harvard was growing increasingly strained. We had thought that we survived the financial crisis of 2009 because Harvard and others had planned to continue participating in our partnership despite widespread economic uncertainty. But over the fullness of time, we faced big challenges that were at least partially attributable to secondary effects of the Great Recession. Specifically, Harvard University as a whole faced significant cost-cutting in the wake of its endowment crash. Dale Flecker, Harvard University Library's associate director for planning and systems, had been leading Harvard's complex library technical environment for twenty-nine years and was deeply respected throughout the library community. We had counted it as a major victory when Dale was quoted (in the press release announcing the Shared Shelf endeavor) as saying, "Images present significant challenges. Having worked with Artstor for years in this domain, we believe that combining forces and know-how offers the most promising approach to these challenges." Then, in an early effort to minimize layoffs associated with the financial crisis, Harvard offered very generous retirement incentives to longstanding employees.[13] Dale was among the first to take the offer. When Nancy Cline, the longstanding librarian of Harvard College, followed Dale into retirement in 2010, Artstor's relationship with Harvard was now owned and managed by new executives and staff eager to look good as the libraries underwent a massive restructuring. *Harvard Magazine* described the difficult environment as "the Libraries' Rocky Transition."[14]

Working with new and stressed people is always difficult, but the discontinuity caused by Dale and Nancy's departure had deeper implications. In leading the plan for Harvard to substitute the cloud-based Shared Shelf for Harvard's own locally built (and increasingly difficult to maintain) Visual Images Application (VIA), Dale had confided in us the key to our success: "You cannot, I repeat cannot, give the catalogers everything that they want." In his twenty-nine years of working in the Harvard libraries, Dale had learned that their passionate and brilliant staff were every bit as resistant to compromise as the passionate and brilliant faculty of Harvard University. He knew that if we let them, they would demand that we build the system around their particular desires and practices. In pulling together the twenty-one Harvard departments that used VIA, Dale had accomplished a rare centralizing of university functions (rare anywhere, but more so at the notoriously decentralized Harvard). Without Dale and with the chaos churning in the Harvard libraries, we struggled to agree on specifications, and the project was delayed. Helen Shenton, who was brought in to lead the libraries from 2010 to 2013, later confessed to me that "Artstor was caught in the crossfire." The head of cataloging for the Harvard Libraries—one of the experts whom Dale had warned us about making excessive demands that would sink the project—was put in charge of managing the relationship with us.

Our partnership with Yale also grew somewhat strained, mostly because it had fallen into oblivion. Unlike Harvard, where Shared Shelf was slated to replace a centralized and valued system, Yale had envisioned Shared Shelf as a means of building a collective approach to digital asset management across a university that by its own account, "lagged compared to other universities in digitizing their resources in the past."[15] In announcing the newly formed and what was intended to be a well-funded Office of Digital Assets and Infrastructure (ODAI), which was notably created outside of the library, Provost Andrew Hamilton celebrated the possibility of an integrated, campus-wide approach to managing digital content: "Yale will be making a significant commitment to develop the infrastructure necessary to support the creation and organization of our intellectual assets, which, in turn, will enable robust access to, and dissemination of, those assets, both on and off campus."[16]

This new Yale office, ODAI, was announced on September 26, 2008. Two weeks after the announcement, in the wake of the Lehman Brothers collapse, the Dow Jones suffered its largest weekly drop ever. By the end of the academic year, Hamilton had left Yale to take the role of vice chancellor at Oxford. ODAI lost much of its central funding and was left to navigate between the library, the two art museums, the natural history museum, the art history image collection, and scientists' endless needs for digital research support. Because the Shared Shelf relationship had been established and owned by the now virtually orphaned ODAI, the library decided to develop its own image management platform (using the same open-source software code base that Northwestern was going to develop for its own local use). Earlier in the relationship, the art history faculty had been very happy that all of their Yale slide library images were hosted alongside the Artstor collection. But they grew increasingly frustrated that they couldn't immediately access all the new images that the visual resources staff had continued to produce. That desire, of course, was what Shared Shelf would enable. But in the time that ODAI was losing its Yale-wide mandate, the art history department's image management team had been absorbed into the library. The library wanted little to do with the Shared Shelf relationship that was "owned" by ODAI outside the library. And the art history faculty began to view Artstor as deliberately unhelpful and unwilling to keep its image collection up to date.

The challenges did not end there. We announced that we would create APIs (software interchanges) that would enable Shared Shelf to work alongside the various modules of the community-built open-source Hydra system that Northwestern and Yale were starting to work with; we wanted to convey the same complementary spirit that we had earlier established with the visual resources curators. But places that were under the spell of "open-source is free" resisted subscribing to Shared Shelf. As just one example, we were confident that Shared Shelf was perfect for Columbia. In 2010, working in close collaboration with a former Artstor colleague—Carole Ann Fabian, who had moved on to become the director of the fabled Avery Art and Architecture Library at Columbia—we had received a National Leadership Award from the federal Institute of Museum and Library Services. The award provided funding for Columbia and Artstor to build a data standard for cataloging buildings within Shared Shelf. Over years of partnership with the university, we had also modified our Artstor library software to work seamlessly with a Columbia-developed viewer called Mediathread.[17] And with our dwindling supply of Mellon content funds, we had subsidized two Columbia collections of QuickTime Virtual Reality (QTVR) photography, working with Columbia's art history media center. Finally, Columbia's image collections had been hosted in the free hosting service since the very early days of Artstor, and faculty members (including Jim Beck before his death in 2007) were happy with the combined service. Then, in May 2012, I met with the person who had the authority to approve Columbia's subscription to Shared Shelf, which would serve not only the library and the media center for visual arts but also the dental school, which was also looking for an image management solution. Shared Shelf would cost Columbia $20,000 a year. "I'm sorry," the decision-maker said. "It's just too expensive. We're just going to put two of our programmers on developing a solution." I was tempted to point out the running costs of supporting two programmers in New York City compared to our fees, but doing so wouldn't have gotten us anywhere.

Lessons Learned: What Worked (Artstor)

Before we turn to asking why institutions are so resistant to change and explaining how Artstor and other ventures have had whatever degree of success they've had in forging synthetic partnerships with to institutions of higher education, we should take stock of lessons learned in story of Artstor's two major products. Specifically, in setting up Artstor's digital image library, we learned to:

1. **Recognize that a jolt to a system can provide an impetus for change, but not make our solution the enemy of the status quo.** At some point, digital images were going to replace slides and analog images. To be successful, we knew that we had to be perceived as supporting faculty and staff rather than as part of the menacing change that was bearing down on them. We needed to be seen and respected as

collaborators who respected them and helped them continue to do their work, albeit in an evolving manner.

2. **Catch the wind of pent-up and growing wants and needs that the old infrastructure can't or won't accommodate.** Over the decades, a system had coalesced around the creation of slides for teaching art and architecture, but that system created problems for various groups and left many needs unmet. Faculty and students from other departments usually had little or no access to the slide library; the main library saw the building of book and journal collections, not image acquisition, as its function; and most students were passive recipients of images even as pedagogical trends emphasized active roles for students. Teachers using slides couldn't zoom in, as one can do with a digital image; if they wanted to show a detail, they had to prepare a slide of that detail. Independently, none of these unmet needs would justify building the Artstor library, but together they supported a new model for the creation and sharing of digital images.

3. **Provide familiar transitional steps to convince the wait-and-see crowd.** We were determined to provide a drag-and-drop slide sorter function even though the web-based technology for doing so (in 2003) was complicated to work out. At that time, faculty were accustomed to sorting slides on large table-mounted light boxes in the slide rooms. These light boxes made the slides to be used in a lecture visible (to be seen, slides need illumination from behind) and allowed instructors to easily reorder the slides to build their argument. Re-creating this function seemed essential, but the web protocols at the time only allowed users to rearrange objects by renumbering them and reloading the site (rather than dragging and dropping them). In the end, we used a "thin client" web-delivered software that created various challenges but allowed users to drag and drop images whether they were using a PC or a Mac.

4. **Create shared plumbing that individual institutions
   can't**. In building a large and growing library of images,
   we identified and added content by negotiating with
   individual museums and other image collections in ways
   that local building efforts cannot. Doing so required us to
   understand not only the wants and needs of those who had
   desirable content, but also the legal and technical barriers
   to aggregating and distributing it. Being able to demonstrate
   the promise of content that the local provider couldn't
   access was fundamental to launching Artstor. If the local
   offering had as much potential for offering content as Artstor
   did, our only value-add would have been cost-effectiveness,
   which in itself would not have been a convincing argument.

5. **Align with, and work within, trust networks**. An obviously
   appealing direct-to-consumer offering doesn't need to be
   embedded in a trust network. For example, the simple-to-
   use solution provided by Uber didn't rely upon local taxi
   companies in any way. Uber just skipped over the existing
   infrastructure. However, when introducing new solutions in
   harder-to-change, mission-driven environments, synthetic
   solution providers need to recognize that faculty and staff
   will look to their trusted communities and networks to
   see if an offering is blessed. Thanks to conferences and
   listservs, communities of shared practice are stronger
   than ever with regard to legitimizing—or delegitimizing—
   new players. Working to respect the norms of and thus to
   gain the trust of horizontal communities such as the Art
   Libraries Society of North America (ARLIS/NA), the Visual
   Resources Association (VRA), the Coalition for Networked
   Information (CNI), the College Art Association (CAA), and
   the International Image Interoperability Framework (IIIF)
   was an absolute necessity for us.

6. **Overserve users for the sake of facilitating change in
   change-resistant environments**. Individuals acting under a
   banner of mission that they get to define for themselves have
   few incentives to be open to external offerings. When our

users asked for their own local images to be made available alongside our images, we put them in. While it was more efficient to train the trainer on campuses, we also offered to train individual users, which sometimes included helping them learn how to turn on their computer. Onboarding and overserving cost a lot, but without these efforts, individuals who have their own reasons to resist change may succeed in doing exactly that.

Lessons Learned: What Didn't Work (Shared Shelf)

A new product can fail for many reasons. Most obviously, it might be a bad or unneeded product, a poorly executed product, or even a decent product based on a flawed assumption. It could be the right product at the wrong time. Or it might be a good solution, but it might not be marketed and sold effectively. It might fail because of the quality of post-sales service or because a competitor does a better job in terms of quality, price, or service.

I can have only so much perspective on mistakes that I made, or that we made as an organization. The point of this book is to help our sector realistically approach the key questions of financing and executing services collectively and in a way that can make a material difference in the future of higher education. I believe that documenting as much as I can about the possible contributors to the failure of Shared Shelf represents at least as much of a contribution to the sector as telling Artstor's earlier success story. As CEO, I pushed us to develop Shared Shelf and to keep investing in it over time, even as it was struggling to gain traction. The reasons for its failure are most likely based on my failure to ensure that we executed well enough on one or many aspects of building or deploying the service. There are other lessons to be learned as well. Specifically, we also learned about various challenges faced by new ventures seeking to bring about institutional change:

1. **The do-it-yourself inclination is widespread but is particularly strong among well-resourced institutions.** As

the faculty and staff at the financially strongest institutions continually redefine their work and mission, many are predisposed to building their own solutions, either locally or in consortia. Any service that seeks to even partially displace an existing local solution will run into this resistance and must make a strong case that the solution is better, not just cheaper, because local players are deeply invested in not seeing their own costs. And they are sometimes rewarded with recognition for devising their own solutions. In addition, the isomorphic impulse tends to be to look up, not down. Universities want to be like Harvard, so if the well-resourced places are inclined to local solutions, some others will surely follow.

2. **Discontinuity is particularly disruptive for sustaining change in nonprofit institutions**. When the coin of the realm is recognition of one's accomplishments, every changeover in decision-makers can lead to a dramatic change of course. Because bottom-line financial success measures are not the only focus in colleges and universities and are not systematically passed from one key project player to the next, all leaders set their own mission priorities. New efforts can be successful when they win over key individuals, but if the base isn't widened to include a larger part of the institution, discontinuity in the cast of characters can swiftly destabilize projects and relationships. The discontinuity between our project and the key players at our founding funder (Mellon) and our most valued customer (Harvard) was demoralizing and, in the end, debilitating.

3. **In changing practices that require sign-off from various and variously authorized campus offices, it is extremely difficult to scale up partnerships**. A new service that reaches across budget silos means that the service hasn't been purchased before, which in turn means a lack of standardized buyers and procedures in and across institutions. Unlike the National Student Clearinghouse, which *always* works with registrars, Shared Shelf could

be licensed by the library, departments, or instructional technologists. It also could be used by communications offices, public relations offices, and science labs. Not having one standard buyer makes for a long and complicated sales process because no one sees the need to solve a shared problem. In fact, any one of the potential campus coalition of buyers might see an external solution as replacing the most interesting and autonomous part of their own work.

4. **Establishing an effort that is based on being an institutional shared good is difficult within a democratic decision-making environment**. Even though someone in a leadership role at the eight Shared Shelf partner institutions sought an enterprise-wide solution, it was the case that departmental decision-making, including decisions regarding software, remained largely a democratic and self-determining process. Jason Kovari, our lead contact at Cornell (one of Shared Shelf's biggest institutional users, with thirty-nine separate projects managed in the service), reminded us that he too had to sell the service to users, who had the freedom to choose from many software solutions that they can utilize, buy, or spin up themselves.

5. **Although raising capital is difficult, the relationship risks in how one chooses to do so can be distinct from the business/investment risks**. At first, Harvard saw us as a compatible partner, but having deployed capital for our work, it eventually began treating us like a vendor. The reputational risks became incredibly dangerous for us. We had believed that having Harvard to testify to our value would help us in the marketplace; but as we discovered, their potential to criticize us publicly would also have a powerful effect. Once things became complicated for whatever reason—our fault, their fault, no one's fault—the problem became ours. After the original players left the scene, our having taken capital from consumers in the marketplace changed the terms of the relationship in unexpected and not always pleasant ways.

6. **A thesis can be right, but the organization might not be capable of creating and implementing it—and early enthusiastic buyers may not represent the market.** At the same time we were pursuing the LexisNexis model of moving from content to workflow tools, another organization that licensed content through libraries also began expanding into the management of research data: the enormous science publishing firm, Elsevier.[18] In a 2016 presentation describing Elsevier's and other companies' expansion into tools that support data creation, curation, and processing, Lorcan Dempsey, a well-respected strategist in the library community, noted, "Workflow is the new content."[19] By this he meant that while the traditional work of libraries focused on acquiring content in one form or another, they were now facing a future where the work of assembling, managing, and integrating data and evidence from their campus faculty and from other sources might become the primary activity of the library. Artstor was tiny in comparison to Elsevier; we thought we could expand in ways that were theoretically compelling but that required more reach and clout than we had. The enthusiasm of long-standing partners such as Harvard and Cornell led us to believe that we were capable of expansion. But these partners knew us very well, and they were outliers in their desire to take an enterprise-wide approach to digital asset management. The rest of the market didn't feel the same way, and if we'd done more research, we might have realized that the market to support humanistic collections workflow was not deep, even if the idea was taking hold in the sciences.

7. **Goodwill and mission alignment go only so far when a product is capital intensive.** At the same time that Artstor was bootstrapping its cloud-based asset management service, another small startup—Dropbox—was doing the same. In 2008, as Artstor put together the $1.2 million in funding from the Shared Shelf partnership, Dropbox raised $6 million

in funding from the venture capital firm Sequoia. Artstor gained an extra $750,000 from the IMLS grant in 2010; at roughly the same time, Dropbox's Series B funding in 2011 provided the company with $250 million of working capital. I remember describing to Artstor board member Greg Avis the process of trying to get grants in which we promised to do work that regularly required more effort to complete than the grant paid for. "At a time when the cost of capital for most growing businesses is pretty close to zero," he sighed, "for you it's pretty close to infinite. It's almost impossible to get, and when you do get it, it costs you more than it's worth."[20]

———

In building the Artstor image library, we created a new and trusted set of relationships in which we provided a service that otherwise would have been resolved locally. In developing Shared Shelf, we tried to do so but faltered. In chapter 3, I describe how understanding the powerful web of institutional change resistance is essential to those who are deciding how to forge these types of solutions.

3

The Hard Reality of Observed Practices

INSTITUTIONAL RESISTANCE TO CHANGE

In March 2013, I had coffee with W. Taylor Reveley III in the president's house at William & Mary. Taylor had served on the Mellon Foundation board since 1994 and had been a great friend to me and to Artstor since its founding. "Heaven only knows," he had written me at one point, "how many mountains you've had to climb, and deep abysses you've had to bridge." After a pleasant and wide-ranging conversation over lunch, he asked who else I planned to see on campus. Having failed to convince the library staff to meet with me to discuss Shared Shelf, I had set up a meeting with the visual resources curator, who was based in the art history department. Taylor knew that William & Mary had not subscribed to the Artstor image library until a full seven years after its launch. When I mentioned that I was off to the art history slide room, where the faculty and staff had been implementing their own local image management system, he smiled and wished me luck.

My experience at William & Mary proved to be no different from my experiences at Northwestern and Columbia. Because I had grown accustomed to a very long sales cycle and had come to accept the process of trying to convince people across various departments about possible new ways of working, I hadn't given much thought to my impending sequence of meetings at William & Mary. One might *theorize* that organizational leaders define or at least shape the actions of those below them in the hierarchy, but I was used to the *practice* of trying to sell change within colleges and universities, and I knew that the president of a university was not relevant to the work of convincing staff to subscribe to our service. Taylor was never going to *order* the art historians to buy or use Artstor. He was never going to *order* the librarian or the director of academic computing to buy Shared Shelf (even though he, like all college and university presidents, recognized the serious and growing problem of increased costs and wanted to reduce redundant spending whenever possible). Looking back, I recognize that I never even asked myself why the president or the provost wouldn't direct staff to license a product that was (a) good enough for the most discriminating schools, which many schools usually aspired to imitate; and (b) affordable and showed every sign of being able to save the institution a significant amount of money.

A Theory of Change

In 2009, I was submitting a brief article to the *Stanford Social Innovation Review* on lessons learned with respect to introducing change to change-resistant institutions in my work at Artstor. I asked the noted sociologist Neil Smelser (1930–2017), who was spending a year in residence at the Russell Sage Foundation a few blocks away, if he would look at my draft. After reading it, he said, "It's interesting. Let me ask, though: What's your theory of change?"

My brow tightened in irritation. What did he mean? I wasn't trying to create a grand theory. In my article I had distilled a few lessons about how to convince faculty to change their behavior and how to get staff to pay for a service that they had been inclined to provide on their own. These lessons were pragmatic; there was nothing theoretical about them.

I had a bit of a history of being defensive about the importance of having a theory. Twenty years earlier, just as I was starting on my dissertation, I had confessed to one of my advisors, Lawrence Manley, "I'm worried because I don't really have a theory of literature." Larry responded, "I should hope not. You're what, twenty-five years old? I sure hope that you don't have a theory of literature. Pay attention to what the texts are actually saying. And then say what you have to say."

Now, as I write this book five years after leaving Artstor, I see why Neil Smelser was absolutely right to ask about my theory of change—not because it related to the operations of Artstor, but because having such a theory represents an essential part of outlining a path for ventures intending to forge synthetic solutions with colleges and universities. I needed to sort through the evidence of what my colleagues and I learned as practitioners—and then do something with the evidence. And that calls for theory. As the philosopher Ernst Cassirer argued, contextualizing evidence from individual observation requires theory to give meaning to the particular experience: "The aim of theoretical thinking . . . is primarily to deliver the contents of sensory or intuitive experience from the isolation in which they originally occur. It causes these contents to transcend their narrow limits, combines them with others, compares them, and concatenates them in a definite order. . . . Thus, every separate event is ensnared, as it were, by invisible threads of thought, that bind it to the whole."[1]

Burton Clark (1921–2009), one of the leading sociologists of higher education, was highly suspicious of academic research on the subject of institutional change in colleges and universities that drifted into theory while staying removed from practical experience: "Researchers write mainly for one another," he wrote. "They publish articles in journals that practitioners do not read." The lessons learned by doing things, he concluded, should come first and *then* be supplemented by theories to contextualize the lived evidence:

"We who study university change can reduce the research-practice disconnect. . . . We can reason inductively from the experience of on-the-ground practitioners. We can give primacy to the hard reality of observed practices in defined settings. . . . In the complex realities of practice, we can pursue what works."[2]

At Artstor, I was immersed in the inductive learning that Clark advocated as the only way to find what works. But without a theory, those who want to provoke change (and those who support them) are left to hope that they will find the perfect person to back, align that perfect person with the perfect team, and work on the perfect problem at the perfect moment in time. A theory of how pragmatic intermediary organizations can synthesize change in colleges and universities will help those who want to change higher education do more than keep their eyes open for heroes.

According to former Hewlett Foundation president Paul Brest, some funders believe that they should not burden nonprofit leaders by asking them to articulate a theory of how they are or will be successful: "These skeptics are implicitly analogizing grantees to idiots savants—individuals who are able to do complex calculations, such as finding the square root of any number, in their heads without knowing, let alone being able to explain, how they do it. [The writings of one critic of asking grantees for a theory of change] imply that even if his grantees could explain their strategies, they are so busy doing good that it would be wicked to make them take the time to do so."[3] Brest surely believes in backing excellent operating leaders, but he was skeptical of approaches to philanthropy that rely only on a funder's good judgment in identifying those needle-in-the-haystack heroic operating executives.

When I wrote my article on bringing change to change-resistant institutions, I hadn't defined a change-resistant institution, or even defined what an institution is. If pressed, I probably would have said that institutions stick around; they endure. William & Mary, for example, was chartered in 1693. Institutions have columns outside of their main buildings, and these columns have two functions: to hold up heavy structures and to symbolize that these structures are associated with thousands of years of tradition. Both of these functions relate to enduring, and enduring has a significant element of change-resistance built in. Thus, my sense would have been that outlasting change seems to be a central feature of an institution.

I also hadn't felt the need to explain why institutions are important because I had been trained at the Mellon Foundation, where the prevailing ethos was that supporting the work and missions of institutions was central to everything we did. Institutions, we used to say, were conservative in all the best senses; they defended and supported functions such as basic research even as the world of markets wanted quick fixes and products. I thought of institutions as dedicated to a set of public, rather than exclusively private, goods: institutions promoted the expansion of civil rights and opportunities for marginalized people and voices. They supported civil society and kept chaos—the stronger version of change—at bay. I didn't need any definition beyond that as we started working on Artstor. Our belief in the value of enduring institutions anchored our defense of them, even as their resistance to change frustrated us on a daily basis.

Not defining institutions but working to support them meant never having to think through the difference between institutions-as-organizations (such as the institutions with columns outside of their buildings) and other, less concrete institutions (such as "the institution of marriage"). Even though many of us think of institutions as organizations, theorists are more likely, and more helpfully, inclined to talk about institutions as value-shaping communities that surround and enfold individuals. Sociologist Victor Nee defines an institution as "a web of interrelated rules and norms that govern social relationships, [and] comprise the formal and informal social constraints that shape the choice set of actors."[4] According to economist Douglas North, "Institutions are the rules of the game in a society or, more formally, are the humanly devised constraints that shape human interaction."[5] Two sociologists with a more anthropological bent, Roger Friedland and Robert R. Alford, conceive of institutions "as both supra-organizational patterns of activity through which humans conduct their material life in time and space, and symbolic systems through which they categorize that activity and infuse it with meaning."[6]

In the early days of Artstor, I always thought of the material connections first. For example, I thought of the University of Michigan as the institution that Artstor was trying to change and to help. It was a place, it hired people, and it had an identity, albeit a sprawling one. But as we gained experience, we began to see that the "web of interrelated rules and norms that shape the choice set of actors" was not generated by the university as an organization or as the center of a web. We learned that the University of Michigan isn't just one institution. Instead, it's a loose federation of suborganizations. Some of these suborganizations were just organizational units, but others functioned as institutions in their own right, with their own rules of their own games.

Proposing a theory of bringing efficient and effective change to these institutions and nestled institutions entails understanding how the organizational structure of a college or university functions. Economist Herb Simon (1916–2001) wrote that organizations are designed to be efficient and effective: "The commandment, 'Be efficient!' is a major organizational influence over the decisions of the members of any administrative agency; and a determination whether this commandment has been obeyed is a major function of the review process."[7] But we didn't encounter this commandment on campus. Instead, we encountered groups of passionate individuals who saw the institutional priorities or imperatives issued from on high on behalf of the institution (that is, the college or university) as basically irrelevant to their decision-making process. Why?

The most obvious reason why a university doesn't function as an efficient business is its nonprofit structure. Unlike for-profit firms, whose first priority is to pay back investors and produce returns for shareholders, universities do not focus exclusively on the financial bottom line. Instead, they focus on their mission. Nonprofits are essential in providing society with desirable public services that the market will not support. In other words, regular markets will not support many important mission-driven activities, and so we support those organizations (both through tax breaks and through donations) in their quest to determine how best to carry out the activities that are not defined by profit maximization. In contrast, classical economic theory is based on a unifying priority-setting mechanism for corporate decision-makers. Economist Michael Jensen presents a particularly emphatic defense of how "value maximization states that managers should make all decisions so as to increase the total long-run market value of the firm."[8] In responding to the emerging school of thought that businesses should also consider the interests of their employees, their customers, and society at large (the theory known as *stakeholder value*), Jensen doesn't see how any efficient outcomes could result:

> Managers would have no way to know how to best benefit society, and furthermore there would be widespread disagreement on how and what to do. Moreover, if adopted, stakeholder theory would do further damage. It would literally leave managers unmonitored and unaccountable in any principled way for their actions with the vast resources under their control. Now that's a disaster.[9]

So at least in this colorful celebration of the central guiding role of profit-seeking in for-profit organizations, the decision-making of managers in the for-profit realms must be consistently aimed at increasing the organization's financial bottom line. Of course, some economists (and some activist investors) argue for corporate social responsibility and other approaches to valuing the needs and wants of other stakeholders. Still, as a general principle Jensen's lens is useful for dramatizing the core principle of for-profit priority setting that could never be the ordering principle in organizations—such as colleges and universities—where profit-seeking or even economic efficiency will never be the primary priority.

We also need to consider the motivations that drive the decision-making of individuals. Even though for-profit firms specify an overall goal for the firm, not everyone who works in a for-profit organization is driven only by the desire to make money. People choose their careers for all sorts of pecuniary and nonpecuniary reasons. People often just prefer to work in a certain atmosphere or on a certain set of problems and are willing to choose careers that pay less because of the perceived person/job fit. The mix of motives of all people needs to not be oversimplified, but we can acknowledge that in comparison to those who work in for-profit firms, many workers in nonprofits are more likely to "infuse [their activity] with meaning," as Friedland and Alford put it, and to tilt their personal decision-making scale more toward the symbolic realm than the material. That balance is not precisely parsed, and as we will see in the next section, their motivations can be more confused and conflated than people might think. For the moment, what matters are the implications for how complex nonprofit organizations do, or do not, precisely guide their employees' decision-making.

If decision-makers in nonprofits are less motivated by profit maximization than those in for-profits, and if their decision-making is not guided by the single objective of maximizing the value of the enterprise, then how do they make decisions? In *The Theory of Social and Economic Organization*, Max Weber suggested that people in organizations can be inclined to focus on value markers that are close at hand rather than more distant ones. Weber argued that when presented with overarching goals ("absolute value"), most people will focus on the actual choices that life presents to them. They act on "marginal utility" as they arrange various subjective wants based on how urgent they are, and then do whatever feels most urgent. According to Weber, "Absolute values are always irrational."[10] In a college or university, where employees are not necessarily unified in the pursuit of organizational value maximization, we might assume that some other directive from on high guides their work, but Weber suggests that real people make decisions based on what they see as valuable in their near vicinity.

In implementing Shared Shelf at Cornell, we learned the hard way how fragmented one university could be. The absolute value and cost savings (for the university as a whole) of one shared, economically and programmatically efficient platform for managing and sharing digital images were far less meaningful to departmental decision-makers than the software's functionality in the very particular context of how they would use it, how comfortable they were with it, and how it conformed to the personal preferences of opinion leaders in the department. Despite the enthusiastic support of the Dean of the Libraries and her colleagues, Shared Shelf was only one option for autonomous collection managers (including faculty members) across the campus. To each decision-maker, the idea of aligning with a university-wide direction was irrational. As Jensen notes in his typically trenchant support of the need for a profit motive as a guiding principle, the absence of one unifying objective function "allows managers and directors to invest in projects that destroy firm-value whatever they are (the environment, medical research) without having to justify the value destruction."[11] In nonprofits, such concerns can be core—and by no means indicative of "value destruction." Jensen's dramatic defense of for-profits' unified vision isn't relevant to institutions where the mission is paramount, but his extreme view of what shirking leads to highlights how, in mission-driven organizations, straying from any centrally issued goal is an inevitable consequence of multiple and varying missions. In a nonprofit organization, following one's own vision may not be shirking and may not "destroy firm-value." But the tendency of departments or individuals to do so makes collective institutional action unlikely.

What, then, guides the decisions of real people in colleges and universities? Some very useful theories identify the forces that shape the decisions that happen within and at different levels of the institutional ecosystem.[12] In general, social scientists' perspectives on institutions have evolved in the past thirty years to recognize the interplay of people's choices and the power of organizational structures rather than giving undue weight to either of the two. The pioneering work of sociologists Paul DiMaggio and Woody Powell in the 1980s and 1990s led to the theory of *new institutionalism*, an approach that begins by recognizing the interplay between people and the structures that people build and choose to inhabit and, occasionally, change:[13]

> Theories that make individuals primary tend, at the extreme, to become open-ended, solipsistic, and voluntaristic approaches in which the entire world is renegotiated in every social interaction. . . . Theories which make organizations central tend either to overstate an omnipresent, disembodied power which enables elites to discipline and punish without resistance, or to assume that they

have extraordinary latitude to make strategic choices determined only by their access to material resources.[14]

In the case of colleges and universities, the dynamics between individuals and institutions are particularly complicated and woven in a way that makes them extraordinarily resistant to change. Specifically, a number of different threads are interwoven: (1) the relationship between individuals and the suborganizational institution (e.g., decision-makers who are more tuned into the material and symbolic priorities of their own department than to the university as a whole); (2) the relationship between the subunit and the larger organization/institution (e.g., the relationships of the library, the athletics department, or the biology department to the university); (3) the relationship of individuals to other horizontally structured institutions that entangle them in the norms and mores of their peers across the country and the world; and (4) the relationship of the suborganizations (such as departments or units) or the larger organization to other, similar suborganizations and supraorganizations across the landscape. All of these relationships provide norms and/or rules that shape the material and symbolic choices of individual decision-makers. These choices may be expressed in very concrete terms (metrics, rules, policies, reward structures), and they may fundamentally affect the ways that individuals see their life stories playing out. Understanding—or, really, theorizing about—the dynamics of these four different pulls (described in the following sections) can help us better understand the challenges that an externally provided solution confronts when trying to achieve acceptance on campus. The alternative to understanding this fabric of change-resistance is to just shrug one's shoulders and say, "Well, you know how institutions are." And that doesn't help.

The Individual-Organization Split

Although people who work for nonprofit organizations are legally and ethically entitled to reasonable compensation, they have made a choice to live by the rules of the nonprofit game known as the *non-distribution constraint*.[15] Unlike working for a for-profit firm, working for a mission-driven nonprofit means that no matter how successful you are, you will never have what for-profit entrepreneurs call "a liquidity event," because (a) you hold no equity in the enterprise and (b) the nondistribution constraint dictates that while the organization can legally generate surpluses, such profits cannot be distributed to staff or trustees. There will be no IPO and no profit-sharing. In exchange for the tax advantages they receive from society, these nonprofit organizations are responsible for aligning the motives of staff and managers with society's needs rather than with traditional market rewards.[16] As Vladislav Valentinov explains:

> A nonprofit organization, of whatever type, is essentially a response to the difficulties in adapting monetary motivations to nonmonetary ones. A nonprofit attempts to overcome these difficulties by "switching off" the profit motive and replacing it with a "mission," which is invariably formulated in terms of specific outputs and thus represents the object of nonmonetary motivation.[17]

This nondistribution constraint offers nonprofits a number of important benefits, including a signal to the public of some degree of trustworthiness. The idea that the staff members at nonprofits can be trusted is a positive one—and by and large, they can be. Economist Burt Weisbrod charted how for-profit nursing homes used more sedatives than did nonprofits, where the staff are willing to invest more time and energy in the well-being of nonsedated residents. This trade-off between the quality of care and the cost of labor is just one example of why nonprofits' nondistribution constraint contributes to an aura of trust.[18] And yet there is also a big problem here. The idea of the constraint is that talented people are signaling their commitment to the organization's mission by accepting lower compensation than they might find in a for-profit firm. But in some cases or to some degree, the nondistribution constraint also reinforces some nonprofit decision-makers' freedom to promote their own particular vision in the decision-making process.

This trade-off of some income for personal satisfaction is a consumptive rather than a productive activity, even if this personal satisfaction is derived from service to others. Think about it for a moment: a person who chooses to work for a nonprofit organization may have noneconomic motives that mix altruism (saving the world, doing good, helping others) and self-interest (more interesting work, better work environment, less pressure). And for at least some of them, the pursuit of a mission (especially given the sacrifices they have made to do so) reinforces their determination to pursue that mission in the way that they believe is most effective. Here, the catch-all idea of a mission that is only vaguely and generally defined can lead to managerial discretion that then defines, by practice, what the institution is *actually* about. For entrepreneurial managers who have chosen to trade off some amount of income for mission fulfillment, one motivation can be the opportunity to define the actions that are prioritized. And with the creative act of mission authoring can come the single-mindedness of people who feel entitled to decision-making rights as recompense for their sacrifice.

In this way, the governing principle that defines a nonprofit—its limits on financially compensating individuals even if the individuals are successful—creates room for managerial priority setting, an activity that might be seen either as creative expression or institutional rebellion. The belief that managers (who have decision-making discretion) will align their priorities with a vaguely defined mission or the overall financial well-being of the suprainstitution requires quite a leap of faith. It is just as likely that an individual manager's own vision will define the void left by the ill-defined and too-broad governing notion of the organization's mission. It is not quite the disaster that managerial discretion represents in Jensen's view of for-profit firms, but it does help to clarify the challenge of aligning decisions within nonprofits to overall institutional priorities.

The Department-Organization Split

The idea that a given college or university is not one institution but rather a loose affiliation of many institutions linked by a logo and a sweatshirt color likely will not be surprising to those who have seen academic and nonacademic departments at work. Academic departments have their own norms that can be distinct from the overall institution's. Given the prominence of faculty (and faculty governance) in campus decision-making, we should recognize that faculty norms set the tone for much of the campus even if they are not always on the front line of decision-making about products and services. The rules of the game for faculty governance are an unusual feature of the landscape of the academy; the boundaries of faculty decision-making rights are not precisely demarcated, which sometimes creates disputed zones of authority between the suprainstitution and subinstitutions such as academic departments. Let's first summarize the power of faculty governance in norm-shaping and then examine how the institution of faculty governance can shape the decision-making capacity of other groups on campus.

The current norms of faculty authority were articulated in the American Association of University Professors' 1966 Statement on Government of Colleges and Universities:

> The faculty has primary responsibility for such fundamental areas as curriculum, subject matter and methods of instruction, research, faculty status, and those aspects of student life which relate to the educational process. On these matters the power of review or final decision lodged in the governing board or delegated by it to the president should be exercised adversely only in exceptional circumstances, and for reasons communicated to the faculty. It is desirable that the faculty should, following such communication, have opportunity for further consideration and further transmittal of its views to the president or board. Budgets, personnel limitations, the time element, and the policies of other groups, bodies, and agencies having jurisdiction over the institution may set limits to realization of faculty advice.[19]

In advocating for shared governance rather than a strict delineation of what "belongs" to the faculty or the trustees, former college presidents Gene Tobin and Bill Bowen have suggested that some tasks should be parsed out, with faculty responsible for decisions about "selection, advancement, and termination of peers" and trustees responsible for "investing institutional resources." They go on to note that there are, of course, "innumerable decisions to be made in the vast territory between these two bookends."[20] This vast territory is often the scene of tension, whether the question concerns how much authority faculty should have over choice of teaching tools or platforms or is about what is included in the AAUP's broad inclusion of "those aspects of student life which relate to the educational process." Tobin and Bowen emphasize their central belief that these questions must be worked out together, but they also understand how antagonistic the relationship between faculty and administration can become.

Given the ambiguity that hovers over the domain and limitations of faculty decision-making, it seems likely that other people who have chosen to work in this environment also hold fast to their freedom to pursue mission-driven goals and see a significant role for themselves and their units in defining and carrying out the institution's mission. Some assertion of this decision-making authority can be in the service of supporting faculty members' autonomy. "We love Artstor," a university staff member said at one point, "but there's one faculty member who hates it and insists that we build him his own database or else he's threatening to take a position at another university." For such a staff member, Weber's marginal utility might be defined by how well he can support the faculty member's view of what falls within the realm of faculty governance. Others, who view the overall institutional mission definition as vague, too general, or too distant, might define their own realm of rights. In fact, some faculty and staff may not feel any sense of loyalty to the suprainstitution. A blog posting from a popular blog summarizes some of this tension:

> Do we really owe our institutions loyalty? I feel loyalty to my profession, as vexed as it is, because I think what historians do is valuable and worthwhile. I feel loyalty to my friends and colleagues in academia, because we have to stand together in intellectual and professional solidarity in a world that neither understands nor appreciates what we do. . . . But I don't feel particularly loyal to the institutions that have employed me.
>
> Given the realities of the academic job market in the humanities for the past 40 years, and the ever-increasing demands for

winning tenure, it may even be reasonable to see ourselves in an adversarial relationship with our employers. . . . Maybe the absence of institutional loyalty on my part has to do with the fact that I've worked for institutions that deployed the rhetoric of loyalty selectively, when they wanted to extract more unpaid work out of the faculty, for example. Then, we were one big "family," but when I went to my "family members" for protection and redress from other "family members" who were treating me badly, I discovered the limits of that rhetoric on "family."[21]

In sum: faculty (and to some degree the staff) set their own rules rather than follow any supposed institutional/organizational imperative. In addition to laying claim to governance rights in the ambiguous space defined by Tobin and Bowen, how else do they define their norms?

The Alliance of Individuals and Their National Peers

In my Artstor days, I spent a lot of time with campus visual resources curators not only because they could vote for or against subscribing to our services but also because they had, via their listserv, immediate access to a community of peers that stretched across the country. One wrong move on our part and hundreds of subscribers to the listserv, in the same position of influence across the country, would learn about their colleague's outrage. In the fragmented world of a campus, employees tend to find their peers in other institutions rather than in the organization that signs their checks. A person might be the one visual resources curator, the one lacrosse coach, or the one scholar of Korean history on campus, but they belong to a transinstitutional community that they can access via listservs, conferences, and other physical or virtual spaces where community members gather. Because Artstor was trying to earn the trust of an evolving community of digital image users, we went to the Visual Resources and Art Libraries conferences. We also attended all the library conferences, the digital library conferences, and the instructional technologists' conferences. Because our buyers served faculty, we went to the College Art Association and the Society of Architectural Historians' conferences, and then when we wanted to let teachers of literature and culture know that they might already have access to Artstor, we went to the conference of the Modern Language Association (MLA).

These decisions were obvious; these conferences were the places to find the people whom we wanted to support the decision to subscribe to Artstor. But the conferences also are the central manifestation of the trusted communities that have the potential to shape the norms and values of their community.[22] According to sociologist Charles Perrow, professional and scholarly societies can calcify their members' generalized norms:

> Professional and trade associations are another vehicle for the definition and promulgation of normative rules about organizational and professional behavior. Such mechanisms create a pool of almost interchangeable individuals who occupy similar positions across a range of organizations and possess a similarity of orientation and disposition that may override variations in tradition and control that might otherwise shape organizational behavior.[23]

If associations can lock accepted practices into place, Greenwood et al. note that they also might serve as a vehicle for reshaping values:

> Associations can legitimate change by hosting a process of discourse through which change is debated and endorsed: first by negotiating and managing debate within the profession; and, second, by reframing professional identities as they are presented to others outside the profession. This discourse enables professional identities to be re-constituted.[24]

They propose that the means for promulgating such a redefinition is the process of "theorization":

> Theorization is the development and specification of abstract categories and the elaboration of chains of cause and effect. Such theoretical accounts simplify and distill the properties of new

practices and explain the outcomes they produce. In effect, theorization is the process whereby localized deviations from prevailing conventions become abstracted . . . and thus made available in simplified form for wider adoption.[25]

According to Jim Grossman, executive director of the American Historical Association, academic societies have a specific type of power. They don't hire people, but they do "convene, legitimize, and inspire." In other words, they set norms because the people who comprise the institution *are* the institution, even though they are constrained by the segments of their norm-setting population that dominate the community's culture. "If we tightly adhere to the norms of the people who researched the culture of the Early Modern period in a particular time—the first half of the twentieth century," says Carla Zecher, executive director of the Renaissance Society of America, "we will die out. Expanding what is studied and by whom and to what ends is what will keep the field alive amidst changing societal demographics and ideas." In chapter 4, I return to the challenges associated with *affecting* the norm-setting of the self-governing cross-cutting institutions that differ from vertical organizations. But for the moment, the point is that horizontal communities such as associations and societies inevitably shape the norms of what constitutes success for their members—via what they accept as papers at their conferences, whom they reward with fellowships or prizes, and what they select for publication. As an example, recall the Northwestern innovators who were invited to give keynote addresses at museum or library conferences to celebrate their trailblazing work in documenting the Dunhuang caves (see pages 46–47).

Stasis in organizational practices is reinforced by reward structures that, once set, are notoriously difficult to alter, but horizontal institutions can potentially play a role in bringing about change. For example, as digital scholarship emerged in the early 2000s as a creative force for changing the nature of humanities scholarship, the assessment and reward structures lagged. "Faculty members in humanities disciplines have been pioneers in many forms of digital scholarship and teaching," wrote Scott Jaschik in *Inside Higher Ed*, "but many have complained for years that some of their departments don't have a clue how to evaluate such work, and that some senior scholars are downright hostile to it."[26] In 2012, the Modern Language Association released its Guidelines for Evaluating Work in Digital Humanities and Digital Media, "designed to help departments and faculty members implement effective evaluation procedures for hiring, reappointment, tenure, and promotion."[27] The existence of society-sanctioned guidelines have not overwritten the existing standards and reward structures, but they are likely, over time, to play a role in changing the system from within.

As Tobin and Bowen note,

> Traditionally, much of academia has been organized vertically, with the department as the key, largely self-contained unit. Going forward, we suspect that much more horizontal structure is going to be required, because decisions of many kinds are going to transcend department structures . . . Discussions of options . . . will often cut across departmental lines and at times across campus and even institutional boundaries.[28]

But membership organizations aren't the only institutions that reach across. In writing about how the National Institutes of Health (NIH) helped to shape systemic attitudes concerning the racial diversification of faculty, legal scholar Susan Sturm notes how a funding agency can carry change across a network:

> Institutional intermediaries use their ongoing capacity-building role within a particular occupational sector to build knowledge (through establishing common metrics, information pooling, and networking), introduce incentives (such as competition, institutional improvement, and potential impact on funding), and provide accountability (including grass roots participation and self-, peer- and external evaluation).[29]

As Sturm notes, funders have the power to influence via material means in ways that associations do not: "Public or quasi-public organizations [can] leverage their position within preexisting communities of practice to foster change and provide meaningful accountability."[30]

The executive director of the Whiting Foundation, Daniel Reid, has sought to strengthen the rewarding of teachers and scholars in the humanities who are engaging with the public outside of the academy. Like the MLA's work to provide guidance and norms for evaluating digital scholarship, the Whiting Foundation seeks to influence the reward structures that shape the behavior of teachers and scholars. Without the significant funding power of the NIH and without the bottom-up buy-in from the community that MLA channeled, Whiting's method has leaned on working within the established vocabulary of rewards. "Since we don't have a lot of money," Reid notes, "we realized that awarding fellowships even of modest amounts might have disproportionate impact for committees seeking to evaluate candidates. Does it mean a lot to those who are determining the reward structure for faculty at Princeton, where significant outside grants are quite common in the humanities? Probably not. But at the University of Maine or the University of Arkansas, prestigious institutions where outside humanities grants are nevertheless rarer and public service is a natural concomitant of the schools' public status, a faculty member who wins an award vetted by their peers in a national competition is a big deal. And that's where we think reward structures can be nudged to recognize, reward, and encourage the behavior—the approach to scholarship—that so many within the profession, so many students, and so much of the public actually want to see, but which often doesn't 'count' or 'fit' within the reward structures of yesteryear."[31] In subsequent phases, Whiting has sought nominations via scholarly societies, amplifying the signal by sending it through horizontal as well as vertical institutions. Within the academy, promotion and tenure rules of the game are among the most change-resistant structures, so these strategies to evolve them will require patience and time.

Those who have the power to effect change in these structures are often those who have progressed through the steps of progress defined in earlier times. A department chair (or a swimming coach) will have an identity that is shaped by their role in a department, their role on a campus, and their role in a transinstitutional community. Whether the shared norms of these communities support change or not, they also can serve as gears for advancing the material agendas of individual decision-makers. DiMaggio and Powell note how structural similarity within a field can facilitate career creating: "Personnel flows within an organizational field are further encouraged by structural homogenization, for example, the existence of common career titles and paths (such as assistant, associate, and full professor) with meanings that are commonly understood."[32]

Relying on the norms and rewards of a horizontal network of peers to build a career is, of course, no sin. But in attempting to understand what makes higher education so change-resistant, we are trying to dig deeper into the various influences on the individuals who have to buy into a new approach to problem-solving. So far, we have noted that they might feel liberated to pursue their own version of the organization's mission because they've elected to work in a mission-driven environment rather than a company that pays more. Then we proposed that faculty governance provides a model for asserting decision-making rights. Now we are arguing that horizontal institutions have a particular soft-power role in shaping the behaviors and beliefs of individuals connected across the sector. But because institutions shape both the symbolic and material norms for their individual constituents, we also need to recognize that identifying with the reward structures of horizontal communities provides a channel for individuals to advance materially. For example, the head football coach at a Division III college might aspire to become the coach at a Division I university. But to achieve his own goal of moving up, he must meet particular metrics of success that may or may not align with the desires of the school's administration. Similarly, faculty members at a school that requires faculty to teach four or five classes a term might aspire to a post where they need to teach only two or three per term. To advance in this way, professors might prioritize their research over their teaching. The rewards of material advancement can take many forms, and there's nothing wrong with an individual having the freedom to pursue these rewards. But the individual's goals (pursued through horizontal community channels) can pull against the overarching goals of the local institution while advancing rewards for individuals acting on the basis of self-interest.

As we struggled to get community buy-in for Shared Shelf, we sought out the open-source—and transinstitutional—software community that was forming to create its own asset management modules. We committed to building our software in sync with their APIs (software exchange protocols that would allow our software to work with their open-source modules). We offered to host hackathons to develop new solutions together. But we regularly found that the libraries (such as Columbia's) that were making commitments to the Hydra open-source "community" wanted little to do with an external solution like Shared Shelf. The underlying reason may have been the values of the open-source community. But their rejection of Shared Shelf may also have been based on the visibility and material advancement that goes with being champions within their community and heroic innovators on their campus. Regardless of the motivations, going up against the norms of a new and passionate horizontal community can be a formidable challenge for an outside agency offering a synthetic solution.

Interinstitutional Department-to-Department Alliances

As part of resetting how we understand the interplay between individuals and institutions, DiMaggio and Powell build on Weber's famous image of the iron cage; for Weber, the iron cage was the unconsciously constructed structure created by efficiency-seeking within capitalism that constrains individuals' freedom to make choices in bureaucracies. Bureaucracy in the quest for economic efficiency is real, DiMaggio and Powell assert, but it only begins to define the shaping of modern institutions. They argue that bureaucratic organization structures have long been established and are now similar across organizations. "Today," they write, "bureaucratization and other forms of organizational change occur as the result of processes that make organizations more similar without necessarily making them more efficient."[33] The result, they contend, is *isomorphism*, which "forces one unit in a population to resemble other units that face the same set of environmental conditions." These organizations may have started out trying to differentiate themselves by being effective in formulating their own responses to the work that they do. But "once disparate organizations in the same line of business are structured into an actual field (as we argue, by competition, the state, or the professions), powerful forces emerge that lead them to become more similar to one another."[34]

This diagnosis applies generally to institutions of higher education and even to their suborganizations, including academic departments, athletics departments, alumni offices, and libraries. In fact, many of the attributes that contribute to isomorphism are particularly strong in the academy:

> The greater the reliance on academic credentials in choosing managerial and staff personnel, the greater the extent to which an organization will become like other organizations in its field. Applicants with academic credentials have already undergone a socialization process in university programs and are thus more likely than others to have internalized reigning norms and dominant organizational models.[35]

This unintended consequence of institutional self-definition—hugging closely to the behavior of peer institutions—is reinforced unconsciously as similarly selected individuals are indoctrinated into processes and structures that may feel locally defined but are also shaped by these extramural norms. Remember that mission-driven environments allow for a multiplicity of objective functions, from preparing undergraduate students for particular professional roles in everything from filmmaking to accounting to dentistry to helping them define their own view of the meaning of life. In environments with such idiosyncratic goals (among participants and for the institution as a sum of disparate parts), it makes perfect sense that aspirations are defined in alignment with whatever extramural field-defined norms are already the most celebrated. As sociologists John Meyer and Brian Rowan note:

> The more ambiguous the goals of an organization, the greater the extent to which the organization will model itself after organizations that it perceives as successful. There are two reasons for this modeling. First, organizations with ambiguous or disputed goals are likely to be highly dependent upon appearances for legitimacy. Such organizations may find it to their advantage to meet the expectations of important constituencies about how they should be designed and run.[36]

These organizations are competing in a fog and without any unified bottom line. So they look to what the next peer is defining as success. Hundreds of institutions want to be Harvard, even at the expense of their own particular strengths, limitations, and local context. To prepare the institution for widespread change, these isomorphic forces and the structures that reinforce them need to be identified and considered.

How are these comparisons made? In traditional for-profit markets, profits and losses are continually tabulated, as are the stock prices of a traded firm, to measure its overall market value. Although all data, including data about the financial bottom line, can be manipulated, everyone is inescapably drawn to metrics even (and perhaps especially) when an organization's activity is hard or impossible to define. In some areas of higher education, most notably intercollegiate athletics, results are highly visible: an 11–2 record in football is very different from a 2–11 record. Fundraising campaigns have specific targets; admissions rankings celebrate the average SAT scores of or the number of valedictorians in their entering cohorts. When we move into the less discrete aspects of the work of colleges, we still find a search for quantitative clarity: faculty tenure and promotion committees consider tabulations of how many times a work was cited (a key component of gauging the impact factor of journals); students rate professors in the classroom. As we think about which forces strengthen the weave that makes colleges and universities resistant to change, we need to acknowledge the power of the measures that provide trophies for prestige. Research universities aim for the prestige of joining the American Association of Universities (AAU), which follows a specific formula for tracking research productivity. Another enormous focus is rankings, whether *U.S. News and World Report*'s various rankings of undergraduate colleges or the National Research Council's ranking of departments and programs of all kinds.[37]

Of course, institutions can choose the measures that they are going to play to. For example, they might decide to improve their contribution to their students' social mobility after reading the Opportunity Insights project, which tracks individual colleges' effectiveness at lifting their students' economic status,[38] or they may seek to improve (or, in certain cases, seek to exaggerate) alumni giving rates to game their *U.S. News* rankings.[39] Hungry for the attention of students and funders in a highly competitive environment, colleges and universities rely upon clear and specific marks of distinction, which may or may not align with behaviors they want to encourage. Those behaviors may not foster aspects of the mission they want to pursue; they almost certainly move in the opposite direction of controlling costs. "Competition in higher education," Larry Bacow notes,

> drives costs up. It does not reward the least-cost provider. Institutions actually compete by advertising their relative inefficiencies. Promoting low student–faculty ratios is just another way of advertising that you are the most labor-intensive institution around. Note that institutions rarely promote the fact that they have the best learning outcomes, but they do advertise small classes, easy access to faculty, lavish facilities, and multiple opportunities for students to engage in an endless number of student organizations and activities.[40]

For better or for worse, metrics may propel certain institutional objectives. But until there's some incentive for *lowering* the cost to students, families, and societies, local or positional victories for individual institutions—as real as they are—inexorably contribute to society's growing anger and mistrust of the sector and the people in it. These victories provide narrative endpoints for faculty, deans, coaches, and staff, but they reward individual behavior that may well push against the collective good of the sector.

Data, Myth, and Mission

Rankings and measures provide a map for a competitive strategy. At first glance, we can see how colleges and universities compete in the service of these metrics: for students, especially students who can pay to subsidize the organization; for athletes or for high test-scoring students who will lift their institutions' *U.S. News* rankings; for faculty stars and the funding that such recognizable performers sometimes bring; for donors and grants. And while they experience the material effects of these competitions, they don't have stock prices and they are adept at not going out of business. They play in many markets, but as durable nonprofits they are shielded from some of the resetting effects of the marketplace. Some force, or forces, guide their moves more than the invisible hand does.

The philosopher Ernst Cassirer, cited earlier to explain how a theoretical perspective enables the concatenation of individual data into a connected web of logic, also wrote about an alternative language to the theoretical mode of viewing the evidence of the world:

> Mythical thinking . . . does not dispose freely over the data of intuition, in order to relate and compare them to each other, but is captivated and enthralled by the intuition which suddenly confronts it. It comes to rest in the immediate experience; the sensible present is so great that everything else dwindles before it. . . . It is as though the whole world were simply annihilated. . . . This focusing of all forces on a single point is the prerequisite for all mythical thinking and mythical formulation.[41]

The concrete and real-world effects of the mythical imagination are central to understanding how colleges and universities work—and how they don't.

Twenty years ago, Bill Bowen and I published *The Game of Life: College Sports and Educational Values*. In that book, we presented data related to the precollege, in-college, and post-college lives of 90,000 students from three different decades who either played college sports or did not. Our research had a strong empirical basis because we thought it was the only way to address policy questions on a topic connected with such strong emotions. For example, to respond to critics of college sports programs who argued that things were better in the good old days, we wanted compare students from the 1950s to today's students via studying what their attributes were in college and by collecting information about their post-graduation occupations, earnings, subsequent education, civic involvement, and life satisfaction.

In short, we had hoped to provide an empirically based discussion that would privilege facts over myths. In terms of emphasizing an empirical approach to the subject, the book was successful, perhaps to a fault; the *New York Times* described it as "a book that could have been a bombshell had it only been written in a language other than that of an actuary's manual."[42] And while those who wanted to change the balance of athletics and academics at their institution may have read and cited it, it's safe to say that it instigated little change in the system. Highly specialized athletes in thirty or forty sports continue to enjoy a very significant admissions advantage to the most selective colleges and universities. The 2019 "Varsity Blues" scandal (in which celebrities were caught paying bribes to college coaches and faking high school athletics records for their children) shows that if anything, our book (and studies like it) ended up serving as a how-to manual for understanding the rules of the game—legal or illegal—within the sports recruiting complex.

Our goals of informing the debate and even changing some of these practices ran up against a series of deeply entrenched myths. Despite the common usage of the word, a myth isn't necessarily a story that isn't true. Rather, it's a story that connects something current to some deeper and symbolically generative past. Anthropologist Bronisław Malinowski saw a hundred years ago how myth can shape institutional choices: "The function of myth, briefly, is to strengthen tradition and endow it with a greater value and prestige by tracing it back to a higher, better, more supernatural reality of initial events."[43] College sports are justified on the basis of the myth that they matter.

One enduring myth of college as a means of lifting the station of poor students—the Horatio Alger myth—periodically is taken seriously when colleges and universities are considering their obligation to accept and support low-income students. Such myths splice together the aims of an otherwise fragmented campus. But for most departments and units, few consolidating or institution-wide myths guide the work. That doesn't mean that mythology doesn't play a determining role in decision-making; it just means that in lieu of guiding myths, individual actors are left with the watered-down version of mythology: mission.

Early in his long career, sociologist Burton Clark proposed that a coherent institutional story—an "organizational saga" or myth— guided every decision in colleges such as Swarthmore and Oberlin. According to Clark, an institutional saga

> makes links across internal divisions and organization boundaries as internal and external groups share their common belief. With deep emotional commitment, believers define themselves by their organization affiliation, and in their bond to other believers they share an intense sense of the unique. In an organization defined by a strong saga, there is a feeling that there is the small world of the lucky few and the large routine one for the rest of the world.[44]

Today, very few unifying institutional sagas exist. In 1963, Clark Kerr outlined the disparate German, English, and American roots of the complex organization that he labeled the "multiversity." With all the various post–World War II societal expectations for creating new knowledge and preparing citizens for a wide range of pursuits, the momentum was clearly shifting away from a unified saga like that of Swarthmore. According to Kerr, "A community should have common interests; in the multiversity they are quite varied, even conflicting. A community should have a soul, a single animating principle; the multiversity has several."[45]

While a few mythical narratives like the passions evoked in a full football stadium or the memories evoked by seeing a familiar sweatshirt might loosely hold together the dispersed fragments of community spirit in the multiversity or multicollege, few other myths function as shared sagas for the disparate activities that are pursued, supported, and justified on a campus. What, then, fills the void? Besides a very few campus-unifying myths, to what do individual agents or groups turn for a narrative to justify their work? A less intense version of a unifying saga can be found in the now requisite story provided by a mission statement. And a focus on a vague aggregated mission leaves individual decision-makers with the most flexible of storylines.

College and university mission statements are notoriously fuzzy. Northwestern, for example, doesn't spell out any specifics: "Northwestern is committed to excellent teaching, innovative research, and the personal and intellectual growth of its students in a diverse academic community."[46] Harvard doesn't even attempt a mission statement for the university as a whole. Missions are roughly the same across universities and similar to that of Iowa State: "Create, share, and apply knowledge to make Iowa and the world a better place."[47]

The mission statement itself is often elaborated in a vision or strategic plan that can articulate a set of initiatives or directions that may provide more clarity about activities for the upcoming five years. But in general, the notion that mission-driven actors within a college or university are envisioning anything like the same mission seems hopeful at best. With all the pulls on individuals that we have seen, the Weberian "absolute value"—remote to begin with—is hardly clarified by a mission statement in any way that can be used to guide management priorities.

Those of us who work in, or with, the complex communities that constitute colleges and universities have spoken of the importance of attending to our mission. Knowing that universities (like other nonprofits) cannot and should not make decisions solely on the basis of what the world's markets will support, we have placed our confidence in the idea of mission as our strategic keystone. We defend our enterprise as mission-driven, and we write about the dangers of mission-drift. Though we often criticize mission statements as both vague and overreaching, we do believe that they have some utility:

they are intended to inspire staff, to articulate why we undertake some activities even though they may be detrimental to our financial bottom line, and to help enterprising faculty, administrators, and staff decide whether a given activity fits or not. However, the idea of using a mission statement to guide operational decisions opens the door to all sorts of problems in nonprofit operations.

In noting that nineteenth-century novels are filled with characters like David Copperfield who plot, invent, and narrate their own life story, literary scholar Peter Brooks wrote, "The plotting of the individual or social or institutional life story takes on new urgency when one can no longer look to a sacred master plot that organizes and explains the world."[48] The unifying organizational saga for individual colleges or universities has gone the way of the unifying narrative of the Church's "providential plots"[49]—that is, plots that are guaranteed to have meaning because they fit into some greater plan. In the case of the novel, with no such divinely coherent plot functioning as an ordering narrative structure for life, characters from Don Quixote to David Copperfield gathered the foundational fragments of other characters' stories to create a life story of their own. The same can be said of the story of a college when there's no unifying saga that guides the actions of all the campus characters. We may want to believe that mission guides decision-making at colleges and universities, but given the vague mission statements intended to include of all the varied objective functions of the multiversity, it's as if these statements have been created through Mad Libs, the word game in which one player fills open gaps with random nouns, verbs, adjectives, and adverbs: "_____ University seeks to prepare _____ for lives that are defined by _____. While serving _____ and honoring _____, _____ University aims for the highest _____ for its _____, _____, and _____."

With a grandiose but vague mission statement in place, how do the people who populate institutions write their own version of the organizational story? Individual decision-makers have a lot of freedom to justify decisions because the institution's mission provides no providential plot at all. As they seek prestige for themselves or their units, by way of targeted metrics or forums that will reward their innovations or initiatives even if carried out with no collective organizational goal in mind, the story of why and how people can make their way in the dark forest of tangled objectives is left to them to write. Meanwhile, the overall and difficult-to-alter direction of the institution is ascribed to something beyond the realm of human influence—to fate. As Paul DiMaggio has noted, institutions are said to "take on a life of their own."[50] Colleges' and universities' resistance to change feels beyond anyone's control. The relentless working of the system seems to be determined by something bigger than the people involved. The ever-increasing costs of college (and thus ever-increasing tuition costs to students and families), foreseen by Bill Bowen in 1968 as continuing to rise faster than the inflation rate, represents one aspect of the institutional reality that is beyond anyone's control. The consensus seems to be that nothing can be done about it. Individuals shrug their shoulders and go about living their lives, defining the institution's story—or at least the priorities in their particular corner of the institution—in their own terms.

As an individual college or university expands its ambiguously defined basket of goals, it devolves the formation of guiding narratives to its suborganizations. Only rarely can it cohesively promulgate anything like a foundational myth. To the degree that it has organization-wide priorities, those priorities are either aimed at maintaining the appearance and reality of organizational unity or ensnared in transinstitutional tapestries that reflect a race for legitimacy and prestige. Rankings and arms races are the "rational myths" that harden these major avenues of change-resistance. Meyer and Brown describe them as "highly institutionalized and thus in some measure beyond the discretion of any individual or organization. They must, therefore, be taken for granted as legitimate."[51]

Once the rules of the game for material advancement are established, the weave that connects organizations across a field serves only to tighten them. Ambiguous definitions of success get distilled into very real conversations about compensation. On the symbolic level, the decision-makers' and decision-influencers' writing of their own story is shaped by the norms and mores of their communities of peers across the sector. No one is charged with countering the trajectory of colleges and universities, even as these various participants know that the current path does not lead higher education to a good future. All these levels of change resistance must be engaged if those proffering new, shared approaches are to have a chance to collaborate with the creative authors of solutions within institutions to create a new story.

A theoretical framework about the nature of the problem is only a prelude to a theory about the strategy to address it. The material and symbolic stakes for campus decision-makers can't be ignored or obliterated. In the next chapter, we turn to teasing out what it takes to intervene in the stories that institutional agents live within and are inclined to write for themselves.

4

Rewriting Myths

INSTITUTIONAL ENTREPRENEURS

In January 2004, the investment committee of Middlebury College's Board of Trustees concluded that the committee should not continue to play the hands-on operating role of deciding which investment managers to hire or fire for the college's endowment. According to John Tormondsen, a Goldman Sachs partner who served as chair of the investment committee, "We could see the results of our trying to do private equity on our own—which weren't great—and we knew that a volunteer approach wasn't going to be effective at identifying and getting access to the best funds, negotiating fees, and monitoring them on a real-time basis."[1] The committee was also concerned that the college wasn't large enough to build an investment capacity in-house. If they did try to do so, they knew that attracting investment staff to the middle of Vermont would be a challenge, and the office would have a difficult time meeting regularly with the investment managers who passed regularly through New York or Boston. They considered basing an investment team in those cities but knew that paying for talented staff in those markets would require salaries (and bonus structures) that were out of sync with the compensation of almost all of the college's employees.

Another option was working with Investure, a consortium being created by Alice Handy, the former University of Virginia chief investment officer. Investure had just signed up Smith College as its first client. Handy and her colleagues proposed an outsourced chief investment officer model to Middlebury, asking the college to entrust Investure with investing and managing the college's entire endowment. As Middlebury considered Investure, Tormondsen had a long discussion with the world's most widely respected endowment manager, Yale's David Swenson. Swenson's advice was clear: Middlebury should accept the costs and the challenges involved and hire its own investment staff.

Swenson's primary concern was the *principal-agent problem*. In his book *Pioneering Portfolio Management*, Swenson explained this dilemma: "Nearly every aspect of funds management suffers from decisions made in the self-interest of the decision-makers, not in the best interest of the fund . . . The wedge between principal goals and agent actions causes problems at the highest governance level, causing some fiduciary decisions to fail to serve the interest of a perpetual life endowment fund."[2] It wasn't that Swenson didn't respect Alice Handy; on the contrary, he thought very highly of her. But Swenson just didn't believe that an outside agent would, in the final analysis, place the college's interest over its own interests.

Despite Swenson's advice, Tormondsen and his colleagues were intrigued by the experience of David Salem, a member of their investment committee. Salem had started The Investment Fund for Foundations (TIFF), a pooled vehicle for nonprofits that sought to put parts of their endowments into a basket of different hedge funds. Salem believed that sophisticated investing required a significant organization with people geared to particular tasks. Even given Salem's experience, the committee was considering until the last moment whether to go it alone. In the end, Handy's presentation clinched the decision. "She was direct and open," noted Ron Liebowitz, the newly installed president of Middlebury. "She knew how to deal with Middlebury's quirks. For example, we had representatives from the student investment club in on the search and she knew exactly how to talk to their concerns."[3]

Four years later, when the 2008–2009 endowment returns of leading colleges and universities were circulated, the news was expected to be bad. Institutions that were fortunate enough to have significant endowments depended on a 5 percent payout from their endowment to support their programs; the market drops associated with the Great Recession would have a very significant impact on their operating budgets. And indeed, the data were discouraging and upsetting. The median college and university endowment had shrunk by 19.1 percent.[4] Many of the most respected endowment offices saw dramatic losses: Harvard's endowment declined by 27.3 percent, Yale's by 24.6 percent, Stanford's by 25.9 percent, Princeton's by 23.5 percent. Middlebury College, however, fared appreciably better; its endowment declined by 16.7 percent.

Why did Middlebury perform appreciably better in such a terrible market crash? Along with Smith College, Dickinson College, and Investure's other four clients, Middlebury had approved a strategy of buying S&P 500 long-dated puts—that is, contracts that would allow them to "put" or sell the S&P 500 index at a set price regardless of the market value when they chose to activate the contract. This short trade or hedging strategy had required investing $31 million (roughly 3 percent of Middlebury's endowment) to buy these put options, which would expire on a certain date and could lose all value if they were not used. The puts would, in effect, serve as insurance against possible market declines. The declines did in fact materialize in 2008–2009 after the collapse of the subprime mortgage market and the failure of major banks. In the end, the hedging strategy saved Middlebury $59.3 million while allowing it to remain heavily invested in the equity markets that had continued to rise until the significant downturn beginning in September 2008.

As we've seen, it isn't unusual for colleges and universities to go it alone on almost every function of the organization. Campus decision-makers fear that many of the vendors that serve higher education are likely to put their own well-being ahead of their clients'—exactly the sort of shirking behavior that the principal-agent dilemma recognizes. Swenson had warned Tormondsen that the natural inclination of outside investment managers was to focus on acquiring new customers (and the concomitant fees) rather than to focus on managing Middlebury's funds.

Swenson's skepticism of outside agents represents a widely accepted theory for resisting the outsourcing of college and university functions of all kinds. This theory of not delegating the college's fiduciary responsibilities to a firm that has its own priorities has served Yale well; Swenson and his colleagues built the best long-term endowment record in the country. And yet if carried to its extreme, the principal-agent problem could lead a college to grow its own spinach for the dining hall and raise its own trees to turn to pulp for making paper towels. Which reasons and situations might allow a college or university to trust an outside provider? The Middlebury trustees had no theory of change to counter a powerful and supported theory for *resisting* change. Their ultimate choice was a good one, but were they just lucky? If we want to learn how trusted intermediaries, such as Investure, can overcome the do-it-yourself instinct of faculty, staff, and trustees, then we need to take apart the lessons of experience and see if we can construct them into a pattern that illuminates these experiences and provides lessons and guidance. In other words, we need a theory—a set of hypotheses that allows us to identify the conditions and behaviors that can make hard-to-change institutions open to change. Without such a theory, every success looks like a magical accomplishment of improvisation and individual talent, and we come away with no map for suggesting an effective way forward. In this context, the principal-agent dilemma seems to be one of the more rational reasons to resist external solutions. If external solutions proffered by outside agents cannot be trusted, then it makes perfect sense for responsible, mission-driven individuals to choose the path of institutional self-reliance.

We have seen how individuals facing decisions about how best to carry out their work in colleges and universities can be influenced by the norms and rules that they absorb from the tapestry of institutions and communities in which they are embedded. In some cases, surely, individuals in a department or a unit write their own life story in harmony with the larger narrative of their college or university.

That link might result from participation in campus activities, friends in other departments, personal connection to the founding myths of the institution, or an interest in moving into campus administration. But as agents (authors) of their own story, they usually write that story under the influence of the psychic, symbolic, and material rewards that are most apparent and most meaningful because they are fostered in the norm-setting communities that are remote from the edicts of central administration. A community that affects their priorities can be a department or it can be a far-flung set of peers connected by a listserv and an annual conference. Through such networks, college and university decision-makers absorb and pursue both material concerns and purpose-justifying symbolism. The result of these subinstitutions and the administrations of the overall organization sharing their rules of the game with their peers is that colleges and universities, in loving competition with one another, follow each other like birds flying in precise formation.

Middlebury's decision to invest with Alice Handy's new firm, Investure, provides an illustration of how this durable and change-resistant institutional fabric can be pierced.

The Institutional Entrepreneur

When Alice Handy decided to leave the University of Virginia after twenty-nine years, she made a list of the ten elements that she was looking for in her next opportunity.[5] The list included working with nonprofits, working with "bright and talented" investment professionals, and being "a flexible and curious" investor. She also wanted to "work with a small group of individuals—20 or fewer" and "have fun," traits that are often associated with start-up entrepreneurs. Start-ups sometimes even codify (as Facebook did) an ethos of "moving fast and breaking things," a mode that usually doesn't sit well with conservative and change-resistant institutions—the places that start-ups usually profit by breaking. Recall David Swenson's chief concern with outsourcing: an agent's objectives may not consistently align with the institution that engages with them. As the agent working with organizations that values objectives beyond maximizing profits, a start-up firm serving higher education faces the *vendor versus partner problem*: because it is viewed as a potentially disruptive force seeking to overturn the established order of operations, the start-up may gain customers but never gain trust. In discussing why firms sometimes prefer in-house innovation, economist Eric von Hipple observes that "when a user develops its own custom product, that user can be trusted to act in its own best interest. When a user hires a manufacturer to develop a custom product, the situation is more complex."[6] How did Investure manage to establish trust and position itself in partnership with its clients?

Handy's long career at the University of Virginia had not always focused exclusively on endowment management. At various points in her career, she had overseen the University of Virginia's "insurance, payroll and travel advances, and registering the university's fleet of vehicles with the state. . . . the university's securities lending program, debt financing, and the golf and resort complex."[7] Her focus on understanding institutional needs, behaviors, and processes prepared her to position Investure as a partner rather than as a misaligned asset-and-fee gatherer. From the beginning, she offered to provide cash management services for the clients' operating funds, knowing that Investure's scale and relationships with custodial banks could be more effective than a school managing its cash on its own. She also established an internship program to bring students from consortium members into the firm, and most important, she established regular meetings of the consortium's chief financial officers at Investure's offices. She and her colleagues actively utilized the members of the colleges' investment committees as partners and contributors.

Building any new institution—and particularly an institution that seeks a place in the forest of other institutions—isn't an easy process. In a 1988 article, Paul DiMaggio designated a new domain of institutional sociology by defining a category of *institutional entrepreneurs*. According to DiMaggio, "Creating new institutions is expensive and requires high levels of both interest and resources. New institutions arise when organized actors with sufficient resources (institutional entrepreneurs) see in them an opportunity to realize interests that they highly value."[8] These actors build something new through the collaborative development of good solutions that serve the interests of all parties.[9]

Handy and her colleagues at Investure knew enough about the workings of their institutional partners to realize that the existing boards were more than just the clients that hired them. In the world of the elite private equity and hedge funds, identifying the most successful investors is one challenge and gaining access to their investment vehicles is another. Handy and her colleagues knew many such managers and could have asserted that they knew best about everything. But they didn't. Instead, they listened to and allowed the members of various investment committees to coauthor the story of Investure. Their contributions to the building of the Investure investment portfolio became one of its founding myths of origin: "Through Smith we got access to Stonehill, through Middlebury we were able to get into Appaloosa, we met Cerberus through Dickinson," Handy noted. "And when it came time to think through the puts strategy (and figure out how and when to unwind it), the committees were right there with us, figuring it out. For all kinds of reasons, we knew that we'd do better with them as partners than as passive clients."

In the early 2000s, one couldn't be working to build an innovative organization without being aware of the theory of *disruptive innovation* articulated by Harvard Business School professor Clayton Christensen. According to this theory, established firms are so focused on maintaining their current customers via current methods that they disregard how any other customer base might matter to them. As they use the methods and models that were designed around their existing customers and services, they are exposed to being disrupted by new firms that introduce initially imperfect innovations that aim to serve and draw away marginal and underserved customers. Over time, the new organizations iteratively improve their products before eventually undermining the larger organization's core customer base. In Christensen's theory, the innovators peck away at the market around the fringes where no one is paying attention, winning over customers that the dominant market has underserved. General Motors was famously a loser in this game: the

Toyota Cressida grew into the Lexus before GM even understood how it had lost its Cadillac buyers.[10]

Christensen's model of disruptive innovation is one of the dominant theories in understanding the strategy of start-ups. But not all entrepreneurs follow the Christensen model and set out to disrupt or overturn all that came before them. According to organizational theorists Raghu Garud, Cynthia Hardy, and Steve McGuire, institutional entrepreneurs must be "skilled actors who can draw on existing cultural and linguistic materials to narrate and theorize change in ways that give other social groups reasons to cooperate."[11] Smith College investment committee chair Nealie Small, who had managed a wide variety of investment manager relationships in her role as chief investment officer of Scudder Kemper Investments, noted that "Alice and her team shared their business strategy and their compensation discussions with us in a way that I'd never seen; it's as though the curtain that usually lies between client and manager had been lifted and we were part of her organization."[12] Dickinson College investment committee cochairs Thomas Kalaris and Jennifer Reynolds noted that Alice showed an understanding of their own work as fiduciaries for the college: "She knew the processes that we would have to deal with. She knew how the finance committee would be thinking about liquidity and how to think about and how to fund the payout. She knew campus politics. She knew that we would have debates about environmental sustainability. In the end, we bet on Alice."[13] As she created her new firm, Alice Handy conveyed a compelling story of why Investure would be a partner, and she told it in their language and in a way that responded to a range of genuine institutional needs.

Scholars of entrepreneurship Daniel Hijorth and Chris Stayaert have recognized the importance of the capacity to tell a story in any kind of entrepreneurship: "Entrepreneurship as a dialogical creativity is located in between the possible and the impossible. . . . Convincing others—directing desires, organizing resources, dealing with obstacles—and sharing images of 'what could become' is done in small narratives to which people can relate."[14] Considering the license that decision-makers in colleges and universities have to author their own version of the institution's mission, the importance of the entrepreneur's storytelling sophistication is a central juncture of influence.

The particulars of selling into mission-driven organizations where each constituency relies on its own myths rather than one shared saga requires the sort of coauthoring in which the Middlebury, Smith, and Dickinson College committees participated with Alice Handy. The buyers weren't looking just to buy into someone else's vision. Instead, they wanted take part in authoring that vision. To gain entrance into the symbolic universe of mission-driven actors within institutions, institutional entrepreneurs have to "create a whole new system of meaning that ties the functioning of disparate sets of institutions together."[15] In the context of myth-fueled institutions, these external story writers aren't just telling an amusing story to get their foot in the door for a quick sale. Creating a new system of myth via storytelling—what literary scholars call *mythopoesis*—requires knowing the old myths well enough to be able to invent a new world or myth by creative reuse of pieces of old myths. The *Star Wars* saga draws from fragments of earlier myths, including World War I's dogfights and trench warfare, medieval sword fights, and the timeless quest of a hero as he seeks to overcome the dominating presence of his father. But the power of *Star Wars* to attract audiences comes from its weaving together of these mythological components to create a new but familiar universe deeply imbued with the resonance of familiar symbolic patterns. Institutional entrepreneurship in the myth-dominated world of colleges and universities must be believably familiar to local participants in the same way. In being entrepreneurial, actors cannot do anything they please. As organizational theorists Raghu Garud and Peter Karnøe note:

> As embedded actors, they can entertain certain possibilities and not others. If they deviate too much from existing approaches, they may trigger counter-reactions that could thwart their efforts. On the other hand, if they do not deviate enough, they may not

be able to galvanize a collective and generate momentum for their initiative. Entrepreneurship, from this perspective, is a process of mindful deviation.[16]

If storytelling were the only challenge, for-profit entrepreneurs would have achieved a stronger foothold in the academy. What else can we tease out of the project of institutional mythopoesis?

During the 1990s, the investment strategies used by managers of university and foundation endowments evolved because they recognized that as a perpetual fund, they could trade off liquidity (the need to access funds at short notice) for the potential of earning greater returns over the long run. Universities and foundations recognized that their total return strategy—an investment approach that sought long-term capital appreciation as a source of producing a regular payout—allowed them to invest in private companies. The leveraged buyout and venture capital investors with whom the endowments invested did not have to focus on providing returns in the next quarter or even the next year. Instead, investors used pools of this patient money to invest in new, growing, or restructuring companies that targeted greater annualized returns over longer periods of time. To be sure, there were trade-offs in this style of investing: the performance of these investment managers would not be truly evaluated until the companies were sold or listed on the public stock exchanges. Judgment and ongoing assessment of the managers were required to gauge these funds' performance.

At the same time, endowments began to invest in absolute return funds and hedge funds, which use a wide range of investment strategies with the goal of performing in ways that are less tied to the ups and downs of the public markets. These strategies include short selling equities and bonds as well as investing "long" for positive returns, investing in arbitrage strategies around mergers or discrepancies between asset prices in different markets, and using quantitative strategies based on world market movements or macro theories about how political or economic forces will shape asset prices. On the one hand, some of these hedge funds performed very well in both up and down markets. On the other hand, some were secretive about their investments or their investment strategies, employed theoretical models that many investment committee members couldn't understand, charged high fees, could choose to lock up capital for long periods of time, and employed high degrees of leverage that could put the deployed capital at unreasonable risk.

Along with private equity, hedge funds are often categorized as "alternative assets." Institutions that had invested in alternative assets in the 1990s had done very well, but the work was not easy. As Swenson noted in *Pioneering Portfolio Management*, identifying and betting on the right managers meant more in these harder-to-understand investment strategies. Getting into the right funds and tracking their performance was a labor-intensive, knowledge-intensive activity. As these investments came into wider use among the sophisticated endowment managers at the large universities in the 1990s, the investment activities of most small colleges remained lodged in the volunteer investment committee of the Board of Trustees.

Committees were becoming aware of their own limitations. "It has become clear," Smith investment committee chair Nealie Small wrote at the beginning of the process that culminated in the hiring of Investure, "that a small, in-house staff cannot provide sufficient expertise, and a volunteer Investment Committee is not nimble enough to deal with quickly changing markets. A review of research in the industry and discussions with Cambridge Associates, a leading independent investment and financial consulting firm, has led us to conclude that Smith would have to have access to a larger team of professionals, with a higher level of expertise, if we wish to produce stellar performance in the current environment."[17] The investment committee at Dickinson College came to the same conclusion: "The three of us on the committee all worked in investments; we knew how hard it was. Basically, we knew how lucky we had been to make any of the right investments and that the endowment needed full-time attention to get it right."[18]

Scholars of strategic management Royston Greenwood, Roy Suddaby, and C. R. Hinings propose that certain types of contextual changes act as jolts that might spark institutional entrepreneurship by disturbing the socially constructed field-level consensus. When things are stable, "practices are reproduced by regulatory and interactive processes." But there can be jolts to the system, and they take the form of social upheaval and "technological disruptions, competitive discontinuities, and regulatory change."[19] At the end of the 1990s, it was a jolt to the endowment management ecosystem that investing in alternative assets had become a necessary strategy for endowments to meet their return targets. The jolt gives an opening; instigating change around one of these jolts requires an understanding of an institution's priorities and why a particular solution can address a particular institutional need.

The first question to ask in the face of such a jolt is whether the solution can be addressed locally. Might the solution to a change opportunity be conceptualized and addressed by local institutional resources? It makes obvious sense for local staff to solve local problems; that's what they're there for. As we've seen, Middlebury didn't have local staff to oversee its investment managers. This gap certainly makes the choice to look outside easier, especially because the responsibility being borne by the members of the volunteer board was making those board members uneasy. But what happens when local staff are eager to take on a problem, as in the case of the campuses that resisted Artstor? Seeking the significant resources they needed to digitize their slides had led some staff and institutions to ask Mellon for $1 million, which built our awareness of the problem. Others cheerily sought to plunge in on their own, despite the massive scope of the problem and the solution. In 2007, a staff member at SUNY Albany, the only large institution to cancel its Artstor subscription in our early years because they concluded that the subscription cost too much, posted on the Visual Resources Association listserv that it was ready to build its own digital image library:

> Having missed every wave of automation, digitization, and other computer-aided advance in visual resources, the University at Albany's Visual Resources Library has finally secured substantial funding to build a digital image database and web-based

delivery/presentation system through an internal grant program. This funding represents eight years of outreach, research, proposal writing (and rewriting), but we have finally received support for our project.

The requested funding will cover storage space, storage back-up, web server space, a database server, a database application, power supplies to these servers, racks for the servers, funding for the extra labor required, and two imaging and cataloging stations, although we have built in enough flexibility into our proposal to account for any unexpected expenses . . . There are very few constraints—I have the funding, our campus runs all of the major database server platforms (SQL, Oracle, UNIX), and we have nothing to transfer into the database from an older application. If you could send me your "dream set-up" descriptions and jus-tifications I would really appreciate it.[20]

Given the enormous scope of the task and unable to achieve its goals, the university soon resubscribed to Artstor. What we had taken on was a very big job, one that was best accomplished on a scalable and networked basis.

Consider, for example, the problems associated with the admis-sion, education, and career preparation of PhDs in the humanities. In the pre–COVID-19 era, only half of the students who'd received a graduate degree in history were getting any sort of job in academia, and of those, two-thirds were hired at teaching-intensive institutions even though most PhD programs are heavily focused on prepar-ing students for the type of research career that very few PhDs will have.[21] Those who built careers outside of the academy had been trained for specialized research, and while they can (and do) change paths and find jobs elsewhere, the institutional culture of gradu-ate education has maintained certain foundational subinstitutional myths about what constitutes the preparation of PhD students. Advi-sors often don't support their PhD candidates, or don't know how to support them, if they mention pursuing anything other than an academic career. Clearly, the transinstitutional system of PhD educa-tion, built around the established norms of institutions, is hardened against change. Organizational theorists Cynthia Hardy and Steve Maguire explain the *paradox of embedded agency*:

> If actors are embedded in an institutional field and subject to regulative, normative and cognitive processes that structure their cognitions, define their interests, and produce their identities . . . how are they able to envision new practices and then subsequently get others to adopt them? Dominant actors in a given field may have the power to force change but often lack the motivation; while peripheral players may have the incentive to create and champion new practices, but often lack the power to change institutions.[22]

The systemic challenges in PhD education are indeed difficult, but the solutions to those problems do not rest on local myth rewriting. Isomorphic pressures overshadow local impulses for reform: institutional decision-makers find themselves thinking, "If we take fewer students, someone else will just take more" or "If we change our graduate curriculum to support students in exploring career paths other than academic ones, we will lose the 'best' students to our competitors." Distinguishing a local challenge from a systemic challenge is an important step in determining which problems are best taken on with the help of organizations that are focused on systemic change. No institution is going to resolve an issue where the first mover advantage is actually a disadvantage. Internal entrepreneurs are particularly challenged by the paradox of trying to change a system while playing by its rules.[23] A look at the exasperating history of PhD reform or a conversation with an underemployed PhD recipient will confirm this conclusion.[24]

In short, the dense tapestry that we described earlier—local and transinstitutional norms define rules of advancement and mission-fulfillment for individuals—constrains change within an organization. No one gets rewarded for collective action, either within the institution or across institutions. Working as an agent for any change that isn't sanctioned means pushing against the rules of the game, a Sisyphean task that can crush the motivation to succeed. Change resistance within a sector-wide context cannot be resolved by people in dominant positions just "behaving better." Pierre Bourdieu, the sociologist who perhaps did more than anyone to delineate the complex intertwining of social, cultural, and economic capital, describes how even those in positions of dominance are, in a sense, trapped:

> Domination is the not the direct and simple action exercised by a set of agents ("the dominant class") invested with power of coercion. Rather, it is the indirect effect of a complex set of actions engendered within the network of intersecting constraints which each of the dominants, thus dominated by the structure of the field through which domination is exerted, endures on behalf of the others.[25]

Bourdieu may be using dramatic turns of phrase to make his point, but his point is real: the mix of various sets of values, some economic, some about manners, some about preferences that are formed by individuals and subcultures in intergenerational dialogue, are not easily disentangled. No one knows how we got here, and a lot of people know that the system is not working well. But how can we create replicable models for introducing and sustaining change?

The External Solution: Fitting In

To convince mission-driven staff and faculty, an outside entity needs to be able to explain why its solution has the potential to be *by its nature* better than the solution that would be the logical outcome of a local approach. Its new synthetic mythology must also make rational sense. Setting up a mission-driven, market-driven synthesizing intermediary is worth it only if (given enough time and enough good execution) your approach will be able to address an institution's problem distinctly better than the institution could do on its own. Alice Handy was able to tell stories that resonated with the complex politics of campus life, but she also was confident that the challenges of asset allocation and portfolio management had become too complicated for an institution without a significant team of specialized staff. In Artstor's case, we knew that the need for images of primary source materials was limitless. Because art is being created, discovered, and photographed in new ways (from new angles, with different light) every day, it was just a fact that no one institution could amass all that it needed on its own in the way that an aggregated and networked resource could. If local players can address the need by themselves, they will and they should, and an external provider is not the better answer. Where the scale of the optimal network is clearly beyond the reach of what would be built locally, institutions will find it harder to reject the narrative of an external solution.

An Ambitious External Entity with Aligned Aims

Having been immersed in the Mellon world of respecting the enduring and fad-resistant nature of institutions, I had mixed emotions in the early days of Artstor. Early on, I had argued that one of Artstor's major objectives was "to save colleges and universities money." However, my colleagues convinced me that we shouldn't set a goal that we ourselves could not tackle directly; we could proffer solutions, but only they could make the decisions both to rely on Artstor and then to seek to reduce or avoid other costs. Exasperated by the difficulty of convincing people of the obvious benefits of a collective approach to creating a digital image collection, my colleagues and I felt at times the allure of the disruptive innovation. But we didn't want to disrupt institutions of higher education—we wanted to support and sustain them, even though sometimes it felt like we wanted to help them more than they wanted to be helped.

Artstor (and Shared Shelf) sought to work within the system. At the same time, we promoted an alternative model to the status quo. Like the work of Investure, our work was fueled by a belief in co-creating with the institutions. In comparing US and European entrepreneurs in the for-profit markets, Raghud Garud and Peter Karnøe argue that US ventures are inclined to aim for "breakthroughs" rather than "bricolage." Bricolage connotes "resourcefulness and improvisation on the part of involved actors . . . characterized by co-shaping of emerging technological path as actors . . . [seeking] modest yet steady gains."[26] The search for breakthroughs, on the other hand, has a major drawback:

> Specifically, an approach that attempts to generate a break-through can end up stifling micro-learning processes that allow for the mutual co-shaping of emerging technological paths to occur. That is, actors in the US may have failed, not despite, but *because* of their pursuit of a breakthrough. Bricolage preserves emergent properties. It is a process of moving ahead on the basis of inputs of actors who possess local knowledge, but through their interactions, are able to gradually transform emerging paths to higher degrees of functionality.[27]

Garud and Karnøe conclude that "attempts at coming up with breakthroughs risks alienating those with vested interests,"[28] and that bricolage may be the better choice. This mutual co-shaping is a necessary component for building trust between an outside service and a college. Given the barriers of norms and myths that reject such entreaties, the external institutional entrepreneur must start with significant investments of time, effort, and understanding to establish mythopoesis. The making of new myths is not the work of smooth-talking salespeople. If the solution to a significant problem is optimally addressed on a larger-than-local basis, then mythopoesis should occur on a significant scale, too. George Lucas created a galaxy far, far away, and J.R.R. Tolkien invented entire languages and a history that stretched over eons, both of them seeking to give their creations the appearance of long-standing mythical worlds.

How can a new firm trying to help mission-driven institutions create similarly rich stories and establish legitimacy? Garud et al. explain how Sun Microsystems sought to create new technology standards for the web by giving away its JAVA language so that it would become the dominant internet code standard.[29] Like establishing technology standards, selling services to colleges by establishing new myths requires convincing those colleges that you are aligned with them. Sociologist Mark Suchman notes that legitimacy can be elusive and difficult to manipulate, but "self-sustaining once it is established." For example, if one is seeking legitimacy on the basis of a solution being practically effective, claiming that it is "the right thing to do" may not win over skeptics. "Crass pragmatic appeals," he notes, "may debase lofty moral claims, and hollow moral platitudes may signal shirking in pragmatic exchanges." The balance is difficult to achieve, but it is possible: "Better integrated, more firmly established regimes tend to hold these diverse legitimacy dynamics in close alignment, for example, by defining certain arenas in which self-interest is considered morally laudable, or in which social conscience is considered personally rewarding."[30]

We saw how Alice Handy achieved this goal by establishing internships for consortium institutions' students as a clear signal: "We are with you." At Artstor, we regularly invested in significant projects that we did not expect to bring in many or even any new subscribers. For example, when the staff at the Metropolitan Museum asked us to collaborate with them, we launched a service that provided images that scholars could use in publications for free. The project cost us time and upkeep, but it signaled to our campus constituencies that we had their well-being in mind. Like Sun Microsystems giving away its software in order to establish a market and a set of standards, we were ready to show that we were willing to spend money to build a new myth that aligned with our collaborators'. We were on their side; our mission was to support their mission. Our story was their story.

One of the founders of the now widely esteemed Central Park Conservancy in New York City, Artstor board member Lewis Bernard had intuited the need for a newly created organization to look like a very old organization. "We worked very hard to recruit Trustees whose names were known as supporting Lincoln Center or the New York Historical Society," Bernard said. "We knew that the Conservancy needed to look like it had always been there—and had always been something that people wanted to be a part of because of its legitimacy." The Conservancy was actually an innovative public-private partnership, but clothing it in the language of the old myths of New York society was one of the keys to gaining the community's trust.

The value of offering new products and services from outside of the institution might be very strong, but the barriers to acceptance—across institutions, norms, and reward systems both symbolic and material—are very high. Making the mythopoetic case for symbolic alignment is a start, but how does an outside agent not only gain entry to the stronghold but also leave with a signed contract and a check?

Establishing legitimacy might seem to require a heroic leader—someone capable of developing a new story that a change-resistant institution will make its own. As Garud writes, entrepreneurial agency is located "in a few individuals who have the full-blown ability to discover, create, and exploit opportunities that lie beyond the reach of most."[31] In commenting on an early draft of this chapter, Alice Handy did not see herself as a heroic figure. "I wish you would give more credit to the team," she wrote. Handy was making an important point: if an external organization is created to provide a scalable service to higher education, then the successful launch of that service requires experienced and talented people from different domains. This requirement was inherent in the Investure promise to identify, gain entrance to, and monitor the performance of various private equity partnerships and hedge funds. Given the lack of measures to gauge the current performance of these investments, experienced staff was needed to look deeply into the funds' holdings while still being able to gain insights into the investment managers' personal and professional plans.

Investure also needed staff members who were fully onboard with the ethos and mindset of being partners to the investors. Bruce Miller, who eventually became Alice's successor as CEO of the firm, reminded me that his original charge as director of private equity investments was not his only charge. His compensation was based not on the performance of Investure's private equity investments but rather on Investure's overall performance. In selecting colleagues, "we go through a lot of candidates," he told me,

> to find those who are ambitious enough and knowledgeable enough to understand what the GPs [general partners of the

private equity funds] are doing and who also are inclined to buy into our "whole firm" approach. Most of the good ones want to be compensated on their own individual calls; that doesn't work here. We need people who are self-possessed enough to listen to the team and step back from "his" or "her" ideas when someone else's preferred investment (in real estate or bonds or gold or whatever) is better for the effort. I went for a year in 2006 without making any investments because it didn't feel like private markets were the best bet for the Consortium's money. And while in some firms, it would have looked like I wasn't doing the work that I was hired to do, that's exactly what Alice wanted me to do.[32]

The idea behind Artstor—that every college in the country shouldn't scan its own slide of the *Mona Lisa*—was extremely simple. It was also ridiculously complicated to carry out. Like Investure, we had to find people who resonated with both the mission-driven work and the market-supported mode we were working in; those who worked on the front lines had to be able to talk about Fra Angelico or Chinese porcelain as well as proxy servers and the quirks of disabling pop-up blockers in different browsers. And indeed, throughout the organization we had extraordinary people who were accomplished in their fields and ready to venture out to change the sector. Gretchen Wagner, our general counsel and executive vice president, devised our intellectual property policies in ways that won over the entire community. Max Marmor, formerly the art librarian at Yale, was our first hire after Gretchen and discovered and brought in all of the original collections. Carole Ann Fabian had worked at the Getty, had led the art library and the academic computing center at SUNY Buffalo, and had served as president of the Art Libraries Society of North America (ARLIS). Nancy Allen had been the collection manager at the Museum of Fine Arts, Boston and had been awarded the ARLIS prize for distinguished service to the field. Bill Ying had been the chief technology officer at Columbia University's Fathom Ventures and was a tireless teacher and visionary. Dustin Wees had been in charge of cataloging at the Clark Art Institute and was loved and trusted by the visual resources community. Megan Marler, who came from Luna Imaging, a pioneering image management software firm, led all of our user support and all of our strategic partnerships around Shared Shelf. All of these people were talented politicians who ventured into rooms filled with skeptics everywhere they went; they put their reputations, which they'd built while embedded in institutions, at risk because they believed that Artstor could do something that was both helpful and important.

And they didn't bring only knowledge and networks to what we did. They led the way. In June 2007, we proposed to the board that we make a fundamental change in the way that we served our clients by allowing users to download full-screen-sized images for use in PowerPoint. Until that point, we had allowed users only to download postcard-sized images; they could use very large images only while working within the Artstor software environment. That system was deeply frustrating to many of our users. But I had been resistant to changing that policy for a number of reasons. First, I was concerned about our content providers; many of them were still very anxious about how providing images to Artstor would affect their business model. Second, I worried that some subscribing institutions would download the images that they wanted and then cancel their subscription. Third, I feared that we would no longer be able to track usage, which had provided us with valuable data for marketing our work. When a teacher (or a class full of students) clicked on an image in the Artstor environment, that click was added to the user statistics that were helpful in winning new subscribers, content contributors, and funders. If we allowed users to download bigger images, we wouldn't be able to count usage anymore: a professor who used a hundred images in a PowerPoint presentation semester after semester in an introductory lecture class of three hundred students would post that PowerPoint to a course website and the students would click on it repeatedly to study for midterms and finals. Under the new system, our user stats would record only one use despite these multiple engagements. For all these reasons, I believed we had to be cautious, even though many professors had voiced their frustration during my campus visits.

In the spring of 2007, Gretchen Wagner and Louise Kelly (who led our user data analytics effort) came to see me. They told me that we had to allow bigger downloads or risk losing our users. We talked through all the concerns described above. We could see answers to some of the problems, but certainly not to all of them. When we wrote the board that June, we spelled out the history of the issue:

> We have known from the outset that restricting the size of images that could be downloaded from the Artstor Library to 400 pixels (roughly a reference-sized image, suitable for use in a student paper or for study) would have two implications: (1) content owners would gain comfort from knowing that Artstor was taking measures to prevent inappropriate uses of their images; and (2) some number of our users would be frustrated because they would not be free to use Artstor content in whatever software environment they might choose. Our strategy was to build a trusted space first, and then to determine if—as time went by—it made sense to modify the constraints because it is always easier to loosen such restrictions rather than to tighten them.[33]

After presenting the data from user surveys and discussing the risks, we concluded that our key goal was to demonstrate that we were truly acting as partners to the campuses we had set out to serve:

> Allowing larger downloads for most of the Artstor collections will not only better meet the needs of individual users, but also generate significant goodwill among our participating institutions. While we have made a lot of progress in this area over the past two years, taking a step like this would demonstrate that we trust participating institutions and view them as partners in our larger aims. There is certainly a level of business risk associated with opening up our locked environment; on the other side, there is also business risk with local efforts forging ahead without us and viewing Artstor with indifference or frustration due to incompatibility. Over the longer term, our ability to sustain our place will depend on our users deriving continuing value from Artstor.[34]

The board approved this change, and it was a crucial moment in Artstor's development. Usage increased dramatically and local do-it-yourself efforts lost their strongest argument against Artstor. Now we could work with local staff in supporting their users in the ways that they wanted to. This strategy decision changed—and most likely saved—Artstor. It happened because the Artstor staff knew the right answer and had the wisdom and courage to tell the organization's CEO that I was just wrong.

In other words, the idea that institutional entrepreneurs are always heroic leaders is ultimately misguided due to the complexity of interacting with so many campus constituencies in so many languages. Of course, any successful business requires the leadership of someone like Alice Handy. But it also requires a model that can address the complexity of the task of change.[35] Doing something difficult at scale requires a lot of people with particular expertise who can participate in the myth co-creation, the mythopoesis that builds a bridge between an outside entity and internal organizational constituencies. Myth-building requires a great deal of mutual care and respect from both sides. And yet, as we saw in chapter 3, it isn't always possible to tell where campus decision-makers' symbolic imperatives end and their material concerns begin. Having the ability and the interest in coscripting how an external agent and local faculty and staff can co-create together is necessary but not sufficient for changing organizational practices.

The Importance of the Market Test

JSTOR, the archive of scholarly journals that is beloved by scholars and students around the world, was invented and developed by Kevin Guthrie (following Bill Bowen's original insight that even 1994's scanning technology was good enough to free libraries from storing miles of bound back issues of journals). My memory of the earliest test of JSTOR is that it went incredibly well. It was 1995 and Kevin would sit down with an impatient senior scholar of American history in front of a terminal that contained the back issues of a journal such as the *American Historical Review*. The faculty member was there at the behest of his university president, who had told the president of the Mellon Foundation that yes, of course, the school would be happy to help with a test of this "thing." Kevin would then ask the professor what he was working on, and the professor would respond with something like, "banking regulation in Iowa during the Polk administration." Kevin then typed those words in and hit the ENTER key. As relevant journal articles dating back to 1895 appeared on the screen, the professor's grouchiness evaporated. "I didn't know that Trimble had written that. Wait, when was the Nute article published? Hold on, let me just write down that reference." I used to tease Kevin about how easy his job was, because when I sat with a professor to demo Artstor, the response would be something like "Why on earth don't you have a pre-restoration picture of the inscription above the leftmost spandrel of the apse of the chapel of a small town outside of Orvieto that might have been done by a follower of Cimabue? Without that, this thing is really not going to be helpful."

When an innovation is so immediately and apparently valuable to key campus constituents, as JSTOR was, it might seem that an entrepreneurial firm can take a shortcut and avoid collaboration with on-campus staff. Early on, it seemed likely that JSTOR would pass the market's test and be able to sell subscriptions. But even so, JSTOR's management still chose to establish an environment of trust because they knew that they needed to forge a collaboration between very skeptical constituencies of suppliers (publishers) and consumers (libraries). If they had neglected to build that balance, delicate questions of intellectual property might have exploded. Moreover, the ecosystem was interconnected: the end-users who wanted the journals also wanted the journals' publishers (such as academic societies) to be protected. Armed with this knowledge, Kevin and his colleagues invited libraries to become partners from the beginning. They also had to create a partnership with the scholarly societies—the horizontal institutions—that owned and continued to create many of the journals. Doing so in a way that balanced the parties' interests and addressed the societies' fears was essential to establishing a mission-driven project. Many of today's disintermediating ed-tech firms, from Course Hero to ResearchGate, may not be interested in building that trust. If their offerings are compelling enough to disintermediate the institutional partners that organizations such as JSTOR or Artstor seek to enlist, they may succeed financially. But they also may not stand the test of time if their community-spanning projects run into trust-damaging and/ or legal complications. Pragmatism can be powerful, but legitimacy and pragmatism together might be more durable.

Acting in ways that demonstrated that we saw our mission as intertwined with those of our users affirmed that Artstor could share—and even collaborate in rewriting—the symbolic stories of the campus. Doing so had concrete ramifications for our business model as well. It advanced our young organization's material security, which we needed to survive and to continue fulfilling our promises. The symbolic co-creation made our service worth paying for. The words of our intentions were shown to be more than just words when we took actions that made enough sense to our buyers on campuses to continue to sign up and write checks to support our work. The testing of ideas happens as William James famously noted, when those ideas are shown to have worldly meaning: "If you follow the pragmatic method, you cannot look on any such word as closing your quest. You must bring out of each word its practical cash-value, see it at work within the stream of your experience." It's necessary, but not sufficient, for synthetic solutions to align with the symbolic goals, local myths, and life stories of decision-makers on campus. To thrive, however, the solution needs to do more than pass the symbolic test; it needs to provide sufficient tangible value for the decision-maker to choose to allocate scarce resources to the external provider. Passing this market test is the key to getting past the perhaps hidden, perhaps unconscious psychodrama playing out in the heads of the decision-makers who are pondering whether to buy or to build. When they sign the check, they are casting their lot with a joint venture, and they are going to be judged on how well the jointly constructed solution works out.

The material interests of staff or faculty don't—and shouldn't—end with a commitment to a mutually beneficial relationship with an outside provider. Decision-makers who write synthesis into a campus's story can also write their own material advancement into the new story. In the case of Artstor, coalitions of supporters on the organizational buying side figured out how the shared undertaking could help them create a new institutional success story. Brian Shelbourne, the visual resources curator at UMass Amherst recognized that Artstor, which provided images from a wide range of collections that could support the rapidly growing interest in using images in fields from religion to law, could help him construct a new future for the institution and for himself. "Of course, I'll always take care of the art historians," he said. "But I also know how to make this kind of content work—in classrooms, in research, on course websites. If we [visual resource curators] insist on limiting ourselves to art history, we're dead. If we remind the library and academic computing of all the things that we're good at, we can be valuable to them and to everybody they serve." Today, Brian is head of the digital scholarship services at the UMass Libraries.[36]

US colleges and universities will thrive as dedicated and talented faculty and staff seek (and find) efficient and effective solutions. When decision-makers conclude that an external co-creator can provide better value and are willing to commit institutional resources to it, they are doing more than signing off on a contract. They are also reconciling their local, unit, or departmental goals with what should be an overall organizational mandate to contain the unsustainable cost model associated with endless go-it-alone projects. They are fitting in with a *need* that often isn't used as a guiding narrative. Before they write the check, they may be telling themselves a story that, in their particular case, cost concerns *must* be sacrificed in the name of fulfilling some particular version of their mission. After they commit to a joint solution, they fit into the larger story, like an individual tile in the mosaic of organizational cost effectiveness.

Some challenges are so significant that they cannot be reconciled within the organization, and the solutions need to be sustained even through discontinuity. In 2014, Investure faced a test of whether its story was working for the consortium institutions or just for individuals. Ten years after the Investure Consortium was created, I was serving on the Smith College board's investment committee as it debated a proposal from Investure to raise the fees that the college paid to Investure. The trustees who had been there when Smith began working with Investure—Nealie Small, Pat McPherson, Ann Kaplan, Nina Scherago—had completed their terms or rotated off the investment committee. As a result, the investment committee was mostly new, and some members were skeptical of Investure's proposal to increase its fees, which had for ten years been far below market rate in recognition of the central importance of Smith in creating the consortium. The committee had been very happy with Investure's work, but nobody likes writing bigger checks.

At the same time that Smith was debating the issue of increased fees, our work at Artstor was getting more challenging. Our relationship with the Mellon Foundation was based on an arm's-length distance. Shared Shelf wasn't gaining customers as fast as we had planned, and some of the original partners, including Harvard, had experienced a complete turnover of the personnel with whom we'd worked. The new people saw us as vendors; we felt that they were squeezing all they could out of us, and we knew that our reputation was at risk if we didn't do whatever they wanted. The balance of our symbolic and business-driven relationship with the original institutions that had joined us to collectively create Shared Shelf was tilting away from being a shared symbolic undertaking and was increasingly becoming a stressed business relationship. Since its beginning, Investure had held an annual dinner with the investment committees of the consortium institutions. In the fall of 2014, as the Smith board considered the Investure proposal to raise fees and even whether to continue its relationship with Investure, I sat next to Bruce Miller, then one of the Investure senior partners, at the dinner. "Our senior people, we're all fine," he said. "The firm has thrived and so have we. But we need to keep our young talent. They're so good. If they go other firms, they'll make a lot more money. So, we can either add clients and lose the focus of the Consortium so that we can pay them, or we can raise the initial members' fees to something like the rate that is now everywhere out there as market rate."[37]

Bruce's comment made me remember an early Artstor presentation to a large joint meeting of the Visual Resources Association (VRA) and the Art Libraries Society (ARLIS) in 2004, a few weeks after we announced the Artstor fee structure. "Why are you charging us so much money?" someone asked half in anger, half in sadness. "Do you have any idea how small our budgets are? I thought that the Mellon Foundation was trying to do something helpful." Earlier in my life, I had thought that I was going to be a professor and had never thought that I would lead the sale of a product. But I knew that our fee structure was not only fair but also important to our buyers. "We don't for a second expect the art history department or the art library to pay for Artstor," I responded. "It's a campus-wide resource, and it has to earn its place in the campus-wide library. But even more important: I think that you *want* to be paying us. We are asking you to trust us to help you do work that is big and difficult and central to your mission. The last thing you want is for us to make commitments to you and not have a plan for keeping our promises." We knew that when colleges made the decision to pay for our service, they were recognizing that relying on us—in partnership—was better than trying to solve the problem by themselves.

Getting this financial buy-in is essential because campus-based decision-makers don't hold up signs or switch hats when they are switching from their mode of writing their own mission to planning their own material path forward. As mission-driven agents, they mix the personal and professional, which includes eliding their professional and personal narratives of success. People come in packages, and they are rarely capable of disentangling their various motivations in such an environment. Agreeing to pay for a service goes beyond symbolic buy-in, allowing market discipline to align external providers and internal priorities. The outside firm needs to be paid in order to do what it does and do it well.

Smith eventually agreed to Investure's proposed fee increase. I saw Alice at a board meeting a few meetings later. I apologized that the process of agreeing to the fee increase had taken quite a while and had included a fairly extensive effort to re-underwrite the firm and Smith's relationship with it. "Totally fine," Alice replied. "It's just process. It's just process." Later, when reading a draft of this chapter, she mentioned that maintenance of relationships with Investure clients is ongoing: "It is hard work to maintain the initial enthusiasm and remember what it was like before the relationship. It needs to be constantly renewed."

At Middlebury and other colleges joining with Investure, the decision was made by the trustees. However, most day-to-day resource allocation decisions aren't made by trustees, whose livelihood isn't an issue. This is not to suggest that they did not care about the outcome, their performance, and the perceptions of their performance. But their material interests were farther from the do-it-yourself decision than the staff's interests. Nonetheless, the trustees still had to reflect on whether their enjoyment in doing the work (and their confidence in their own capacity) outweighed other considerations. These boards—without material interests intertwined with the decision—recognized that they had too much to do in their day jobs and so decided to pay someone else to do what they believed was best for the college.

As the partnership with Investure advanced, the boards were able to monitor its value and results because norm-setting intermediaries helped them understand what was happening. Unlike many harder-to-measure parts of campus life, investment performance is conducive to good measurement. The National Association of College and University Business Officers (NACUBO) tracked Investure's performance for each of the colleges and located those data in the national landscape. The investment committees knew the results of having outsourced the management of their endowments.[38] Over time, if higher education is to make any material progress on the cost crisis, the most important measure will likely be the net price for college tuition. Fuzzier measures of "excellent progress" might be worthless or even counterproductive.

Building and establishing shared solutions that save institutions money requires building services that last and partnerships that focus on saving higher education money. Investure's experience points to another important baseline: outside solutions must remain aligned with campuses' needs even as people on both sides change. Discontinuity in staffing can, of course, affect consortia as the partnership's dynamics change. In 2014, the first Investure clients withdrew from the consortium as their organizational priorities (concerning investments in fossil fuels) were no longer aligned with some of the investment vehicles that Investure used to generate returns; Swenson's original warning concerning the principal-agent dilemma came to the surface due to a difference in investment values, not a misalignment of self-serving motives. Middlebury and Dickinson remain Investure clients, though at some point they may alter their needs or priorities as well. "I always knew that these relationships might not last forever," Handy notes. "When an endowment grows large enough or when paths diverge, there needs to be a way out. We were built with that eventuality in mind." With its endowment reaching nearly $3 billion, Smith decided to build its own in-house team in 2020. Investure seems to continue to thrive after Handy's retirement in December 2018, a transition that could have led to discontinuity in the narrative arc of the firm's history.

When new mission-driven and market-supported intermediaries get past the cultural myths of the person or departments whose partnership they need, they get inside the walls of the institutions. They get to where people are ready to talk about business in a place of shared interest. When they arrive, first as emissaries establishing trust and then as partners, both they and the decision-makers who had earlier tried to repel them from the walls realize that they aren't engaged in a battle. Instead, they're on the same team. Both parties can share a mission by crafting a story in which they can all be on the right side.[39]

For institutional entrepreneurs, the traditional conquering hero model isn't the right one. Any external provider selling to colleges and universities—collaboratively or disruptively—might understandably bemoan the confusing landscape of conflicting life stories and institutional myths into which they've stumbled. It's natural to be conscious of and frustrated by such a dramatic set of behaviors that resist change, especially when there's some suspicion of latent careerist motivations on the part of the potential buyer. But in the end, if they see the story as a heroic duel that comes down to "us or them," they aren't going to win because the institutional defenses that reject aggressive invaders are just too strong. Those battling for change from either inside or outside of the organization have to realize that the battle metaphor is not an appropriate one. Weaving the outside organization's story into a campus's tapestry requires re-creating and rewriting what the people within the institution had thought to be their fate, not conquering them.

I've argued that there are a few stages in the synthesis that aligns the work of outside organizations with the work of those on campus. First, it only makes sense to gear up for this work if one is taking on a problem that's sufficiently complicated. Then, it's of central importance to build a team of specialists geared to the task and passionate about compatible work. The work of symbolic alignment comes next, as the outside team is able to do the hard work of proving to users that this new solution is optimally aligned with a new narrative that addresses both local stories of success and serves the organizational need for cost efficiency. I've also argued that gaining a shared financial commitment to the solutions is essential both to forge a genuine co-authoring of the solution and to sustain that narrative through times of personnel changes. The new narrative has to be durable because the way that nonprofits enable individuals to define their own mission leaves projects unusually exposed to rewriting when the personnel who make contractual decisions change.

Sustaining the new narrative, jointly created by the campus constituencies and the outside team, long enough to build trust and have an ongoing role in the work of the campus should not rely on a notion that enthusiastic change agents can will the project into being. Instead, a successful synthetic service provider needs to be able to hire and retain talent who can then overserve opinion-leading individuals and organizations in a system where isomorphism is, for better or worse, an almost irresistible force.

This kind of work requires money. Building this kind of enterprise requires a capitalization ecosystem that can support it, and while pieces of such a system exist, this unusual kind of venture clearly does not fit into traditional boxes for creating and sustaining the normal market firms. In the next chapter, I turn to the profound financial challenges associated with carrying out system-changing work.

5

The Incomplete Financing System for Mission- and Market-Compatible Ventures

By 2015 it was pretty clear that the denouement of Artstor's story as an independent organization was approaching. I was having lunch with George McCulloch, a founding partner of Level Equity, a growth equity venture capital firm. George had joined the Artstor board only six months earlier. I was trying to explain to him why the Mellon Foundation had decided not to provide any funding for Shared Shelf. I summarized our history with Mellon, explaining its role as the funder that had created our organization. I also said that I felt that Artstor had been doing everything that it had set out to do, and that we had been talking with Mellon since 2007 about what we needed to do to secure growth equity for our new product. But now, fifteen years into our organizational life and with Shared Space having a difficult time getting traction, the foundation was not only resisting the idea of providing any funding for Shared Shelf but also urging us to merge with—really, be absorbed by—our much larger cousin, ITHAKA/JSTOR. I was part of the way through recounting the fifteen-year history when it became clear that George, not I, was going to be the one making sense of it all.

George asked me about the Mellon leadership over the past fifteen years. I explained that Bill Bowen had stepped down from the Mellon presidency in 2006 and was replaced by Don Randel, who had been replaced in 2013 by Earl Lewis.

"Yeah, that one," he said, referring to Bill. "He took all the upside. Nothing left for the next guy except for downside risk. Lender's dilemma." My blank expression made it clear that I had no idea what he meant. "If someone lends you a hundred dollars," he explained, "it's your problem. If they lend you a million dollars, it's their problem. All they want to hear from you is that everything is fine, that you don't need any more money. They don't want to hear about all the cool things that you could do with more money; they just don't want to own any of your risk."

George was completely right. The path to Artstor being absorbed into ITHAKA/JSTOR took some time, and like many founding CEOs I had a difficult time letting go. The Artstor library of images, which had become a valued part of the work at two thousand institutions, moved into the very safe hands of ITHAKA/JSTOR. The new product—Shared Shelf—was putting a serious strain on our organization, but ITHAKA/JSTOR seemed glad to be getting it, too; Shared Shelf would give them a cloud-based workflow and publishing platform that it could provide to libraries as one part of its large array of highly valued services. ITHAKA/JSTOR also took over some of our headaches (such as Harvard's demands), and even though I didn't miss those struggles, it was still painful to hand over promises that I had made to someone else to fulfill.

In retrospect, what is striking about that conversation with George is that he grasped the situation so clearly, and his analysis was exactly right. He had seen this kind of scenario before in companies in which his firm had invested. But at Artstor, the "upside" that Bill and the Mellon Foundation of the early 2000s had captured wasn't the upside—an increase in the market value of a financial asset—with which George was familiar. Bill and the Mellon Foundation hadn't received a penny in financial returns from the tens of millions of real dollars that they had deployed in creating and nurturing Artstor as an organization. Instead, the "upside" of Artstor's early success was a metaphor; Artstor's success reflected well on the Mellon leadership that had created it. George was using an analogy based on comparing behavior of investors in his world of investments with the motivations of philanthropic "investors." The patterns of human and institutional behavior that George recognized from his investing world allowed him to understand the dynamics in this realm, where philanthropic goals were clearly not the same as those of a financial investor. The metaphors showed the similarities, but there also had to be differences.

In creating Artstor, Mellon hadn't needed to parse whether it was investing in an organization that was akin to a profit-seeking car dealership or metaphorically investing in (that is, donating to) a mission-driven church-like effort. If it had done so, it would have recognized that on the one hand, the foundation was providing significant start-up financing for a venture that would sell digital content and services to other firms. In this mode it was creating a market-driven entity that would offer the benefits of scale, sell on a business-to-business basis, and seek to capture the value that was embedded in the fragmented do-it-yourself campus efforts of creating and managing digital assets. On the other hand, the foundation would have realized that by providing support for a major new initiative to broaden and democratize awareness of our collective cultural history, it was in essence providing philanthropic funding to bolster colleges' and universities' efforts in areas of study (the arts and humanities) that aligned with the foundation's values.

A logical question would have been: What units of measure should the foundation use to measure its return on this mixed investment strategy? Because the foundation hadn't specifically parsed the different goals of its investment, it hadn't created any structured basis for determining whether to provide additional funding for the enterprise once the original founding personalities had left the foundation. And yet one of the first lessons that we learn in our middle-school math classes is "Keep your units of measure straight." Unfortunately, in organizations that provide capital for mission-driven but market-supported ventures, it's pretty common not to know how to keep one's units of investment or return straight. This chapter is about those units of investment, the paths of organizations that need investment capital to thrive, and the investors who may or may not know how to calculate the various returns that they are seeking.

In creating Artstor as a scalable solution to a systemic need, the foundation had made a strategic investment in the well-being of the higher education community. The return on that investment was going to be counted not in money being returned to the foundation but rather in the material and symbolic value that would accrue to the institutions and individuals in the community. Matt Bannick, formerly managing director at the Omidyar Network (the social good corporation established by eBay founders Pierre and Pam Omidyar), writes about how the thinking at the Network evolved after it made several attempts to use philanthropy to address social issues. Because it was so difficult for the Network to measure the success of gifts and grants that they had made, they turned to investing in companies whose work would, by its nature, make the world better. In other words, they would rely on the mechanism of the market to determine when an organization was successful. If a company's business goal was to create a better battery to store energy generated by solar panels, then environmental benefits would accrue as a byproduct of the business aim, which could be measured in traditional market measures of market share, revenues, and profits. For a few years, they invested in for-profit ventures with such aims. But after some time, the Network started to question whether a firm's financial success was always the right measure for gauging its portfolio of social-good investments. As Bannick wrote:

> With time, we realized that this insistence on risk-adjusted returns would cause us—and the impact investing industry as a whole—to systematically under-invest in creating the conditions under which innovations—and entire new sectors—could be sparked and scaled. We realized that if we truly cared most about sector creation, then we needed to develop a way to

account for the total value creation of the firm, including sector value creation as well as the firm's direct social impact and financial returns.[1]

In this chapter, I review the various ways in which reconciling the accounting of a social-good investment is a jumbled mess. If Bannick is right, then the financial accounting of invested funds should count the value of opening up a new sector of investment that others had avoided because of the risks. The costs avoided by institutions that benefit from a venture that provides a shared solution should be tabulated as part of the total value creation. This idea—accounting for the firm's total value creation—embraces a systems approach in which the synthetic service–providing firm and its investors are aligned with (rather than extractive from) its market. To take a systems approach, there first needs to be a system. And to have a system work toward a given end, the system needs to have a shared goal.

Faster Cures: Sharing a Goal as Prerequisite for Systems Change

Financier Michael Milken had been funding cancer research for twenty years when he was diagnosed with advanced prostate cancer in 1993. He was surprised by how little he knew about that disease. "Even more surprising," he wrote, "was the lack of interest in the medical community. The National Cancer Institute didn't fund much research on prostate cancer because they received few grant applications. Physician-scientists weren't submitting the applications because there appeared to be little funding available. It was a vicious circle. The field was so moribund that one young investigator was told by his mentor to avoid the 'career suicide' of prostate cancer research."[2]

In many ways, Michael Milken was in a very unusual position when his doctors told him that he was likely to die within two years. He had just emerged from two years in prison, the result of a financial career that some see as one in which he "threw off great ideas all day long"[3] and others deem to be a story of "the use of the underworld tactics of the con and the shakedown . . . in the world of finance on a national and international scale."[4] Whether his finance skills had been deployed in virtuous or villainous ways, it seems clear that he had unusual insight into how systems work and an unusual ability to tell stories to take advantage of opportunities that the financial system enabled. As someone who had a capacity for understanding systems, his cancer diagnosis and daunting prognosis focused his mind not on vague support for research but on the process of coordinating systemic efforts to create and deliver cures to patients. As he tried to determine why there was no particular sense of urgency to address a problem that he had suddenly found to be a matter of life or death, he recognized that each of the renowned cancer research institutes "considered the others to be competitors rather than collaborators in cancer research."[5] At the same time, in the for-profit world of large pharmaceutical companies, "industries weren't allocating enough research funds to cancer drug development because they didn't think the return on investment would justify the risk."[6] Medical research was bounding along in ways that interested and rewarded researchers, and drug companies were focused on investing primarily in safer, bigger products. There was no systematic approach to advance the specific goal of creating and delivering cures for prostate cancer to patients.

Milken's solutions partially relied on his capacity to provide money and, more important, to facilitate systemic approaches. "The problem wasn't a lack of financial capital," Milken said. "It was a lack of human capital. . . . Surgeons, medical oncologists, radiologists, biomedical researchers, and other scientists had too little communication outside of their respective specialties. . . . Another concern was that researchers were spending far too much time writing applications for grants."[7] In his notorious earlier career, he had transformed the finance industry by dramatically expanding the use of junk bonds, which were issued by companies with lower credit ratings, and which thus paid investors higher rates of return to compensate for the risk that the investment represented. In that context, Milken had written about how the financial system determined how access to capital did, or did not, enable people's ideas to be translated into action:

> My studies showed that access to capital—the lifeblood of business—had always been restricted. In medieval times, it vested in royalty and the church. With the 19th-century revolution in manufacturing, capital access broadened to a small group of industrialists and their bankers. And even as late as the 1960s, capital was controlled by a few large financial institutions that doled it out to their privileged clientele, who invariably were male, white, and "established." As one of the most highly regulated industries in the nation, the banks were encouraged to provide loans only to borrowers perceived as "safe."[8]

Whatever one's opinion of Milken's career in finance, it is clear that he brought a significant understanding of systems to his work on delivering cures for diseases. He looked at the various players and their motivations for deploying or utilizing capital and set out to tinker with the system so that capital could support the motivations of the players involved under the umbrella of shared system aims. Ultimately, his systemic approach to prostate cancer proved effective both for the field and for him. After making substantial progress in the 1990s on aligning researchers, doctors, pharmaceutical companies, and government funders associated with prostate cancer, Milken moved beyond his own disease (which had been chased into remission) and created an organization called Faster Cures, which focuses on "working to build a system that is effective, efficient, and driven by a clear vision: working with our partners to build a patient-centric system."[9]

What Milken had seen when he focused on the world of medical research and drug development was a fragmented landscape of different players with different goals and little systematic effort to collaborate or coordinate around what might seem like an obvious goal: providing cures for patients. Larry Bacow's insight that "there is no natural constituency for cost control on a university campus" is true of the entire higher education sector taken as a whole. US higher education aims to serve many ends—to prepare students for all segments of the workforce, to conduct the world's research, to be all things to all seekers—but can we really point to any systematic effort to reduce the cost structure of the enterprise and hence the price of tuition? While there is a natural constituency for controlling costs—students and their families—they are oddly without a coherent voice. Throughout the sector, their voice is fragmented by the wide diversity of ends that they are seeking from college. In going to college, some are seeking a kind of church (e.g., personal growth, learning, satisfaction), and others are seeking a kind of car dealer (e.g., material or social advancement). Believing what they have been told—that they are investing financially in their personal financial advancement—they accept the terms of the transaction.

In the case of schools with competitive and selective admissions, students and families don't complain about the price because they are buyers with little leverage. Their voices are not unified and harmonized to challenge the cost of the enterprise in the way that Milken sought to align various players in the medical system, including patients, to respond to a clear and compelling need. Students and families are treated as—and hence they act as—buyers in an elaborately constructed market where the sellers have hard-to-track strategies that bestow hard-to-track benefits. In this chapter, we review the existing half-established and fragmented mechanisms that could support the creation and nurturing of organizations that could do the hard work of reducing the cost of college. We begin with an important and perhaps obvious realization: the goal of fundamentally changing the cost structure of US colleges and universities will never be achieved if we don't collectively agree that doing so is important. Capital flows only when those who provide funds know the end to which those scarce resources are being deployed; if we don't agree that lowering the rate of cost increases associated with producing a college education (and hence the price paid by students and families) is a shared goal, then we surely won't achieve it.

Educational innovation is funded in a variety of ways: locally, coincident with faculty or staff doing their daily work and devising a solution to a problem that they encounter; with support from a college or university's own funds via institutional or individual philanthropy; or from outside-the-system return-seeking investors. For-profit educational firms that may mix strategies of institutional collaboration with the possibility of ultimately disrupting their institutional partners raise private venture capital based on the promise of high growth. In the tour of synthetic intermediaries, we have seen different models: the National Student Clearinghouse was funded by an enormous for-profit firm, Artstor's and TIAA's start-up capital came from foundations, Investure was floated by its founders and initial clients. These organizations operated in unusual circumstances. They each had enough capital to get off the starting line, establish a value proposition, and receive a positive market signal in the form of earned income when their services proved themselves to be useful.

This chapter's key question—How do we finance these synthesis-seeking intermediary organizations?—rests on the need for collective and systemic thinking toward a defined, shared, and urgent goal. The good news is that pieces of a financing system exist, having been developed as various players inconsistently pursued inconsistently defined goals. These components offer a few models that could become clearer and more focused with collaborative planning.

We start, however, with a relevant story of a rapidly developing systemic approach to student-centricity in higher education. A loose network of people and organizations are aligning their efforts to develop a systemic approach that starts with the proposition that higher education doesn't currently serve students well enough. In this way, it recalls the emerging strategy in medical research of focusing on patient-centricity. Still, its vision of the future has some significant gaps.

Throughout the 2010s, a coalition of frustrated higher education leaders, technology entrepreneurs, and reform-minded funders began to develop a systemic alignment for a potentially disruptive approach to higher education. In 2011, Clay Christensen and his coauthors had turned their focus to higher education; their book *Disrupting College* described how online education would disrupt the change-resistant system of colleges and universities:

Plugging a disruptive innovation into an existing business model never results in transformation of the model; instead, the existing model co-opts the innovation to sustain how it operates. What this means is that, generally speaking, the disruption of higher education at public universities will likely need to be managed at the level of state systems of higher education, not at the level of the individual institutions, which will struggle to evolve.

This emerging disruptive innovation [online education] also presents an opportunity to rethink many of the age-old assumptions about higher education—its processes, where it happens, and what its goals are—and to use the disruptive start-up organizations to create institutions that operate very differently and more appropriately to address the country's challenges.[10]

At the same time that *Disrupting College* was published, Arizona State University and Global Silicon Valley hosted their first joint conference, known as ASU-GSV, to bring together educational technology firms, investors, and higher education funders. For firms in the educational technology sector (commonly referred to as "ed tech"), the dominant model of change grows from Christensen's conclusion that colleges and universities cannot or will not change their models with their consumers in mind. Many in the ed tech community believe that today's colleges and universities need to be disrupted.

This growing effort to restructure higher education includes not only the traditionally market-driven firms who see in global higher education a $70 billion market but also the mission-driven agents who worry about the lifetime opportunities of students who face ever-rising tuition (and concomitant loan burden), half of whom will carry this loan burden despite falling short of gaining a college degree. And of course, as we have seen throughout this book, many people and institutions have some mix of these material and symbolic motivations. These players come together at ASU-GSV, which counts among its sponsors the Gates Foundation; the Walton Family Foundation; the Chan Zuckerberg Initiative; ed tech/publisher giants such as Pearson, 2U, and ETS; and other firms too big not to be interested in a $70 billion industry, including Google,

Amazon, Goldman Sachs, and KKR. What are the unusual circum-stances in which these charitable foundations and investment banks work together?

In 2016, the Lumina Foundation, one of the many sponsors of ASU-GSV, announced its first *impact investments*, not grants but rather equity investments in for-profit firms. Having been created from the $770 million proceeds from the sale of the USA Group to Sallie Mae, the Lumina Foundation has set a singular goal: to increase the proportion of Americans with high-quality degrees and other credentials to 60 percent by 2025. Lumina's clarity of mission focus is highly unusual among foundations that tend to work in a number of areas with a more diffuse set of objectives. The reason-ing behind the foundation impatience rests on the fact that six years after they start attending four-year institutions, only 62 percent of US college students have graduated.[11] In addition, after four years of attending a community college, only 28 percent of students have completed a degree.[12] Like Christensen, many in the ed tech com-munity, including Lumina, feel that traditional institutions are fall-ing far short in serving students. They've concluded that it's time to stop believing that institutions are the right vehicle for bringing about change and have instead decided to invest in models that they see as directly supporting students. Lumina's first such investment was in Credly, an alternate credentialing service that, according to Lumina, "empowers organizations to officially recognize individuals for demonstrated competencies and skills"[13] and aims "to spur social innovation in postsecondary learning."[14]

Credly enables people to mix academic credits from traditional institutions with those from online courses and work or military experience. Lumina's clarity of goals leaves it agnostic to the gov-ernance structure of organizations or firms that might help to accelerate student degree attainment. After investing in Credly, the foundation also made equity investments in fourteen other for-profit firms that provide services to students (whether or not those firms work with or around colleges and universities).[15] John Duong, who led Lumina's direct investing in companies, spelled out the clarity of its goals:

Many students getting an education are doing so with some career aspirations in mind, and it is the learning institution's job to help them. They're not like, "Hey, I'm just going to go and learn"—which is fine if you have that luxury—but the majority of people going into school are trying to get the skills necessary to get them to a better professional career track and pathway.[16]

Investors like Lumina are bound to be less dogmatic about the mechanisms for creating a focus on student-centricity—less concerned with whether the organizations that can help are for-profit or nonprofit, or whether the effort is campus-based or external to the system. This approach certainly makes sense given their frustration with the pace of the system's service to students, but as students' concerns come to the fore, these different providers will, of course, have different priorities. Workforce success has always been part of the college equation, though it isn't the only reason to attend college. The priorities and actions of the investors and firms that define the terms of student-centricity will affect the colleges and universities with whose work they intersect.

Historian Steve Mintz, a longtime advocate for making colleges more efficient and effective, has suggested what the stakes are for colleges (especially those in difficult economic situations) when working with these firms:

> Campuses have, in the past, outsourced a host of services previously provided in-house, typically involving janitorial and food services, and are increasingly partnering in areas like student housing. The looming financial challenges posed by the [COVID-19] health crisis will, I believe, encourage new kinds of outsourcing—reflecting institutions' lack of internal capacity and resources. And this will require campuses to figure out whether these third parties are truly strategic partners or predators.[17]

In the emerging student success system, investors like Lumina are seeking what they see as desirable social change both by making grants and by deploying capital to educational technology ventures. As these firms grow, they can become candidates for capital infusions from venture capital and private equity firms, investment banks, and large corporate investors.[18] Within higher education, a consortium of like-minded public universities have also formed a collaborative approach (the University Innovation Alliance) to supporting student success.[19] Whatever their various or mixed motives, providers of capital are nurturing this emerging system of supporting ventures that aim at serving students' success. The focus on students' progress rather than institutions provides a clarity of vision and a growing sense of differentiated roles for various types of agents. Those who seek to sustain institutions as institutions have less clarity regarding who should do what.

The foundations, university leaders, and entrepreneurs who are forging collective approaches to supporting the degree and career aspirations of students and families have worked systemically within an institutional landscape that usually is anything but systemic. Is there hope for expanding their system to bring the well-being of institutions as a topic at the table, lest colleges and universities be reduced to strictly transactional service bureaus for students-as-consumers? Attempting to answer this question brings us back to the flawed MIT consent decree case (see chapter 1). In that case, collaboration among nonprofits was deemed to be problematic because it was considered unfair to the market of students. If the purpose of higher education is designated solely as workforce preparation for the personal benefit of that market of students, then the enterprise could get stripped down to its bare bones. The disruptive players who can provide or assemble credentials will rise while institutions that serve as engines of basic research and other public goods will be devalued. In addition, the values of non–market-driven academic pursuits will have to yield to Christensenian disrupters. Of course, it isn't only the actions of outside agents that generate the institutional agnosticism of the student success movement. The actions of colleges and universities contribute to the anti-institutionalist sentiments when they fail to communicate their research and research implications in ways that the country understands, when tenure is defended on the basis not only of academic freedom but also on the basis of a degree of job security that few others in the country still have, and most of all when they defend the need for higher-than-inflation cost increases without end.

The student success movement that aligns funders and firms with the goal of student career advancement rests on a defense of the rationale for investment in higher education formulated sixty years ago by economist Gary Becker. He proposed the now widely accepted notion that the decision to invest real dollars in one's own human capital through educational attainment should be valued as a financial investment. This idea is in some ways much older than Becker's formulation of it and is so evidently sensible that it needs no theory to justify it. College education advances one's career in various ways: by adding value through classroom education and the life training gained through cocurricular education as well as through the networks of connections that students build in college. And the returns to gaining a degree are well established and certainly deserve to be valued. But over the years, the aspect of Becker's formulation that has increasingly been emphasized is that the financial returns justify the financial investment. Colleges and universities have increasingly relied on this formulation as the annual sticker price of tuition at private institutions has increased from $30,000 to $40,000 to $50,000 to $60,000 and beyond. As subsidies from states for public education have declined in real terms, the amounts paid by students and their families in the wide range of public institutions have also grown. Loan burdens vary by stage of education (for example, those borrowing for medical school borrow more, and logically so, because they have higher expected incomes than those borrowing to pay for an undergraduate education) and by sector (for example, some for-profit colleges have exploited students and saddled them with large and unproductive loans). Regardless, the loan burden is real, as is the increasing share of family resources required for tuition. As Sara Goldrick-Rab has written in *Paying the Price*, "It is no longer the case that, if students from low-income families work hard, college will be affordable (recall that the average net price for a year at community college equals 40% of their annual family income). At the same time, it is out of reach for middle-class families as well (for whom a year at a public institution ranges from 16% to 25% of their annual family income). When nearly 75 percent of American families find college unaffordable. . . . It is time for a change."[20]

Within the academy, it is known that relying increasingly on the "It's an investment in your human capital that will pay you back via your lifetime earnings" defense has spillover effects. Students are increasingly seen and treated as customers; it doesn't seem irrelevant to think about how the maxim "the customer is always right" might contribute to the ever-increasing level of negotiation between students and professors over grades. And it makes sense that as the cost of college is increasingly defended on the basis of its projected workforce returns, the academic majors that are perceived to enhance early-career earnings have become an increasing focus of students and families. Anything that gets in the way of college as a means of career enhancement is increasingly seen as a problem. In 2022, controversy erupted when Maitland Jones, author of the leading organic chemistry textbook, was fired from his part-time teaching role at NYU because students complained about his propensity for giving low grades in a course that was a prerequisite for those who intended to go to medical, nursing, or other health sciences graduate programs.[21] From the faculty member's side, one can understand why he might feel that it is crucial to uphold high standards in a difficult chemistry course that he sees as essential to the development of chemists; from the students' side, one can understand why it might be frustrating to be paying $80,000 to attend college and to receive a low or failing grade in an organic chemistry course that one must take as a requirement for eventually applying to dental school, without any intention of becoming a research chemist.[22] And although consumer frustration with the cost of higher education has no particular mechanism for making itself heard (in contrast to the increasing patient-centricity in medical research), frustration with and anger at the sector are rising. In a 2018 Pew Center poll, 61 percent of Americans felt that higher education is "going in the wrong direction." Of those, 84 percent blame high tuition costs.[23] In the context of increasing societal skepticism of institutions, colleges are certainly the recipients of society's frustration.

In short, the cost of college engenders more and more frustration; consequently, students are encouraged to see college almost entirely as workforce preparation, and faculty are seen as the barrier to change. Anger toward higher education finds various outlets. Surveys by the Pew Charitable Trusts and the Association of Governing Boards also reveal a rising concern about free-speech issues and the political bent of faculty. The tension around these issues may be entirely separate from society's growing irritation at the rate of college's rising costs, but this tension may also be attaching itself in the public's mind to their perception of an enterprise whose cost structures provoke an accelerating level of frustration.

The Venture Philanthropy Model

In seeding new ventures like Artstor, JSTOR, and ITHAKA and in supporting early-stage efforts like Sunoikisis that it had discovered through grantees like the Associated Colleges of the South, Mellon had been acting ambitiously. The foundation was trying to use grant funds to spark and support the infrastructure of sector-wide change. During the 1980s and 1990s, other foundations had been identifying junctures in other complex systems problems, such as urban neighborhood revitalization, where markets were failing to solve societal needs. When they identified points where they thought that they could make a significant difference, some of these risk-tolerant philanthropies set out to try new approaches to philanthropy to work on big challenges that regular market investors shy away from.

The Ford Foundation's creation of the Low Income Support Corporation (LISC) in the 1980s was a particularly successful example of the creative use of capital. By using outright grants in combination with deploying funds that might eventually be repaid to the foundation, Ford built a new intermediary organization that could sit between those knowledgeable about urban neighborhoods (Community Development Corporations) and financial investors who didn't know how to navigate investments in neighborhoods where they hadn't previously invested. LISC's goals were to connect and foster exchanges between investors and community development corporations in inner cities and to stimulate capital flows in ways that de-risked the investments for market investors.[24] This strategy of creating a new organization (as Mellon had done with JSTOR and Artstor) was one approach to catalyzing change through means other than grants. Another approach, launched by the MacArthur, Ford, Rockefeller, and a handful of other foundations, was to make program-related investments (PRIs) to buttress grant dollars by providing loans with very low or no interest but which they sought to have repaid. PRIs allow foundations to support initiatives that have a path to viability but need hard-to-access capital to get there. Debra Schwartz, managing director of impact investments at the MacArthur Foundation, describes how these PRIs enabled MacArthur to build organizations:

> We have used program-related investments as enterprise-level sources of financing specifically to help organizations double or triple their scale. It is not equity in the sense that they had to pay the debt back to us, but it serves that function of giving an organization money that it can place at risk. . . . The key isn't so much whether it's equity or debt, but that, as a funder, you're providing financing for the organization itself rather than for a project that the organization might carry out.[25]

Although PRIs have been in use since the 1970s, they remain rare, perhaps because grant-making and financial engineering require different skill sets. Program officers are mostly focused on the methods and ethos of giving away money; not many of them naturally think in terms of business models and loan terms.[26] As the Silicon Valley for-profit model became more widely visible during the technology spread of the 1990s, an approach to philanthropy that was based in the grant-making side of the house (and didn't require knowledge of loan contracts) took hold. To understand where *venture philanthropy* came from, it's worth understanding more about the latitude that philanthropies have in determining how to effect change.

With no market measurements to assess their effectiveness, individual and institutional philanthropists are generally left to define their own version of success and their own path toward it. As Joel Fleishman, a leading scholar of philanthropy, has noted, "Every foundation is sui generis, each reflecting the personalities, values, goals, and talents of the key people behind it."[27] Funders have a great deal of discretion in the causes they choose to support and how they provide that support. My conversation with George McCulloch of Level Equity (see page 126) helped me see how a philanthropic organization that was legally required to end every year with $200 million less than what it had at the beginning of the year had acted with the same patterns of pride and reputational self-protection as it would have if it were a bank holding a company's debt. In incubating and funding Artstor, Mellon had ambitiously put money to work with the aim of producing a desired result and had taken on a much more active role than it had historically played in its more traditional grant-making role.

In the 1990s, some foundations and individual philanthropists, particularly those with experience in Silicon Valley, turned to a mode of philanthropy that was explicitly modeled on the investment mode practiced by the firms fostering the spectacular growth of internet and other start-up companies. In a 1998 *Harvard Business Review* article that set out many of the terms of what would become widely known as venture philanthropy, Christine Letts, William Ryan, and Allen Grossman suggested how philanthropists seeking greater impact can learn from the Silicon Valley model:

> The venture capital model emerged from years of practice and competition. It is now a comprehensive investment approach that sets clear performance objectives, manages risk through close monitoring and frequent assistance, and plans the next stage of funding well in advance. Foundations, although they excel in supporting R&D, have yet to find ways to support their grantees in longer-term, sustainable ways. . . . The venture capital model can act as a starting point for foundations that want to help nonprofits develop the organizational capacity to sustain and expand successful programs.[28]

A widely admired model of this mode can be found in New Profit, an operating foundation that raises funds to deploy innovative ventures in K-12 education and social-service organizations. Founded by Vanessa Kirsch in 1998, New Profit set out to "provide social entrepreneurs with just the catalytic supports—unrestricted capital and strategic advice—to help them strengthen their organizations, scale their impact, and take aim at changing the larger systems within which they operated."[29] By monitoring and maintaining close contact with its investments, New Profit aims "to catalyze visionary social entrepreneurs, organizations, and initiatives that can break through and impact the lives of millions of people."[30] Its language and practices, borrowed from the investment world, aim at making the most effective and scalable use of philanthropic funds.

Venture philanthropists recognized that they might learn how to set up expectations for when and how grantees with growing projects might receive additional working capital if they were successful. Then, to monitor these investments, the philanthropists might play a more active role, perhaps by taking a seat on the organization's board, to help guide the organization (and the investment) toward the next measurable stage of success.

In both the old and the new models of philanthropy, supporting the creation of new projects is very much in the interests of philanthropists who are attracted to the idea of serving as "society's risk capital."[31] But when it comes time to provide expansion capital, philanthropists often find it difficult to distinguish between the prospect of supporting a grantee's operating costs (a prospect that is close to anathema for many foundations, which fear creating ongoing dependencies) and providing the kind of capital that the Heron Foundation's Clara Miller describes as "additional capital to expand the original setup to meet expanded demand, to make operations more efficient, or to create new or improved product or program offerings (or all three!)."[32] Miller, who led the Nonprofit Financing Fund before moving to Heron, describes the challenges that plague growing—even thriving—nonprofits seeking to do more:

> There is a period—sometimes relatively short, sometimes over years and years—when the enterprise needs to spend capital on expansion before the quantity and reliability of revenue make the enterprise profitable at an expanded or enhanced level of operation. This is because growth typically occurs in a smooth curve,

while capacity is built in increments that look more like stair steps, with the investment ideally coming in chunks before the growth (i.e., it's hard to hire one-quarter of a chief financial officer when you need a higher skill level in the finance area). . . .

Sadly, the highest-performing and most promising organizations are the most vulnerable to severe growing pains, simply because they're opportunistic and successful, and find more and more ways to grow. Their success means they are the ones most likely to attract more revenue—restricted grants, a dizzying array of government contracts, project funding, an expanded list of willing individual givers. If it's like most revenue in the nonprofit world, it doesn't cover the fully loaded cost of operations, much less the cost of growth. . . .

While some funders instinctively understand the need for equity-like capital grants (small bits are often labeled "capacity building"), these grants frequently target only one part of operations—the computer system or staff training or board development. The reality is that a growing nonprofit needs relatively large amounts of capital to build an expanded operating platform. This more muscular platform, in turn, reliably attracts more net revenue—including but not confined to fundraising income— and eventually makes these and other expanded capacities part of ongoing operations. An occasional lucky grant for capacity building won't suffice.[33]

Although a few funders, notably Heron[34] and the Blue Meridian Fund (which explicitly seeks to "scale evidence-based solutions"), recognize this need for enterprise-building capital, another offshoot of venture philanthropy borrows more than just the oversight techniques from the venture capital world. If PRIs can be repaid, some funders thought, then why can't other venture philanthropy grants be repaid too?

In the late 1990s, the Cystic Fibrosis (CF) Foundation provided funding to a biotech firm that was developing a risky but potentially promising drug. The foundation knew more about the territory than a more generalized biotech investment fund might have known and the staff had a high level of confidence in the research. The foundation eventually invested $150 million in the firm. In 2015, the *Washington Post* reported that

> the CF Foundation sold its rights to future royalties from the drugs for $3.3 billion, the largest windfall of its kind for a charitable organization. The pioneering success of [foundation president Robert] Beall and the Cystic Fibrosis Foundation in the practice of "venture philanthropy" is prompting a growing number of nonprofit groups to explore whether they, too, might be able to benefit their patients, and bottom lines, by investing in similar ways.[35]

Lines begin to blur as mission-driven investment generates a significant return on invested capital, whether as a spillover or as an intention. This blurring of lines is confusing enough to trouble some people: "There's a reason why corporate America exists, and there's a reason why philanthropic organizations exist," says David Cornfield, a professor of pediatric pulmonary medicine at Stanford University. "When that distinction becomes invisible, it becomes very difficult to know where philanthropy ends and venture capital begins."[36] Defining with precision the goals of venture philanthropy becomes particularly confusing when the measures of philanthropic success might be calculated in the units of the market.

Feeling their way around in the obscure forest of venture philanthropy, philanthropists—like the colleges that we are studying—vacillate between the mode of the church and the mode of the car-dealership. These philanthropists are rewarded with "credit" among their peers and the public, but they also recognize that if their charitable contributions end up generating financial success, they can stretch their dollars further. A financially successful public-good venture checks all the boxes. Of course, the robust financial success of a nonprofit shouldn't become a be-all and end-all. Not every soup kitchen that does significant good in the world can or should develop a financially robust business plan, and the financial success of one venturesome grant might whet the appetite of philanthropists who might begin thinking that many or all of their other grants might also aim to be home runs in the financial sense.

The venture philanthropy approach can leave a funder with mixed expectations and no single rubric for establishing the goals of its grants or for deciding when to follow up with more capital. It may be the case that such a strategy is particularly well suited for early-stage healthcare-related funding, where a foundation might have particular information advantages for funding a novel solution. But the need for capital for novel solutions—in education, health, the environment, social justice, and just about everywhere else in the public sector—is far greater than even venture-minded philanthropy can provide. With so much need for capital, a new possibility is emerging (and meeting with both confusion and enthusiasm): tapping into traditional investment capital to take on society's challenges.

Impact Investing: Can Market Investors Do Well While Doing Good in Higher Education?

Since the early 2000s, *impact investing* has served as the umbrella category for a wide range of strategies for providing capital to enterprises aimed at some sort of social good.[37] According to the Global Impact Investing Network (GIIN), "impact investing is an exciting and rapidly growing industry powered by investors who are determined to generate social and environmental impact as well as financial returns. This is taking place all over the world, and across all asset classes."[38] Inherent in the GIIN's definition is the active pursuit of the financial returns that we saw with only the most market-attuned venture philanthropists (as was the case with the Cystic Fibrosis Foundation).

Very different strategies serve as the founding myths of different approaches to impact investing. To use Gordon Winston's metaphors: traditionally, the focus of the investment world has been to build car dealerships. As problems with the environment, global inequality, and public health issues grow, pressure to pursue social benefits grows among those who possess capital and also among firms seeking to do something beyond pursue profits at any cost. But because the well-established system of capitalizing and providing market rewards and punishments to "car dealerships" is not accustomed to accommodating some "church" motives, there's room for success, failures, and illusions in the building of an impact investing ecosystem. Trillions of dollars of investment capital are now deployed under some version of the mantra "you can do well by doing good," but it is not entirely clear that this promise can be widely fulfilled. In this section, I trace the history of this mantra and ask how it might apply to our model of change in higher education. The impact investing world is far from perfect and far from being clear about its goals and capacities, but we can learn from its strategies about what it might take to bring much-needed capital to areas of public good.

In the 1990s, investment approaches that assess companies' environmental, social, and governance (ESG) considerations began to gain traction. Mutual funds that avoided investing in companies in certain markets (such as tobacco) or with certain operations (child labor) were established as mechanisms for investors to invest in ways that were more aligned with their values. In some cases, these investment strategies performed better than their benchmark. If for example, one pursues an investment approach that avoids companies that mine or process fossil fuels, one might achieve strong financial returns during times when oil prices drop. Socially aware investing certainly can generate returns that outperform the market in certain circumstances, but there isn't any universal finding that these approaches perform better or worse financially than investments that don't consider social impact.

Another investment story that significantly boosted the visibility of and faith in impact investing came with a series of investments in microlending enterprises, most notably in the work of the Grameen Bank, led by Muhammad Yunus. Microlending entails lending small amounts of money, usually without any collateral or other constraining terms on which lenders usually rely to protect their interests.[39] These loans support very small businesses, including ventures among the very poor or those led by women who struggle to access capital in traditional ways. While the full (and fascinating) story of microlending is told elsewhere, it's important to note the reverberations of its foundational myth: thanks to the Grameen Bank, capital was used in Bangladesh to open a lending market that traditional investors had seen as too risky. Once capital provided via a PRI from the Ford Foundation and other risk-tolerant philanthropies showed the possibilities of this strategy, the microlending market grew and thrived. This enabled traditional market players who saw diminished levels of risk and the prospect of returns to follow on with new and larger investments. As with ESG investing, this example provided more evidence that the market could be more than a cold and careless forum—that investors could in fact do well (that is, earn returns) while doing good. As Antony Bugg-Levine and Jed Emerson note in *Impact Investing: Transforming How We Make Money While Making a Difference*:

> Commercial microfinance is now a vast industry engaging an array of institutions [including] mainstream investment banks like Morgan Stanley and Citigroup. . . . For many people, microfinance is now the flagship of how for-profit investment that is managed effectively can be put to work to address poverty productively. Others, however, see it as just another way in which investors and greedy businesses exploit poor people. But for all its success and controversy, microfinance is an archetype of impact investment for multiple returns.[40]

Alleviating poverty is, of course, a goal that everyone can agree on. Still, as with any expansion into new territory, the rush to stake out new terrain attracts risk takers of all kinds—both plucky adventurers and charlatans.

With roots in ESG and microcredit strategies, the broad concept of impact investing has taken off: "In 2006, around 100 entities collectively managing $7 trillion were signed to the UN Principles for Responsible Investment; by 2017, there were more than 1,750 collectively managing $70 trillion."[41] The GIIN, using a narrower definition of impact investing, tracks "over 1,720 organizations [that] manage $715 billion in impact investing AUM [Assets Under Management] as of the end of 2019."[42]

Clearly, enthusiasm for the idea of doing good while doing well has grown rapidly, but it has also outpaced the establishment of clear approaches, goals, and norms. Bugg-Levine and Emerson note that those who focus on the early successes of microfinancing might introduce other challenges concerning values, including "the lingering skepticism that many people have about the moral legitimacy of for-profit businesses that sell basic services to poor people."[43] Along with the moral questions associated with mixing these modes come plenty of questions about whether the investment goals of an impact investment can be clearly articulated. Bugg-Levine and Emerson (among others) advocate for particular strategies for blending capital, with different funders playing different roles with different expectations at various stages of building an enterprise. But they recognize too that the subtleties of mixed financing models might get lost as the idea of impact investing circulates widely. The expectations and hopes of those who sell these approaches and those who buy into them can get flattened into unrealistic expectations that the market can solve all social problems and that investors can make profits while doing so. The establishment of different roles for investors with different goals and motives in the impact investing world represents one aspect of how this mode of investing remains underdeveloped and, hence, difficult to utilize to address any particular domain of public good.

The early days of impact investing have focused on poverty (especially in developing markets), urban revitalization, and the environment—areas where traditional market investments have been scarce. In contrast, markets such as healthcare and education have been less frequently targeted by impact investors because the proliferation of for-profit firms seeking to serve institutions makes the realm less appealing for those who intend to use their risk capital to bring investors into a particular sector. However, as Andrew Baxter, Connor Cash, Josh Lerner, and Ratnika Prasad write, the entry of enormous private equity funds such as KKR, Bain, TPG, and Blackstone into the general space of impact investing will likely lead to use of these strategies in areas:

> Th[e] growing entry of traditional investment funds is likely to focus more on ventures for impact in spaces such as education, healthcare and, increasingly, agriculture. In these sectors, there has been a growth of entrepreneurship using technology to develop new solutions to drive impact in relatively shorter time frames.[44]

Beyond the big private-equity firms that have launched impact investment funds, a good example of nonprofit investors can be found in K-12 education, where the Gates Foundation and other foundations and firms have played a highly visible role in shaking up a deeply entrenched and hard-to-change system. In the story of one such firm, Schoolzilla, we find an example of the challenges and opportunities that impact investing represents for mission-driven organizations.

Schoolzilla: A Case of Funding Mission-Driven Work

Incubated inside Aspire (a nonprofit network of charter schools), Schoolzilla became an independent company that created decision-support products for school administrators—dashboards that "integrate multiple sources of student data, including attendance, suspensions, course grades, and more."[45] As Schoolzilla became independent, CEO Lynzi Ziegenhagen had to decide on an organizational model. Frustrated with the decision-making time frame of the nonprofits in which she had been involved, she decided to incorporate the firm as a public benefit corporation (PBC), a relatively new for-profit corporate structure in which "members of the board of directors and officers are required to consider the effects of their decisions on shareholders, workers, suppliers, customers, the community and society at large, the local and global environment, and the short- and long-term interests of the corporation."[46] Otherwise, a PBC's ability to raise capital and obligation to pay taxes are the same as those of other corporate entities.[47] What precisely a

PBC entails and requires has not yet been tested in the courts, but it clearly signals goals beyond seeking profit for shareholders. "And," Ziegenhagen noted, "it's a pretty good brand for working in schools. Not as good as '501 (c)(3)' but it's pretty close." In 2016, the *Stanford Social Innovation Review* cited Ziegenhagen in an article explaining why, despite a growing world of traditional venture capital firms looking to invest in ed tech firms, she elected to work only with mission-aligned investors:

> In raising early-stage capital for the company, she talked with people from about 70 funding institutions, including many traditional venture firms. She was leery of selling a stake in the business—let alone giving a board seat—to any funder that might seek a quick exit. "In the end, I wanted only people who had some structural reason to care about impact, whether it's because they're a foundation or because their funding is dedicated to double-bottom-line organizations," she says. "If we have to make a trade-off between mission and money, or if an acquirer comes along that wouldn't be good for kids, I want investors who will be on the side of mission."[48]

In the years after incorporating, Schoolzilla had to grow or lose its place in the market. Its impact investors identified with its mission, but each investor had its own approach to defining the balance between financial returns and mission returns. Ziegenhagen ran into the challenges of planning in the context of investors who were still figuring out which currency mattered most to them. "If it's your own money, it's one thing," she said. "But if you're investing other peoples' money for mission, you may still be naturally drawn to showing profits sooner so that you have testimony for your next fund."[49] In the natural course of building on its success, Schoolzilla needed a significant reinvention of its platform to allow it to serve sprawling public school districts rather than the charter schools that Schoolzilla had been successfully serving. Rebuilding its successful product and marketing it to a larger and harder-to-sell-to market was a "grow or die" moment for the company. In addition, deciding how to hire and how to grow meant being ready to leap from one speeding train to another. As Ziegenhagen made these decisions, she didn't always know what she had to work with. For example, one investor vacillated on how Schoolzilla should emphasize growth. At one point, the investor suggested that it would provide $20 million in capital. That amount then shrunk to a potential $6 million, and by the time the check appeared, it was $750,000. In 2018, Schoolzilla's staffing decreased from 60 to 23 people and Ziegenhagen was faced with the prospect of "chasing money all the time" to fuel its growth. In October 2019, Schoolzilla sold itself to Renaissance, one of the largest K-12 vendors.

Did having impact investors rather than traditional market investors help in deciding the fate of the company, its products, and its users? Whether it was the company's status as a public benefit corporation or the ethos of the investors, Ziegenhagen was able to sway the sale toward a buyer that she believed was the best fit for Schoolzilla's mission rather than to what might have been a more lucrative exit. Schoolzilla lives on, with its products now included at no extra charge to 2,100 school districts as an enticement to buy Renaissance's much bigger integrated platform of learning analytics; on its own Schoolzilla had reached 149 school systems. "There are some things that only the magic of a start-up can do and make happen in K-12," Ziegenhagen reflected. "But scale sometimes isn't one of them."[50]

In many ways, the Schoolzilla story reminds us that organizations and firms might evolve—indeed, might need to evolve—as they change and as the world around them changes. Paul Brest, former president of the Hewlett Foundation and one of the scholars trying to pin down the form and function of impact investing, argues that this transition shows the value of impact investing. He proposes that impact investing should be gauged on its "additionality": the value that it adds to what regular market investment would have provided. For Brest, this approach provides capital at a time and a stage that may not and probably should not last: "Here, impact investors have played their part. . . . The impact investing story is over, and the enterprise is now supported by customers and ordinary market investors."[51] Like teachers or physicians who have brought their students or patients to the point where they no longer depend on regular interventions, impact investors should be proud of their accomplishments and look for the next opportunity.

When the market should take over—earlier or later—remains a question. K-12 schools are widely considered a public good, and one in need of synthetic innovation, such as Schoolzilla has been providing. When the system in need of collective solutions is sprawling and fragmented (with more than 13,000 school districts in the United States), solutions will need far more capital to grow to scale than philanthropy can ever provide. It stands to reason that a structure that enables capital to flow into new problem-solving ventures is far more effective than a philanthropic band-aid that might get pulled off at the whim of a funder and that may never be capable of providing sufficient growth-enabling capital. This is why impact investing has shown promise in sectors that are risky (or perceived as risky), such as microlending, green energy, and urban renewal.

The Schoolzilla story conveys how handoffs can happen in an arena where goals are widely shared and there's a big market of buyers. Over time, for impact investing to produce financial returns, there needs to be the possibility of recurring revenue if the solution can successfully launch, despite the challenges of working in the sector. We see another example in the medical research arena discussed earlier in this chapter. With a similar outlook as the Faster Cures framework, the founder of the Multiple Myeloma Research Foundation (MMRF), Kathy Giusti, has demonstrated how infrastructure for advancing treatments can be coordinated and constructed, as well as the place of various financing strategies in such a system.

Giusti founded the MMRF in 1997, soon after being diagnosed with multiple myeloma, a blood cancer affecting approximately 34,000 Americans annually. She quickly saw the lack of connections and data sharing among those doing research. Today, the MMRF is widely known and admired for having accelerated coordinated research across labs and for creating the world's largest tissue sample database. She and the organization built out the inter-institutional, interpersonal, and cross-sector collaborations needed to produce treatments for the disease; in doing so, they also provided clarity regarding the variegated role for capital investors and how best to put money to work. Like Milken, Giusti developed a multipronged approach in which different strategies for supporting research and the development of treatments play different roles at the right time.[52] Investors with a particular focus—such as foundations focused on finding a cure for a specific less common disease— have a role in connecting players and filling gaps between them. As Giusti noted:

> The science driving precision medicine—specific therapies developed for narrowly defined groups of patients, often using genetic or molecular profiling—is advancing rapidly. But science is not enough. Exploiting these opportunities requires significant capital. . . . Consequently, new funding models are required in which disease-focused nonprofit research foundations play a central role in raising capital and mobilizing an ecosystem focused on controlling and curing a disease. . . . Since nonprofits are often narrowly focused on one disease area, they know about the relevant scientific research and the promising entrepreneurial activity taking place in that domain. . . . Through its venture philanthropy activities, the MMRF (Multiple Myeloma Research Foundation)'s involvement in deals provides more value to a portfolio company than just money. It provides companies with access to its databank, biobank, and clinical network, as well as the expertise of its scientific and clinical leaders.[53]

The particular work of a small scientific firm will make more sense to a foundation devoted to treating a rare disease than it will to a generalized biotechnology investor. So the foundation is in the position of being both knowledgeable and mission-driven when gauging whether a small firm has the potential to make a difference to patients. According to Giusti, the characteristic that separates the *venture philanthropist* from the *impact investor* is having a reason to prioritize mission advancement over financial returns: "Pursuing a strategy of venture philanthropy requires donors who understand that cures often come from entrepreneurial for-profit companies.

These individuals embrace the idea of making donations that will be used for investments in for-profit ventures aimed at treating or curing a disease and aren't looking for a financial return on their philanthropy." Being "invested" because you or someone you know has a life-threatening disease is very different from being invested when you don't.[54] Giusti goes on to argue, as Paul Brest did, that there's a time and place for regular market investors to do what they do (provide larger tranches of expansion capital) to help growing companies pass the market test.[55] But none of this can happen efficiently and effectively if roles of various players and measures of what defines success for those various players aren't established. According to Matt Bannick of Omidyar,

> Our experience from the past eight years is that impact investors can massively increase the number of lives they touch by concentrating investments in specific industry sectors in specific geographies, and by investing in a range of organizations to accelerate the development of these industry segments.[56]

Accelerating the development and deployment of treatments for a disease represents a clear and distinct goal, but developing the supportive infrastructure for doing so in higher education has been and continues to be difficult because of the absence of shared goals. The goals of higher education are very different for those who see it as a series of various churches rather than a landscape of car dealerships. The developing ecosystem of student success is admirably focused on the return on investment for students who approach college as one would approach a car dealer, who need a car that works as it is supposed to for a fair price. As a society, however, we also need the church aspect of colleges and universities, which means developing the full and complex ecosystem. The system-ordering work that we have seen for the development of treatments for specific diseases provides a map of what we are missing in the quest to fund providers of synthetic solutions in higher education: an alignment of roles that allows various providers of capital to play different roles with different motives at different points, and in doing so, play their part in a framework that supports overarching goals.

Impact investing is not a magical or permanent capitalization strategy for new higher education intermediaries, but neither should the ability to call upon investable capital be reserved as a strategy for supporting those companies that seek to disrupt institutions that society needs. When impact investors advance development of treatments for a disease, they recognize that the firms that they are investing in depend upon underlying basic research that may have been undertaken with federal support from the National Institutes of Health or support from a local university. It's not the place of impact investors to fund that earlier stage of the research. But impact investors in the medical realm don't set out to undermine the institutions that comprise the basic research layer of the system (which can happen in higher education if colleges and universities end up as the organizations disrupted by new ventures). There's generally consensus about roles and goals in medical research, even if provocateurs like Milken and Giusti are needed to remind the players periodically of the big picture. In higher education, the big picture isn't agreed upon, and so different investors enter at different points—and with different motives. Although the student success movement focuses on students' well-being, it also incorporates an understandable frustration with institutions and concludes that it might be better to work outside of them. Indeed, higher education is seen as fair game for firms to feed on. Since the MIT consent decree case, the prevailing attitude is that market rules should guide all aspects of the higher education game, supposedly for the benefit of the paying customers. But the paying customers are also losing out as schools compete endlessly with one another and lack any realistic mechanisms for utilizing shared solutions that could be both efficient and effective.

Institutions can be partners in the development of efficient and effective reform, but the work of building services and embedding them across fragmented mission-driven hosts requires a lot of work and hence requires significant financing. Artstor, with outsized start-up funding from a large philanthropic foundation interested in the arts and humanities, and the National Student Clearinghouse, with start-up funding from a large corporation looking to solve a problem that it knew well, had time to build trust and the resources to be responsive to skeptical campus-based partner-buyers. Other adventurers racing into unknown territory and wishing to merge ideals with pragmatism have a tougher route. The story of one such organization, Switchboard, provides some helpful lessons learned along the way.

Switchboard: A Case That Shows the Limits of the System

With colleges ever more focused on their students' success in finding jobs after graduation, the 2010s saw a proliferation of firms focused on alumni networking, outsourced career services support, and other platforms designed to leverage alumni networks and connections as students transition into the workforce. Large employment-related platforms (including LinkedIn and Burning Glass) and niche career service firms such as Handshake, Track Ahead, Dream Careers, Roadtrip Nation, and dozens of others stepped in to offer job search ("learning to earning") services either by marketing to students directly or through deals with campuses. As these firms point out, career services offices have not been major areas of investment for colleges, perhaps because their work is not counted in rankings like *U.S. News and World Report*'s. These new outside firms see a market opportunity, and they are attracting investment to build networks between colleges and employers, develop assessment tools, and offer services to students, hiring firms, or colleges.

One such firm is Switchboard, which emerged from the enthusiasm of alumni/ae of Reed College. "Reed College alumni are so eager to advise their younger counterparts," reported *Inside Higher Ed*, "that they're donating $40 to the college every time they're asked to help."[57] It's true; alums believed so deeply in the work of Reed that they made a donation each time the new platform (built by a few Reed alums who had graduated in the early 2000s) connected them with another Reed alumnus looking for information, job leads, or a couch to sleep on in a new city. The creators of the platform also were driven by this mission to support students and the college that nurtured them; they had no expectations of frothy IPOs and enormous payouts. As she sought funding to help convert the passion of college communities (like Reed's) into a viable product, Switchboard cofounder Mara Zapeda found that—in higher education at least—being neither fully profit-maximizing fish nor fully mission-driven fowl made it very difficult to obtain growth equity:

> Social impact investors do not typically work in our spaces, and when they do, have narrow theories of change that do not contemplate the kind of system interventions we were making in our respective industries. . . . The current technology and venture capital structure is broken. It rewards quantity over quality, consumption over creation, quick exits over sustainable growth, and shareholder profit over shared prosperity. It chases after "unicorn" companies bent on "disruption" rather than supporting businesses that repair, cultivate, and connect.[58]

Zapeda recognized that whatever Switchboard's strengths or weaknesses as a firm, a clear and significant systemic problem existed. Or, more accurately, there was no system to support higher education service firms that are half-car dealer and half-church. She probably would be best categorized as what New Profit chair Jeffrey Walker and CEO Vanessa Kirsch called a "systems entrepreneur": "Beyond technical understanding of solution X and its application to problem Y," Kirsch, Walker, and Jim Bildner note, "systems entrepreneurs must have a deep understanding of the system or systems they are trying to change and all the factors that shape it."[59] Zapeda recognized that the system of financing hybrid organizations that seek to preserve institutions (whether in higher education, journalism, healthcare, government, or other trusted anchors of our cultural fabric) needs a new model of hybridity. Her manifesto (written with three colleagues) argues that "zebras fix what unicorns break":

> This new movement demands a new symbol, so we're claiming an animal of our own: the zebra. Why zebras?
>
> - To state the obvious: unlike unicorns, **zebras are real**.
> - Zebra companies are both black and white: they are profitable *and* improve society. They won't sacrifice one for the other.

- Zebras are also mutualistic: by banding together in groups, they protect and preserve one another. Their individual input results in stronger collective output.
- Zebra companies are built with peerless stamina and capital efficiency, as long as conditions allow them to survive.

The capital system is failing society in part because it is failing zebra companies.[60]

As Zapeda gathered a network of entrepreneurs and funders who recognized both the flaws of the well-established venture capital model and the desirability of supporting "profitable businesses that solve real, meaningful problems and in the process repair existing social systems," she found herself defining components of a new system.[61] Zapeda's new organization, Zebras Unite, will not change the hard-to-budge structures of venture capital financing overnight. But pieces of systems are already in place, barely visible against the backdrop of the dominant models of capital provision.

Zebras Unite incorporated in 2020 as a co-op, a corporate form used by collectives such as Land of Lakes, Cabot Cheese, and Ocean Spray. Even though most people don't think of the economic significance of co-ops, the largest hundred US co-ops have a value of $228 billion.[62] Zapeda and her cofounders have recognized that for a system to change, it needs the infrastructural components (including the metaphors and images) that allow others to see what a new system can do and why.[63] And they're getting somewhere. Zebras Unite seems to make sense to at least some capital allocators: "I think we should, as investors, take seriously our role in driving some of these destabilizing forces in society," said Rukaiyah Adams, chief investment officer at Meyer Memorial Trust, an investor in venture capital funds and nonprofits. "As one of the controllers of capital, I'm raising my hand and saying, 'Wait a minute, let's really think about this.'"[64]

Zapeda and the other founders of Zebras Unite learned what New Profit's Walker and Kirsch had also been learning: the individual firm struggles without a system, and a system consists of more than a constellation of passionate individual founders and firms. A conceptual system must exist for new models to arise, and the components of infrastructure must be present. Beyond the individual firm and beyond a shared understanding of different roles for different agents in the system, agencies that provide standards, ratings, or rankings help investors and consumers by providing ways of understanding and differentiating the performance of projects or firms. In the case of the MMRF's work of coordinating the building of a tissue database, infrastructure also meant identifying the collective system gaps in information that inhibit progress. How do systems entrepreneurs define and work to facilitate the creation of a new system?

In medical research, Facebook cofounder Sean Parker, accustomed to the fast-moving and failure-tolerant environment of Silicon Valley, attached conditions to funds that he provided to six labs for the nonprofit Parker Institute for Cancer Immunotherapy in San Francisco.[65] As a condition of the grant, the six institutions had to agree to one shared Institutional Review Board (IRB). Dr. Ramy Ibrahim, the institute's vice president of clinical development, noted, "Normally you'd submit to an IRB, then they send questions to the investigator who wrote the (study) protocols, and there's a back-and-forth. Then multiply that by six."[66] With a unified goal, investors and other players can identify problems in the plumbing that can be resolved, as in the case of Parker pushing individual institutions to agree on a more efficient research approval process if they wanted funding. Individual organizational efforts go only so far, as New Profit has recognized: "Sustained, large-scale change demands collaboration across organizations and sectors. Our ecosystem building efforts engage social entrepreneurs, policymakers, philanthropists, and other national and local stakeholders to transform how government (the largest funder of social services) and philanthropy think about how to collectively pursue social change and allocate resources."[67] Conferences and conventions such as Milken's Faster Cures, ASU-GSV, and Zebras Unite's DazzleCon function as sociological infrastructure mechanisms and bring together various agents to sort out who does what and how they interact as components of a system's infrastructure.

It is clear that investors can advance networks in ways that are every bit as powerful as providing capital. In reviewing its impact investment program, the John S. and James L. Knight Foundation recognized that its ability to connect and refer investees also served as a soft-power infrastructure:

> Access to Knight's network provided key inroads for portfolio companies to the marketplace. Respondents cited the diverse networking opportunities via key industry events (74 percent) and introductions (71 percent) as useful conduits to building their customer bases. As one company principal underscored: "Knight has been able to loop us into events . . . sponsoring demos at the Investigative Reporters and Editors Conference this past month or sending us to Newsfoo (Newsgeist) meetings every year or facilitating our presence at the Online News Association Conference, the American Library Association Conference—those are all places where we like to be present and Knight is our only investor who has relationships there.[68]

In addition to the benefits of networks, Bannick noted that infrastructure attracts talent to a potential area:

> Industry players often have common needs that are most economically served in collective form. Infrastructure players advance a sector by addressing these collective needs, thus helping to build a supportive ecosystem for entrepreneurial innovation . . . from industry associations . . . to information exchanges. . . . LACK of infrastructure can disrupt an otherwise burgeoning sector.[69]

Aligning Players and Capital in Support of a Shared Goal

I have proposed that individual specialized firms can potentially provide mission-driven and market-supported services that can forge synthetic bonds with the local culture and practices of individual colleges and universities. Through an understanding how to fit in and respond to local needs, these firms can overcome the barriers

that individuals and individual institutions consciously and unconsciously construct to repel outside solutions. But having explored
the question of whether there are any real models for financing
this kind of change, especially on a large scale, we reach a place
of being daunted. We've seen that the price of higher education to
students and families is problematic and bemoaned, but it isn't seen
as a problem to be coherently addressed. Instead there seems to
be a general acceptance of ever-increasing cost and the subsequent
increase in price to students and/or a growing anger toward and dis-
engagement from higher education. Without a coherent sense of the
need to coordinate an effort to address the cost problem, individual
entrepreneurs, investors, and firms have not been convened to find
their places of collaboration, to differentiate their places in a system,
or to work together on needed shared infrastructure. In general, we
have seen only scattered experiments for merging purpose and capitalization. Philanthropy, a financing system that some people assume
to be a coherent way of building mission-driven organizations, lives
by hard-to-define and idiosyncratic measures of impact and has few
forces acting on the individual "investor" to incentivize the provision
of growth equity or even long-term commitment. That's no one's
fault; the reward system within philanthropy is based on a cultural
capital with different terms of exchange. The other realm, traditional
market investing, works within a system that has undertaken only
the most exploratory experiments in accommodating and taking
account of socially desirable impact.

Many individuals in both of these realms are trying to square the
circle. Increasing numbers of philanthropists recognize that their
grant funds are thoroughly insufficient to address society's challenges, and among the traditional capitalists are plenty of people
who know that the market doesn't have a mechanism for providing
much-needed public goods. Reconciling these very different systems
is tricky enough when considering problems in developing markets;
in these realms, capital holders like the idea of having philanthropists
or impact investors de-risk their own deployment of capital in search
of returns. But in areas that are already populated by regular market
investors and where market-based competition is assumed to be the

law of the land, asserting a place for impact investment runs into challenges. Even if society is depending on sectors such as education, healthcare, or journalism, the integration of mission-driven and market-driven goals is cloudy at best. There are some success stories, though. The Multiple Myeloma Research Foundation finds passion-driven investors who are willing to take risks on novel pharmaceuticals that might fight the disease; Lumina puts resources to work in for-profit firms that might help students navigate the credentials gauntlet. The key question remains, however: What must happen for intermediary institutions that can compatibly help institutions of higher education to be seen as good causes, worthy of mission-driven investment?

Harvard Business School professor Josh Lerner and his colleagues have charted how sustainable forestry provides an example of an aligning of interests that can work. Defining and differentiating organizational roles and aims begins, as we have seen, with a shared goal—in this case, the preservation of Earth's atmosphere. It also begins with an understanding that the project is too big for philanthropy and government alone. As Andrew Baxter et al. note,

> The Global Canopy Programme (2012) estimated that the total annual expenditure on conservation was on the order of $50 billion, of which over 80% was from government and philanthropic sources. Ecosystem Marketplace (2016) similarly estimated the annual flows of private investment dollars into conservation in the low billions of dollars, with the bulk of these funds going for sustainable food and fiber rather than habitat conservation. These expenditures lagged by more than an order of magnitude the required annual expenditures needed to preserve the planet's biodiversity, which Credit Suisse, McKinsey & Co., and the World Wildlife Fund (2014) estimate to range between $300 and $400 billion. Without private investment dollars, this shortfall is likely to persist indefinitely.[70]

Although the need is great and the cause is urgent, if left to their different guiding standards philanthropists and market investors with interests in forestry have no means of reconciling their particular goals since "changes in the rate of timber harvesting frequently affect sustainability goals and financial returns in opposite ways."[71] A piece of the puzzle fell into place in the 1980s and 1990s as innovative investors, including Yale's David Swenson and Jeremy Grantham, founder of Grantham, Mayo, & van Otterloo, identified timber as an investment vehicle that seemed capable of providing consistent returns with a low correlation with other types of assets. Many types of investments all rise and fall at the same time (as markets around the world or different sectors of the economy are often closely correlated to one another). For a time in the 1990s, early investors in timber benefited from very strong returns that were less directly related to the movements of prices in other investment vehicles. As other investors caught on to this strategy and crowded in, timber returns declined. But the idea that forestry can play a useful role as an investment approach for long-term investors was established and continues.

At the same time, climate change became an increasingly urgent focus of conservation-minded philanthropists. Andrew Baxter et al. document how these market-driven and mission-driven players found enough common ground to begin to develop the intermediary organizations (including rating agencies, pooled fund structures, and analysts) to make investment in forestry possible, because "large pools of capital almost by definition must write large checks." They document a "green bond" created by The Conservation Fund's (TCF's) Working Forest Fund. Faced with the opportunity to purchase extensive tracts of land before they fell into private logging hands and lacking the capital to fully fund the purchases, TCF set out to find a vehicle that could both sustain their work and maintain their mission. After exploring various models, including traditional philanthropy, program-related investments, private equity funding, and bank loans, the organization settled on issuing a bond with return expectations set between the low rates that conservation funds generally produce and the higher rates that the market usually requires.[72]

Two other lessons emerged from the TCF case, both related to the work that has to happen to bring such a hybrid system into being.

The first came (as Baxter et al. note) in how and why TCF chose to issue a bond to the open market rather than work with a small group of banks to devise a private placement loan: "One key goal of the fundraising process for TCF was the market education: ideally, if this offering was successful, it would build visibility for future offerings by both the forest conservation industry broadly as well as TCF itself. A private debt offering marketed to a handful of institutions would not accomplish that goal."[73]

The other lesson related to the human capital involved. Selling the concept relied on TCF's organizational leaders being able to understand and then sell the story in the different languages of the conservation world and the investment world. "This combination of skills is certainly not commonplace," Baxter et al. note. "But such pioneers can have enormous positive spillovers in legitimizing an asset class."[74]

In forging such a financing solution, institutional entrepreneurs (like the ones we recognized as being capable of synthesizing change in the landscape of colleges and universities) are needed; they play the role of systems entrepreneurs in the new myth creation, the mythopoesis, of new financing structures. But they can't do it alone. There has to be belief in the need for a system with collective goals in higher education, as there is in the conservation of forests and the advancement of treatments for cancer. We have to ask, though: Is there any reason to believe that there can be a mission-driven financing system when the cause at stake is increasingly thought of as a personal good—or even a luxury item? Preserving healthy forests has a reputation as a public good. Because higher education has increasingly been seen (and defended itself) as a vehicle for personal advancement, are there models in which impact investment has been utilized in arenas that might not have the same level of public support as environmental causes or cancer research? It turns out that even in the world of creative pursuits, systemic structures for investing can be constructed.

As Laura Callanan, the founder of Upstart Co-Lab, has noted, "Farm-to-table restaurants create a market for local, organic, sustainable farmers. Fashion designers build their brand connected to ethical and sustainable practices throughout their supply chain. Video game developers produce titles that help patients manage chronic disease, as well as teach players about issues like civics, peace-building, and empathy."[75] Once she started looking for investable opportunities in what she has defined as the creative economy, Callanan found them hiding in plain sight.[76] Her organization, Upstart Co-Lab, set out to build the field of impact investing in creative ventures and was launched with the support of foundations and individuals who were looking for models "to unleash more capital for creativity, to increase opportunities for artists as innovators, and to enable sustainable creative lives."[77] According to an article about Upstart Co-Lab's work, one such investor invested $100,000 in a bond offering for projects in New York. One recipient was La MaMa, a theatrical organization and performance space in New York City's East Village. La MaMa gained access to a $3.2 million line of credit to renovate its main theater. La MaMa employs only forty-five people but gives opportunities to about 1,500 artists a year.[78]

It will always be impossible to keep our units straight in assessing impact investing. Recall that Matt Bannick from Omidyar has suggested that there are other, very different ways to measure impact that "account for the total value creation of the firm, including sector value creation as well as the firm's direct social impact and financial returns." For instance, La MaMa had sponsored early works of Julie Taymor, who went on to create the renowned stage version of *The Lion King*, which has been seen by 100 million people in over 100 cities in 20 countries.

The creative economy can create a field around investing in healthier food and sustainable fashion, supporting arts organizations, and making video games more ethical. If those who conduct medical research can be awakened to the importance of listening to what patients want and need, can those who care about higher education work together to recognize the consequential choices that higher education faces? Are there ways of aligning a mutualist system instead of only trying to strengthen the individual walls of 3,500 colleges and universities?

In 2017, after Artstor was absorbed into JSTOR, I was fishing around for my next role. Someone introduced me to the leaders of HarvardX, the massive open online course (MOOC) project that was putting certain Harvard College courses online as part of the interinstitutional edX project. As I sat in the HarvardX office on the edge of Harvard Yard, the project leaders said they wanted to establish a financially sustainable model for HarvardX. But they seemed uncomfortable with my proposal to set up a structure to share Stephen Greenblatt's lectures on Hamlet, Charles Fried's course on contract law, and David Malan's class on introduction to programming with other colleges and universities around the country. I suggested that if we helped faculty get past their fears, anger, and do-it-yourself impulses, we could change the cost structure of higher education, not by tearing down institutions but by working with campus constituencies to increase faculty productivity. By utilizing lectures from beyond the local campus—just as art historians were using someone else's slide of the *Mona Lisa*—maybe a professor who had taught three classes a semester might now be able to teach four. It might not be a perfect solution for everyone involved, but it seemed better than watching whole departments close out of financial exigency or even seeing some colleges close. The transition that I was suggesting wouldn't be easy, but it could make a significant difference. The people at HarvardX replied that it all sounded too hard to implement and could be perceived as threatening to the faculty's sense of independence and autonomy. They never called me back for a second discussion.

Throughout this chapter, I've advocated for a delicately balanced new model for funding these mission- and market-compatible synthetic ventures—blending philanthropy, socially minded investors, and the traditional free-market solutions. But one can't make maps when there aren't roads or even rules of the road. We need to agree on a shared purpose, convene those who have a role to play in achieving it, listen to those whom the system is hurting and think about what in turn hurts the system, align the players in the cast, and then chart reasonable and realistic financial models and paths forward. But we have to agree that creating this type of system and the concomitant opportunities for capitalization of worthy ventures matters, and we haven't yet done that in any serious way.

6

The Possibilities of the Collective Curriculum

"The last thing I want," Harvard professor Michael Sandel wrote in an open letter in 2013, "is for my online lectures to be used to undermine faculty colleagues at other institutions."[1] Sandel wrote this amid the furor that arose from an effort by the administration at San Jose State University (SJSU) to utilize Sandel's online lecture course, "Justice," in its own philosophy program via edX. Harvard and MIT had created the nonprofit edX to distribute massive open online courses (MOOCs) the year before the SJSU incident. San Jose State University—a public university in a state that had increasingly cut back on providing funding for public higher education over the course of the 2000s—had seen the availability of online courses such as Sandel's as an opportunity for SJSU to play a leading role in revising the pedagogical model of public higher education. In announcing the plan to use edX courses, San Jose State president Mohammad Qayoumi said, "We look forward to helping other California State University campuses make available to thousands of students the innovative, blended approach to learning developed by SJSU and edX."[2] If SJSU saw itself changing the model of the enormous California State system (which enrolls almost 500,000 students), edX had an even wider set of goals. In launching an ambitious interinstitutional collaboration to create and distribute MOOCs, Harvard and MIT had enumerated a range of goals, including learning about the potential of online education and sharing the work of teachers and scholars with the wide world beyond the academy for free.[3] Among these goals, the possibility of deploying online lectures at other institutions of higher education was clearly on the table. "One of the founding principles of edX is to use the power of technology and online learning to improve on-campus education and to innovate in higher education," said Anant Agarwal, president of edX. "Our collaboration with San Jose State University is a strong example of how well-designed blended learning can engage students and substantially improve learning outcomes."[4]

But by participating (and in the case of Professor Sandel, being a passive participant) in the San Jose State effort, edX had stirred up more than a little resistance. "What kind of message are we sending our students," the San Jose State philosophy department wrote in an open letter to Sandel, "if we tell them that they should best learn what justice is by listening to the reflections of the largely white student population from a privileged institution like Harvard?" A central component of the video capture of Sandel's class consisted of his Socratic dialogue with the largely White audience of Harvard students; in contrast, in 2013 only 24 percent of SJSU students categorized themselves as White.[5] "Our very diverse students gain," the SJSU philosophers wrote, "far more when their own experience is central to the course and when they are learning from our own very diverse faculty, who bring their varied perspectives to the content of courses that bear on social justice. . . . Teaching justice through an educational model that is spearheading the creation of two social classes in academia thus amounts to a cruel joke." The members of the philosophy department addressed their critique not only to their own local administration but also directly to their esteemed colleague across the country in Cambridge. Sandel's plaintive response demonstrated both respect for their concerns and the collegiality of a member of the horizontal community of philosophers: "I strongly believe," Sandel wrote in his open response, "that online courses are no substitute for the personal engagement of teachers with students, especially in the humanities. The worry that the widespread use of online courses will damage departments in public universities facing budgetary pressures is a legitimate concern that deserves serious debate, at edX and throughout higher education."

Four years after this episode, I met with the faculty leaders of HarvardX to discuss possibly taking on the operating role of leading HarvardX. I now understand why the HarvardX leaders expressed little interest in my enthusiasm for using Harvard online courses to craft a synthetic transinstitutional approach to teaching, the core function of higher education. The trauma of the SJSU philosophy department reaching across the country and engaging directly with a disciplinary colleague at Harvard had clearly left scars.

Outsourcing an institutional function is easier when the potential (and eventual) results of doing so can be measured with some precision. For example, an institution that hires Aramark to provide its dining services can compare the costs of providing the service with the cost of employing its own staff and then survey students to determine if the food is as good as it was before. Consider some of the cases that we have explored: Middlebury could measure the advantages and disadvantages of enlisting Investure to manage its endowment funds by comparing the investment results that Investure achieved to the results achieved by other in-house or outsourced endowment managers via the National Association of College and University Business Officers (NACUBO); the National Student Clearinghouse established its value to the participating registrars by being able to centralize a binary tracking measure of whether a student was enrolled or not and a report of those results. But on-campus decision-makers understandably have a higher resistance to change involving outsiders in the functions that are more intertwined with the multiplicity of student, faculty, and societal expectations of higher education. Rejection of outsourcing increases significantly around functions like teaching, where the possibility of precisely measuring either the current or future state of effectiveness is difficult and perhaps even impossible. Understandably the symbolic impulses of those involved—the passions that led faculty or staff to take on a mission-driven career—rise up when material benefits are prioritized above the essential symbolic work. The discrete outcomes of teaching "justice" in different ways might well be exceedingly difficult to measure, but the teachers have little doubt as to why doing so matters.

We can act collectively around clear measures, and the significant progress of public-private systems-building around student success have wisely focused on the clearest measure: degree attainment. As we get deeper into the symbolic forest of education, however, the path gets harder to find. The menu of courses consisting of recorded lectures and adaptive-learning quizzes that gauged whether students had absorbed the lecture material offered by MOOCs seemed, at first glance, to offer the clear and distinct replacement formula that companies like Aramark had supplied when providing outsourced dining services that replaced local dining hall staff.[6] Indeed, San Jose State University's administration was not alone in its enthusiasm for MOOCs' anticipated material benefits. In 2012, Thomas Friedman wrote in the *New York Times*, "I can see a day soon where you'll create your own college degree by taking the best online courses from the best professors from around the world . . . paying only the nominal fee for the certificates of completion."[7] MOOCs suggested the possibility of a Christensen-like disruption by offering to deliver what seemed like teaching (the core activity of a college) in what seemed to be new, effective, and efficient ways. But this quick fix to the material challenges faced by higher education ran aground.

While other domains of activity, ranging from core scholarly research to ancillary activities like college sports, have an established place in the panoply of investments that colleges and universities make, the teaching of undergraduates is both the material and symbolic core of higher education. In material terms, undergraduate tuition and subsidy dollars fund most of the rest of the enterprise. In symbolic terms, there would be no college without the classroom. And while the focus on research accomplishments weighs heavily in the reward structure for faculty at many levels of the enterprise, the classroom represents the space where faculty members structure and present their arguments in a mode far more exposed to scrutiny than their research or service work will ever be. Many faculty members report being far more nervous when standing in front of undergraduates in a classroom than when presenting to their peers at academic conferences.

In chapter 1, I talked about my discussions with Columbia professor Jim Beck, who expressed moral outrage when discussing the quality of some of Artstor's early images. He felt this indignation because he considered standing, alone, in front of undergraduate students as his opportunity to pass along to the next generation the ideas that drove his life's work. Any externally dictated intervention in his teaching—including a library decision that might affect what visual evidence he could use for his presentation—was therefore an invasion of the academic freedom at the core of higher education. While some people think that the concept of academic freedom is basically a restatement of the US principle of free speech, the designed protection of free exploration of ideas in teaching and research relies on a very different code. Joan Scott, a leading scholar of academic freedom, cites the 1894 statement of the regents of the University of Wisconsin as a compelling vision for the code that protects faculty members' freedom:

> We cannot for a moment believe that knowledge has reached its final goal, or that the present condition of society is perfect. We must therefore welcome from our teachers such discussions as shall suggest the means and prepare the way by which knowledge may be extended, present evils be removed, and others prevented. . . . In all lines of academic investigation it is of the utmost importance that the investigator should absolutely free to follow the indications of truth where they may lead.[8]

Wisconsin's and other colleges' and universities' unusual degree of shared governance of their organizations grows out of this core value of protecting the faculty's capacity to explore freely. At the same time, through the vehicle of peer review, horizontal communities—the disciplines—are entrusted with determining which scholarly work constitutes legitimate expertise and qualifies for this protection. Law professor Robert Post clarifies this distinction, in terms that resonate when considering the SJSU episode:

> First Amendment rights are individual, but academic freedom applies to a discipline, meaning a community of inquiry. Knowledge is produced by a community of inquiry, and therefore the right of the discipline is not to be judged by those outside the discipline. The most basic point about academic freedom is that I, as a professor, can only be judged by my peers.[9]

It was into this realm of principle that well-intentioned SJSU administrators blundered by promoting the utilization of Sandel's recorded lectures.

And it was through the horizontal community of their discipline that the SJSU faculty reached out to express their dismay. Consciously or unconsciously, the SJSU philosophy professors knew that the strongest forum to protest the invasion of their academic freedom was the horizontal institution—that their field was the ultimate guardian of behavioral norms. "In the case of the academic professional," Louis Menand writes, "interference by outside political or economic interests is considered repugnant to a unique degree."[10] And while Menand also recognizes the genuine downsides of a sector-wide dependence on slow-to-change disciplines that encourage "intellectual predictability, professional insularity, and social irrelevance," he, like the SJSU professors, believes that without the material and symbolic structures of particular fields or disciplines, administrations will face no constraints in their efforts to achieve cost containment.[11] The SJSU affair highlights one of the many erroneous beliefs of the initial MOOC fantasy that captured public and investor imaginations via edX and its for-profit competitors (Coursera and Udacity) in 2012: that significant changes in the political and financial economy of teaching could happen without the creative leadership of faculty members working within their particular disciplines to frame the positive benefits of the change.

Nonetheless, determining whether and how some sharing of courses—or elements of courses—can increase the productivity of faculty and slow the rising cost of higher education remains a crucial topic for the sector. In 2022, according to the Bureau of Labor Statistics, there were approximately 1.275 million post-secondary teachers in higher education in the United States.[12] Am I proposing that the introduction of a synthetic solution into the teaching enterprise should lower that number to only a few hundred or a few thousand teachers across the entire sector, with each local professor (as the alarmed San Jose faculty wrote), "turned into a glorified teaching assistant"? Absolutely not. The San Jose State faculty were right. The country is well served by a wide and diverse range of faculty members doing their work in classrooms in their own contexts and through their own lenses. In the laboratory of the classroom, students and their teachers wrestle with issues, ideas, and evidence to provide insights into the complexity of life. From these live explorations at varied venues, academic and social innovation is generated.

And yet, because society's interest in subsidizing higher education is limited, the societal and financial pressures on individual campuses increases. The question of how and where we might introduce some effective modes of collaboration seems ever more crucial. It seems almost assured that we are heading to a future in which there will be fewer than 1.275 million post-secondary teachers. The ways that institutions reduce the number of faculty to 1.2 or 1.1 million teachers in the coming years will result from a variety of strategies: the closing of programs, the increasing use of adjunct faculty leading precarious lives, and/or alternate means of awarding college credits to students. This reduction in faculty will be less effective if we don't work toward collectively designed strategies.

The MOOC's primary focus on the organized provision of information via a lecture is certainly one valuable element of college teaching. The other elements include group discussion; one-on-one dialogue with a teacher about a student's ideas, progress, or assignments; lab work on one's own or with peers; discussion and group work on projects or problem sets; field work; completion of homework or assignments; contextualization of the class within an institution's or department's requirements or curricular goals; and of course assessment and grading. These activities take place to varying degrees in different levels of courses, in different fields, and in different institutional contexts. The faculty who do this work bring their symbolic and material concerns to each of these undertakings, and they do so, as we have seen, within various networks of norm-setting and reward-setting communities within their institution and across the horizontal communities of which they are members. We've seen the challenges that arose when Artstor sought to interrupt the relatively linear and established practices of the local slide librarian supporting the art historian. Attempting to even modestly realign teaching practices will bring about even more widespread resistance. Why? Any intervention in college teaching stumbles into a much wider array of well-entrenched and universally reinforced interinstitutional structures of practice. The current rules of the game (and the norms) that structure college teaching are a matter of broad consensus. It's no wonder that SJSU's cavalier and top-down introduction of Sandel's "Justice" lectures was swiftly criticized and easily repelled.

The hype around MOOCs faded when it became clear that they could not provide a magical answer, but that doesn't mean that we should stop trying to find better solutions. In this chapter, I examine some components of the enormous effort involved in finding a working model of interinstitutional collaboration. The edX–San Jose State University collaboration didn't work, but that doesn't mean that others can't.

"Within a mature field," Royston Greenwood et al. write, "the boundaries of occupational and professional communities, though implicitly contested . . . exhibit phases of 'isomorphic' stability. During these phases, practices are reproduced by regulatory and interactive processes." But Greenwood et al. go on to note that the appearance of stability is "probably misleading." Non-isomorphic change occurs when "events, or 'jolts,' destabilize established practices. Jolts take the form of social upheaval, technological disruptions, competitive discontinuities, and regulatory change."[13] Some discontinuities rise like swells on the ocean: Artstor fit into an institutional model of change because of the inevitable and steady systemic opening created by digitization; Investure established a new approach to endowment management based on the growing complexity of managing a portfolio of private equity and hedge funds. But other jolts can be more sudden, and the events of 2020 reminded higher education of how sudden the disruption of a stable system can be.

In the face of the COVID-19 public health crisis, classes (and many other college and university functions) moved online, and physical campuses were shut down. A change-resistant higher education sector consisting of change-resistant institutions populated by change-resistant people proved capable of instituting significant structural change in a few days or weeks. How does this natural experiment, which provided a jolt to business-as-usual, play a role in helping us understand what it might take to advance a model of collective course sharing in higher education?

Mechanisms of a Shared Curriculum

Much has been said and written about the lessons learned from the sudden move from in-person to online classes because of COVID-19 in March 2019.[14] Surveying faculty in the first months of the sudden shift to online teaching (May and August 2020), consultants at Tryton Partners found that "instructors' increased—if forced— experience with remote learning last spring has enhanced their view of how they can use technology to improve their own teaching and to enable student learning. The proportion of instructors who see online learning as effective may still be just under half—49 percent—but that's up from 39 percent who said so in a similar survey in May."[15] Many faculty discovered surprising upsides to teaching online, but they also found the limits of Zoom: "By far the biggest complaint from students and faculty members alike about the remote learning that most experienced last spring was the lack of engagement and interactivity between students and instructors and among students themselves." In the 1840s, President James Garfield had famously said that the ideal college was "[Williams College President and widely admired polymath] Mark Hopkins on one end of a log and a student on the other." While the sudden acceleration of online learning brought an increasing awareness of those parts of teaching that the online classroom was able to support, the Zoom room was also found to be a long way from Mark Hopkins's log.

John Mitchell, Stanford University's vice provost for online learning (2012–2015) and for teaching and learning (2015–2018), has studied the development of online education both before and after the COVID-19 pandemic. According to Mitchell, the switch to Zoom highlighted our knowledge of what can be effective in online education (asynchronous lectures, Zoom for some kinds of discussion, the ability to enlist remote guest speakers). It also revealed noticeable gaps, including, according to Mitchell, "student interaction, office hours, and responsive learning tools."[16] But perhaps the biggest discontinuity introduced by the sudden shift to remote education came in the long established and deeply entrenched structure of assessments and grading. As Tim McKay, University of Michigan associate dean for undergraduate education, notes, the structure of grading is an artifact of the sector's significant growth during the first half of twentieth century:

> This explosive growth was enabled by adopting industrial approaches: standardization of tests, credit hours, degree requirements, and academic majors. The modern academic record and official transcript are deeply influenced by the tenor of these times, shaped as much by the practical needs of record keeping and correspondence in the 1920's as they are by a desire to accurately represent the student experience. The essence of the transcript—a single line recording each course taken and grade received, grouped by semester taken—was designed to allow the transcript to fit tidily into an envelope.[17]

McKay and his colleagues go on to argue for a "transcript of the future," not limited by printing space, that is able to draw on institutional data and combine "a richer record of the student experience along with a portfolio of authentic products of student work." In questioning the vestigial practices around the transcript, they also remind us that grades mean more or less to various audiences and there may well be other, less reductive ways to serve the purposes that the established grading infrastructure is locked into.

The pandemic jolt opened up the possibility that perhaps our long-standing grading architecture may not be as immovable as we had assumed. When it suddenly became impossible for students to sit for proctored exams in large rooms, the system adapted, even if just for a semester. In speaking with other teachers, John Mitchell found that the semester without grades reminded them of the foundational principles of pedagogy:

> I really like the position that many have come to: mastery work. What we have typically done is hand out an exam and what they do on that, that's their grade for the course. But in mastery learning . . . if someone does revise and resubmit, revise and resubmit and they eventually learn everything that's on the assignment, then maybe they should get a good grade. And what I see is a route to a less competitive environment around grades that would help with student empathy and might in the end lead to better student outcomes.[18]

The jolt of the gradeless spring of 2020 didn't stop the world from spinning, but it did point to a set of barriers to a collective pedagogical process: we have to think about how students in interinstitutional shared classes get graded, by whom, and whether it needs to be under someone's watchful eye. To build more distributed (including online) components into the sharing of college curricula and courses, our prepandemic model of grading may need to evolve. For some courses, a portfolio approach might well demonstrate more than a letter or a number that can be rolled into a GPA. One of the many pieces of shared infrastructure needed for building shared transinstitutional curricula and courses is consensus about how and in what mode assessment can serve the purposes that faculty, students, graduate schools, and employers need it to serve. How do we move beyond the pressure-filled and often reductive universal standard that we share today? Synthetic solutions around grading, starting with the redefining of norms, are perhaps best served within particular communities. The medical schools and law schools might know best what actually matters to them, just as employers in various sectors should have a say in what they care about. Changing any set of practices that is so deeply entrenched will be a big job. But that alone isn't a reason not to try.

Chapter 5 described the necessary preconditions for financing enterprises that can design and implement synthetic solutions to shared sector-wide needs. This chapter outlines the necessary preconditions for collective action at the core of the enterprise. These include the foundational involvement of disciplinary communities in determining the symbolic and material conditions for evolving the teaching enterprise in their fields, a consideration of the precedents for supporting collective action in these activities that might inform future mission-driven efforts, and an understanding of the most significant elements of change that remain unresolved even after the innovations of recent years (including consideration of the pandemic-driven acceleration of online learning). In a 2017 survey of college and university trustees, 92 percent of respondents said that college and university business models "had to change," with "lack of faculty support for changing the business model" specified as the biggest barrier to change.[19] If that's the view of trustees, who are most likely to be loving critics of the enterprise, then what must those who view the academy completely from the outside think of faculty's role in advancing or resisting change? The concept of academic freedom—which serves as a bulwark against political interference in the classroom or against financially driven and top-down change—is not self-evident to everyone. And yet the fundamental importance of academic freedom that grants power over the educational program to the faculty need not slam the door on effective and even efficient institutional change. In this regard, it's worth reviewing the very significant progress of Sunoikisis, the interinstitutional classics department introduced in chapter 1.

Sunoikisis: The Role of Insiders in Institutional Change

Like those in the student success movement, Kenny Morrell and his colleagues who created Sunoikisis started with the impulse to ask what was best for students. As Morrell commented in David Kirp's *Shakespeare, Einstein, and the Bottom Line: The Marketing of Higher*

Education, "I want my students to have an extraordinarily rich experience in my discipline . . . and I know that my institution is not in a position to marshal all those resources independently to do that. I've got to get other people involved."[20] He also believed that collaboration would save his field: "Are there going to be fewer full-time roles for classicists in the future? Of course there will be. But all the more reason that we should figure out together who can best do what so that students don't have a lousy experience and lose interest in the field."[21] Finally, he predicted that cost-effective collaboration would save institutions rather than leaving them suitable for disruption and asking themselves, "At what point do families realize that for the money that they're paying they could hire private tutors and pay for whatever kind of support or training their kids need? $60,000 a year? $80,000? $100,000?"

Sunoikisis was devoted to finding ways to improve the experience of students in ways that also made sense for the faculty and the field. By working among, rather than against, the faculty, its leaders were identifying the problems that a deeply collaborative interinstitutional enterprise could overcome. For example, faculty at the participating colleges often found it difficult to take sabbatical leaves even when they had earned them, because when a faculty member takes a sabbatical leave in a small department, it may result in there being no one available to teach required courses or to guide students' senior theses. Sunoikisis created a joint planning process whereby leaves could be covered by others in the interinstitutional network. Moreover, coordination allowed faculty to teach what they knew best: Morrell could teach Greek comedy and his Sunoikisis cofounder, Hal Haskell, could teach Roman architecture rather than each teaching subjects on their local campus that were more distant from their particular expertise and passion.

In short, Sunoikisis began with faculty identifying how change could help them, both for their own sake and for their students'. This effort enabled them to systematically work through the barriers to change in a way that they never would have been inspired to do in response to an administrative directive for financial efficiency. By overcoming the barriers to deep interinstitutional collaboration that are generally attributed to change-resistance on the part of the faculty, they were clearing a path to a large, interinstitutional, and potentially cost-effective shared department. The venture's early and unusual success brought accolades; its leaders were invited to give keynote addresses at conferences. But a number of strong currents pushed against their progress. As we saw early in this book, Morrell's desire to raise additional Mellon support for the interinstitutional effort encountered resistance from a dean who wanted the foundation to support something that would advance their own goals for the campus. As Sunoikisis continued over the years to push against the locally focused impulses of Rhodes or any other college, a later Rhodes dean wrote to the Associated Colleges of the South to express additional reservations about deep collaboration:

> I just wanted you to know that at Rhodes College we were able to sign on to the MOU [the Memo of Understanding between the College and the ACS] as a participant offering courses to other campuses. However, our faculty have not changed our handbook such that we can offer our own students online courses from other ACS institutions. I'm not sure how that needs to be noted on the website. I don't want our faculty to think that this MOU overrides our handbook language about online courses. We're happy to have Kenny teaching, and students from other campuses taking his class. But we don't have a policy that allows students at Rhodes to take online classes for credit from other institutions.[22]

The alignment of players had been central to Sunoikisis's work all along, but the work of aligning the disparate faculty and campuses against the autonomous ethos that dominated campus business-as-usual grew taxing. Because Sunoikisis was a new effort, it lacked supporting infrastructure. "They wouldn't ask the English department to 'self organize,'" Morrell noted. "They wouldn't expect faculty in the regular departments to schedule conferences and programs without release time for the director of undergraduate studies or the department chair, without any administrative support. But for a new, outside-funded venture, they did."

To hold the network together and enable its growth, Morrell knew that the rewards for faculty had to be both symbolic and material. Sunoikisis was building a collaborative community by bringing faculty together during the summer to plan. At the same time, Morrell knew that the new model would need to incentivize change in faculty behavior. Somehow the extra teaching and extramural work had to be recognized, because no recognition system was in place. In addition, institutions didn't know how to calculate the exchange of course attendance and the concomitant credits. Morrell also wanted to provide a reward for good teachers, proposing, "If I open five seats for those in other institutions, in return I would receive $1,000. And maybe there's a $250 incentive for Birmingham Southern faculty as a bounty for providing students so that they wouldn't be incentivized to steer students to their class even if it wasn't the optimal fit." These changes would require an entirely new infrastructure for counting where students landed and who (institutionally and individually) paid into and drew out of the pool. It needed a market-making system to reward and restructure the behavior of students, faculty, and institutions. But Sunoikisis was having trouble even keeping momentum going on the existing project. Morrell and his colleagues still had the multiple components of their full-time day jobs: teaching, research, advising students, and serving on committees.

Sunoikisis was seen as legitimate within the discerning population of faculty whom they were trying to convince to embrace the social change that technological innovation had made feasible. But shifting the systems around those faculty required buy-in regarding institutional change from the other participants in the system, such as registrars, deans, and accounting and technology staff. At one point, Morrell recounts, an administrator at one of the participating institutions warned him, "Don't you speak to my registrar." Even with the support of the most change-resistant players (faculty), Sunoikisis faced many more logistical battles. In 2003, the energy of volunteerism was wearing down, and the terms of the evolved business model (the car-dealer elements in higher education's half-church, half-car dealer model) weren't fully in place.

All involved were finding their way through a dark forest: an inter-institutional model in which faculty were the best positioned to solve the puzzle of producing an effective and efficient shared approach. But there were monsters aplenty in the wood—local institutional change-rejection mechanisms and reward-system structures that lagged behind any change. The limits of the bottom-up "We're all in this together" approach quickly became apparent: the structures of the colleges didn't support new models, and Sunoikisis did not have the resources, the time, or the plan to build market-supported services.

Morrell, Haskins, and their already-busy colleagues at the fifteen Sunoikisis colleges were, in effect, on their own in trying to build a platform for systems change. They were sustaining a field-wide effort on the basis of a network of individual faculty and departmental needs, but they had little "covering fire" to establish the urgency of change against the hard-to-change structures of their individual colleges. While (as Joan Scott has noted), disciplines are the arbiters of which new ideas become accepted as new norms in a field, as institutions they can have conservative natures just like colleges and universities. Without knowing it, and without all of the dedicated resources geared to particular tasks that synthetic service providers have, Sunoikisis was most successful at including the practitioners within a field. But what of the norm-setting intermediary organizations? Were they able to provide support for the many structural changes that were needed? Because change has to be fought for on all fronts, we can consider an example of how a call for a reframing of the norms in one field (music theory) can prepare the ground for systemic change.

As the field of ancient studies was reexamining how it is defined as a field and how it might thrive even as a century-long decline in the study of Greek and Roman language and culture continued, scholars in other fields also stepped back to consider the fundamental symbolic structures of their norm-setting communities. In the field of music theory, Professor Phil Ewell's 2019 keynote presentation at the Society for Music Theory's annual conference reverberated across the field.[23] Titled "Music Theory's White Racial Frame," Ewell's talk preceded the introspection concerning institutional racism that would arise among many academics in the aftermath of the killing of George Floyd by police in 2020. In his talk, Ewell highlighted the explicit racism of foundational German music theorist Heinrich Schenker, often considered "the most influential and original music theorist of the twentieth century."[24] Ewell also took issue with how subsequent theorists had gone out of their way to argue that Schenker's racism had nothing to do with his music theory. A classically trained cellist and scholar of Russian classical music, Ewell had decided that gracious but marginal critique was insufficient. Comparing Schenker's racist political writings with his music theory, he argued that Whiteness pervades a racialized structure of music scholarship: the ideas of nineteenth- and early twentieth-century German scholars, including Schenker, had defined what music counts as excellent and defined the criteria for determining excellence, thereby systematically excluding most of the rest of the world's music. These scholars' racism was not a side-course; it was a defining ingredient in the main course of their work. And, Ewell argued, the symbolic narrative of the field played out in material realities.

"On the one hand," Ewell noted, "music theory, as a field, states that it supports diversity and inclusivity, and with it one presumes racial diversity and inclusivity. But on the other hand, 98.3% of the music that we choose to represent the entire field to our undergraduate students in our textbooks is written by composers who are white."[25] Ewell's critique sparked angry backlash in some quarters, but overall it was well received. As he noted, "Over two years ago, when I began this work, I knew that I'd lose some friends and colleagues once it came out. I speculated that for every friend/colleague lost, I'd gain two or even three more. I was wrong. For every friend lost there have been more like 20–30 friends gained. It's not even close."[26]

As Ewell notes, attempts to adapt the field to align with today's societal and student populations have basically failed. Without changing the frame of what constitutes music worthy of study, he argues, the field has basically said that visitors are welcome, as long as they come to the existing institutional structure and play the game on existing institutional terms. Changing academic and intellectual structures is hard enough as a battle of values and symbols; it is so much harder within change-resistant structures where faculty see their livelihood being challenged. Still, the possible restructuring of departments, curricula, and requirements would be an essential part of remedying a hundred-year-old imbalance that was designed to exclude most of the world's music. In asking how the academy might reframe music theory—or any other discipline—we are also asking how to take on the sensitive set of issues and functions related to teaching that are at the heart of higher education's mission.

It won't be easy for music theory curricula around the country to change to represent the new and more inclusive theoretical framework that Ewell suggests. We've seen that Sunoikisis offered a model for enlisting faculty to define the paths forward, and Ewell used the Society for Music Theory as a mechanism for an intellectual reframing of a discipline. But what other tools for systemic change are needed?

A transformation in the field of music could be supported if faculty in the field coalesce around a narrative that calls for change and the possibility of institutional adaptation. But even if an altered intellectual map offers a rationale for evolving a field, the evolution of teaching within a field still needs other mechanisms for change. One tool that has long allowed academic fields to provide a map for what is worth studying is a remarkably synthetic device: the textbook.

The Textbook as Synthetic Mechanism

In colleges, high schools, and grammar schools around the country, teachers have long relied on textbooks, even though they aren't created locally. With roots going back as far as William James's 1890 *Principles of Psychology*, the textbook has a virtually unquestioned place as a labor-saving, externally provided, synthetic service. Perhaps because of its omnipresence, its potential as a model for both symbolic and material institutional change is underappreciated. Part of this may be due, as Nicky Hayes and Robert Sternberg note, to its deprecated place in the hierarchy of academic reward structures:

> Academics often regard the writing of textbooks as, at best, a second-rate activity. In the United States, many of the larger universities consider writing a textbook unimportant, for tenure and promotion. . . . Devaluing textbooks in evaluations of academic merit sends a dreadful message. It says that we don't really care about teaching large numbers of students. . . . If we really value teaching—and all of the academic rhetoric says that we do—why don't we value the writing of a textbook?[27]

We have seen various fragments of what might support interinstitutional teaching: how MOOCs were once considered a miracle but in truth can contribute only a small part of what is needed to share classes, how the faculty-led collaborative model of Sunoikisis succeeded in many aspects of the social part of a socio-technical change process, and how norm-setting communities (like the Society for Music Theory) may provide a channel for revolutionary rethinking of intellectual frameworks. Let's now consider the role of textbooks in interinstitutional collaboration around teaching.

According to the Open Syllabus project, which compiles reading lists by field, the top three psychology textbooks in use in are *Exploring Psychology*, *Psychology*, and *Social Psychology*. All are written by David G. Myers, professor at Hope College, and all derive from his first book, *Psychology*, published by Worth Publishers in 1986. The dramatically increasing price of textbooks in the 1990s and early 2000s sparked significant societal frustration with textbook publishers, which essentially exploited the lock-in of student buyers that occurs when a professor chooses to adopt a given textbook for a class. This tension began to lessen in the 2010s as publishers offered digital textbooks, printed textbook rentals, looseleaf editions, and other versions that lowered prices for students.[28] Through all of this, Myers's following has remained strong. The 13th edition of *Psychology* was released in 2021. Much of the book's success surely is due to Myers's capacity to keep the work up-to-date and approachable. But the quality of the work is not solely due to the author's intellect;

Myers recalls why he chose to work with Bob Worth, founder of the firm: "Bob told me then that they aimed to produce a few Mercedes rather than a lot of Chevys."

Myers recognizes that creating and maintaining a textbook of high quality takes more than his brain's hard work. In addition to crediting twenty-one faculty who serve as reviewers and consultants, Myers thanks "the innumerable researchers who have been so willing to share their time and talent to help us accurately report their research, and to the hundreds of instructors who have taken the time to offer feedback." Beyond the team of creators, he also credits the publisher (Worth, now a part of Macmillan Learning) for following up on Bob Worth's original pledge to invest in making a Mercedes:

> And they were so true to that word, by making big investments in book development and editing, in the art and photo program, and in design, production, and marketing. They also have had— and Macmillan Learning continues to have—a long-term vision, rather than (as with the companies taken over by private equity firms) short-term cost-reduction/profit aims at the expense of long-term quality.[29]

For many years, Macmillan and other textbook publishers have also supplied a wide set of supporting tools for both teachers and students. Instructors using Myers's *Psychology* can now access a bank of related tests and quizzes; questions to use with clickers (instant survey response tools) to enhance student engagement; faculty guides; video collections; image slides and tables; an instructor's resource manual; lecture guides; MCAT correlation guides; an Achieve Read & Practice online version that combines LearningCurve (an adaptive quizzing engine to help students determine how much information they are grasping) with an e-book; and LaunchPad, which combines the e-book with assignments, quizzes, and exam prep.[30]

As the high level of investment in David Myers's textbooks makes clear, the for-profit sector invests in the quality of a product when it anticipates that high-quality production will likely be one way to overcome student and faculty resistance. Master Class—a company that offers online classes with Spike Lee on filmmaking, Serena

Williams on tennis, and Frank Gehry on architecture—determined that the highest level of production quality was essential for attracting both famous teachers and potential students. "It's an investment idea we believe in," says Deborah Quazzo of Chicago-based GSV Ventures, which invested in an earlier round of funding for Master Class. "It's Hollywood meets Harvard. Education online has not been adequately engaging and it has not driven the type of retention of movies and TV shows."[31] Master Class has a clear field in front of it; it isn't trying to fit in with existing film or tennis classes.[32] Quality, both in terms of content and the production, is an important strategy for helping synthetic solutions overcome the "we can build it just fine here, by ourselves" local response.

By enabling teachers to work with shared resources and not need to invent every assignment from scratch, textbooks have long served as examples of the trusted intermediary organizations described in this book. Textbook authors synthesize the academic material; textbook publishers synthetically create reusable mechanisms. As textbook publishers expand into learning management platforms, a door opens up to suggest that even more sharing could be possible. Phil Ewell recognized the power of this kind of mechanism for the institutions that he hopes to change; with his colleagues Rosa Abrahams, Aaron Grant, and Cora Palfy, he has contracted with Norton to write a new music theory textbook, *The Practicing Music Theorist*. "Instead of thirty Mozart examples," Ewell says, "let's have one, maybe two. Approaching music theory from this nonwhite/nonmale angle, but not to the exclusion of white men, will enrich music theory for everyone."[33] A new textbook that helps reframe a field will certainly be a part of facilitating institutional change; what other pieces of the puzzle need to be put into place to facilitate interinstitutional course sharing?

Interinstitutional Plumbing

From the sublime question of "How many Mozart pieces do we need in the canon?" we turn to the earthly question of how to manage the accounting of students flowing into and out of cross-institutional classes. As we've seen, the collaborative Sunoikisis classics network hadn't fully worked out the transactional infrastructure needed to track interinstitutional student enrollments and to reward the participating faculty. Creating that kind of plumbing is neither a sexy nor a simple investment. Planning and carrying out all aspects of Sunoikisis in the last hour of everyone's day wore out its leaders. In its enthusiasm for the project's early success, the Mellon Foundation sought to scale the effort up to a national level through the foundation's National Institute for Technology in Liberal Education (NITLE), but doing so attenuated the bonds that held the original members together. Some renewed funding did arrive in 2003, but it was not enough to provide the centralized office that colleges needed to implement and track the program's net impact.

Even as Sunoikisis gradually dialed back on its programmatic ambitions, institutional knowledge was building up over time in the liberal arts college community, which continued its efforts to share. Years later, in 2014–2017, Mellon sponsored a program that enabled the leading membership organization for liberal arts colleges (the 700-member Council of Independent Colleges, or CIC) to offer shared upper-level humanities classes across the network. Assessment of the work focused on students' educational outcomes because making the case for shared courses to faculty, students, and skeptics required establishing first that no harm would be done.

After using grant funds to assess the educational outcomes of these humanities classes in 2017, CIC's leaders knew what they needed to do in order to advance the progress of course sharing. In 2019, the organization set out to determine how programs across the network could take advantage of unused capacity in other member colleges to fill a hole in their curriculum or to help students take the courses that they needed to complete a sequence. Gaps in students' records happen for many reasons—they may fail a class, they might need a specific course in their major that isn't being offered, or they may be down a class or two because their athletic program demands too much. Historically, students have filled these gaps by taking a summer course at a community college near home or, thanks to the internet, just about anywhere. This method of filling gaps was a source of concern for all involved because the distinctive value of a liberal arts college education becomes at least slightly interrupted when any class can be glued into a student's transcript. With this new collaborative effort, students could make-up a missing class within the CIC consortium. As a result of seeing students taking classes at peer institutions, faculty members feel less concerned about the dilution of the curriculum.

As a membership organization, CIC was not in a position to create the infrastructure to support such an effort. So the leaders of CIC enlisted a firm then called College Consortium (now called Acadeum). Unlike online program managers such as 2U that focus on hosting online classes on behalf of universities and marketing them to students, Acadeum had chosen to focus on the interinstitutional plumbing to support cross-institutional registration. Institutions that offer classes via the Acadeum system pay fees, as do the students' home institutions. Acadeum handles the transactions in both the financial accounting and the registration accounting. In return for providing these services, Acadeum takes 25 percent of whatever fee is transferred for a seat in a class (as opposed to the 40 to 60 percent share for online program managers). The home institution bills the student at the rate it set for a CIC Online Course Sharing Consortium course, and the student pays the home institution, which in turn pays the teaching institution that is offering the course the rate set by the teaching institution. In this way, both institutions share the revenue that a course generates.

Because home institutions have the freedom to set the rates charged to their students, they can deploy a strategic pricing strategy. For example, some home institutions choose not to bill students during regular semesters by including Consortium courses in their block tuition as a way of making stronger proposals for student recruitment, retention, or completion plans. Through the Acadeum platform, the home institution transfers the portion of tuition that the teaching institution charges the home institution for the course. Because the new enrollment fills an otherwise empty seat, the teaching institution can charge less than the full tuition charge and the home institution can retain the difference. In addition, CIC receives from Acadeum modest revenue that helps fund member programs and services. All payments are automatically transferred through the Acadeum platform and do not require additional institutional billing.

Robb Manzer, a former college provost and Acadeum's chief academic officer, had encountered many consortium-based issues in his work at universities such as Ohio Northern and Nebraska Wesleyan. As Acadeum, based in the ed-tech hub of Austin, Texas, worked to identify the gaps in the system of consortial work, he'd seen how the registrars of the three universities in Abilene met at the train station every few weeks to exchange envelopes with lists of student cross-enrollments. He realized that Acadeum could facilitate the flow of students simply by building connective pipes between registrars' systems. These connective pipes, along with financial reconciliation and some monitoring that allows the participating institutions to report on students' progress, constitute the bulk of Acadeum's services.

Given that the absence of this sort of plumbing represented the major barrier to Sunoikisis's work, I asked Manzer if Acadeum ever considered more significant course sharing, even jointly offered majors. "CIC," reports Manzer, "are the perfect partners. They know how to move forward carefully, to ensure that their members' needs are being met. Ultimately we would like to be that infrastructure that allows this all to take place so that costs are very low and get lower over time. That's the ultimate vision. Looking from the trenches, there's a pretty big problem that this can solve—students can get back on track or have options."[34] In 2020, Acadeum received an investment from Lumina, which sees the firm's capacity to help students make up credits as an element of a system-wide focus on student success.

As a consortium of member colleges, CIC has little incentive to push its members to seek more aggressive sharing of classes, though its system could potentially support that. The key point here is that independent companies such as Acadeum can hustle to identify a systemic gap. Clearly, Acadeum deserves to be rewarded for taking the risk and deploying the capital needed to build the plumbing that neither individual schools nor CIC were willing or able to take on.

Like the National Student Clearinghouse in its early days, Academium kept its pace of change modest, but in 2022 it began to accelerate its fee structure. Will its 25 percent fee, or any new models that it devises, eventually be considered too high a tariff on the institutions? At what point will participating institutions wish that colleges and universities had built an Acadeum-like structure on their own, rather than going to an outside vendor? If missions continue to align, as they seem to do now, Acadeum and individual institutions might be perfect complements, but if profit-seeking ends up being too strong a force, the curve could break in the wrong direction.

As CIC deepened its interest in this strategy of interinstitutional collaboration in 2022, it also began to work with another new, non-profit network for course sharing with the explicit aim of lowering costs: the Lower Cost Models for Independent College Consortium (LCMC), which in turn fostered a company, Rize, that is building a platform for course and program sharing. Under the umbrella of a cross-pollinating and mission-driven collaborative network (CIC), the pursuit of the right synthetic alignment is intensifying. After fostering a solution, an institutional trust network can serve as a motivated and trusted marketing office for the effort, and a modest amount of technical plumbing greatly diminishes the "not built here" suspicion that can adhere to an interinstitutional solution.

By opting to support consortia, including but not limited to the CIC, Acadeum camouflages its business model in the leafy confines of a preexisting trust network. Administrators and faculty at participating colleges are more likely to give the benefit of the doubt to those whom they see as peers. Josh Pierce, the founder of Acadeum, recognized the benefits of Acadeum playing a supporting role and avoiding the work of trust building: "The industry is talking to itself about this as opposed to us knocking on the door and talking to them about it," he said. "We're pretty excited at the fact that industry leaders are starting to work with each other and we're just a player at the table."[35]

Do broader trust networks exist that could bless course sharing on a sector-wide level? By launching his rethinking of music theory in a keynote address to the Society of Music Theory, Phil

Ewell suggested that the horizontal communities of societies and associations could provide a locus for trust-building around curricular change and perhaps around Sunoikisis-like efforts at shared curricula. Academic societies serve as one of the few norm-setting communities that reach across the rigid institutional boundaries that mark the end of one campus and the beginning of another. Societies create and maintain peer-review committees of members for many reasons: to allocate research or travel funds, to nominate new board members, to oversee publications. They also have long been devoted to the validation of scholarly trends and to the dissemination of what is deemed to be significant scholarship (via the society's journal).

Still, it could be natural for societies to play a role in the promotion and collaboration around pedagogy in a more deliberate way than many of them do today. Taking part in activities like sanctioning shared courses and course components would signal the importance of the society's symbolic work of stewarding the future of the field; this is beginning to happen to some societies that had originally focused almost exclusively on scholarly research. As Jim Grossman, the executive director of the American Historical Association (AHA), notes, "To be a historian is to be a teacher." One quarter of the governing council of AHA now comes from teaching-oriented institutions; in earlier times, it was exclusively focused on research publications. Its large annual meeting is steadily shifting (as Grossman puts it) "away from a 'research meeting' to a 'professional development' environment."[36] The more that academic societies recognize, devote time to, and legitimate the pedagogical enterprise, the greater the chance that they can contribute to evolving the norms of the intellectual (symbolic) and material structures of their fields. While supporting research will always be part of their mission, the future of their fields is built—again, symbolically and materially—through the teaching of undergraduates. As a norm-setting trust network, they can—as communities like CIC have done—move their members' collective agenda forward in ways that individuals cannot.

Societies are relied upon to define what constitutes legitimate knowledge within a field, but they don't hire faculty. Colleges and universities control the allocation of faculty lines, and they allocate those lines in various ways, often based on enrollments. Over time, the number of tenure-track positions has declined and may well continue to do so. Societies can either protest such changes (as they sometimes do) with modest effect or ask what they can do to support the collective work of teachers in the field in ways that can have some bearing on the decisions of individual colleges and universities. As Sunoikisis set out to do, they can collectively support the transinstitutional community of teachers and scholars who make up the field. In doing so, they will be acting more as a guild than as a union (which of course they aren't empowered to be):

> Guilds enforce quality standards in an industry or trade, protect members from exploitation, provide financial support and serve as mediators for their members. Labor unions likewise serve their members' interests by negotiating for better working environments and fair wages.[37]

In giving more prominence to teaching over publications, and by working to support collective action around sharing of curricula, courses, and course materials, societies could facilitate the sharing of courses. Their blessing of pedagogical sharing of materials and other aspects of classes could provide a market test for what the field's experts believe should define the field's future.

Although reward structures often focus on research over teaching, faculty worry about the continuity of their teaching when they are contemplating retirement. They don't worry about who will keep up publication, but they do ask, "Will I be replaced in my department by someone who teaches my field in the same way?" Developing interinstitutional curricula that ensure flexibility and depth of offerings to students without the zero-sum game of one local faculty hire meaning the truncation of an intellectual lineage could serve everyone well. In short, we need to build upon the cross-cutting and cross-pollinating capacities of intermediary organizations like academic societies. As the CIC-Acadeum collaboration and the Society for Music Theory–textbook publisher symbiosis show, we need to work on all fronts and develop solutions that resonate within all sorts of horizontal communities to help foster and sustain change in the pedagogical enterprise. And while change will always be hard, change from within the community might not look so bad when participants consider the alternatives.

The Continuing Threat of Extractive Partners

Without bad intent, and with financial investors and critics of higher education supporting their work, for-profit firms are increasingly seeking to extract value from the work of colleges and universities. The 2012 moment of enthusiasm for MOOCs saw another new institutional player leap onto the scene at the same time that Harvard and MIT launched edX. Coursera is a for-profit firm backed in its first funding round by venture capitalists Kleiner Perkins and New Enterprise Associates and supported with courses created and contributed by Brown, Emory, Princeton, the University of Pennsylvania, Vanderbilt, and others. Both Coursera and edX gathered additional college and university partners over time, and both moved toward creating credentials that might be valued in the workplace as a means of monetizing the content that universities were contributing. In 2020 Coursera had an IPO, resulting in a market capitalization of $7 billion. Choosing a different path, edX was financed initially by the universities, with an eye on gaining more trust among members because of its nonprofit status.

In June 2021, the largest online program-management firm, 2U, purchased edX from Harvard and MIT for $800 million. Harvard Provost Alan Garber noted how the universities recognized that they weren't set up to exploit the possibilities of what they had created: "Enrollment in edX courses boomed during the pandemic, which focused even more attention on the value and potential of high-quality online learning. Taking full advantage of that potential will require capital investments at greater scale than is readily attainable for a nonprofit entity like edX."[38]

Critics of the sale, whose proceeds will result in the creation of a new nonprofit organization whose activities are yet to be defined, felt betrayed. In 2012, Steven Mintz, who had served as the executive director of the University of Texas's Institute for Transformational Learning, had advocated for the University of Texas–Austin to join edX rather than Coursera. He later noted, "Those of us who, mistakenly, viewed edX as a model—of cross-institutional collaboration, collective educational research, nonprofit EdTech innovation, and expanded access to a quality education and credentials—have much to ponder. . . . I, for one, feel an acute sense of loss, frustration, and, yes, disappointment."[39]

Mintz and others had led their universities into edX on the basis of prioritizing mission over market. As educational blogger Michael Feldstein noted, the labels were more than misleading:

> It turns out that the other participating universities, after getting less input and worse customer service as "partners" in edX than they would have gotten as Coursera customers, find the noble organization they contributed to . . . was sold to become part of Coursera's most direct for-profit competitor.[40]

Feldstein goes on to suggest what Harvard and MIT learned: not only that edX required capital, but also that it would thrive only as a marketing mechanism for the real businesses that MIT and Harvard aren't, and don't want to be, in:

> To make money off of MOOCs, you need to be in a position to sell other types of educational experiences at a scale that is far larger than MIT and Harvard. You need a sophisticated, multi-level, multi-supplier marketplace. . . . Since MIT and Harvard were never going to build that kind of a business, edX was never going to be sustainable for them. If it was going to have a future, it was going to be at a company like 2U, which helps universities sell online education programs that *can* make money. Selling edX to a large OPM [online program manager] was both a highly logical move and a complete betrayal of everything they originally claimed to have stood for (and against).[41]

In other words, the courses—like Sandel's "Justice"—contributed by institutions such as Harvard, MIT, the University of Texas, Berkeley,

Dartmouth, Rice, and the University of Chicago had been employed to build up an audience of trusting seekers-of-knowledge. The channel that the reputations of these institutions had opened for edX was now going to be used to sell masters' degrees to the public and to mine their user data for other commercial purposes. The video recordings of star professors were extracted from their university contexts and can be deployed in support of 2U's business. "Pretty soon," said former Michigan provost Paul Courant, "publishers or EdTech firms will have all that they need from higher education. Students will buy courses or programs at a rate that colleges can never compete with. If we don't look out, institutions will be hollowed out like empty oil wells or decimated rainforests."[42] Amid the market declines in the first half of 2022, rumors swirled that 2U (now containing edX) might be purchased by Byju, based in India, prompting questions of whether "it could scale back that 'high-touch' model that many institutions have come to expect in exchange for paying 2U millions of dollars through tuition-sharing agreements."[43] Faith in for-profits to serve mission-related goals encounters limits.

As we've seen, Sunoikisis created an impressive transinstitutional community. In the end, however, the links that connected Furman and Davidson, Birmingham Southern and Millsaps, Morehouse and Rhodes, proved too hard to maintain. Twenty years after its founding, Sunoikisis continues to draw faculty together for various workshops and collaborative efforts, but overall it had faced too many barriers to accomplish its ambitious goal of "pav[ing] the way for similarly innovative programs and help[ing] them to expand and transform opportunities all across the country" (as stated in its final grant application to Mellon).

Sunoikisis had been systematically working through higher education's tightly woven barriers to change, and it held promise for defusing the ticking time bomb at the heart of higher education's financial model, which relies on each institution doing almost everything on its own. The effort had succeeded in getting faculty to put the needs of their collective students and their field first and to plan—and act—in coordination. Kenny Morrell knew that Sunoikisis wouldn't result in a magical return to some nostalgic vision of a golden age of growth. Instead, he and his colleagues asked, "Why not band together to give the students what they need and collectively plan the future of the field?"

Like most of my colleagues in higher education, I would be thrilled to see a massive influx of new funds for subsidizing higher education's life-changing enterprises of teaching and research—from the federal or the state governments or from any other source. But this seems increasingly unlikely. The rise of public/private ventures portends more market forces acting on higher education, not some deus ex machina mechanism that allows colleges to fund whatever they like. Financial pressures on students and families, especially student loan debt, will make colleges more responsive to market demands and less focused on the parts of their mission that the market cares less about.

As we've seen in this book, to solve higher education's cost problem we need solutions that reduce unnecessary redundancies across institutions. Mission- and market-compatible synthetic services can and should foster collaborative mission-driven solutions across administrative functions of many kinds, but at the heart of the productivity dilemma in higher education are labor costs and the many challenges that limit productivity enhancements in undergraduate teaching. The resistance to change that abounds among campus constituencies is surely most crystallized among faculty members whose material and symbolic work would be threatened most by shared solutions; in addition, local course design and teaching are considered a good by college presidents, who need to sell the story of the campus's value, often by using ratings such as the omnipresent faculty-to-student ratio, which helps them weave a narrative of quality that is correlated with the level of spending on the production function. Everybody says that they want college to cost less, but few people or institutions are seriously engaged with the question of how to share some part of the weight of designing and teaching college classes. In the end, that is the challenge that we need to overcome, the problem we need to solve.

The proposal to use Sandel's course at San Jose State tripped various alarm wires, including equity concerns, which must be consciously centered in any attempt to synthesize efficient and effective shared solutions. During the course of the pandemic, sociologist Richard Arum and his colleagues at the University of California–Irvine happened to be conducting a longitudinal study of various curricular and extra-curricular components of an undergraduate liberal arts education. When the pandemic hit and students were taken away from their somewhat more equalized campus environments and returned home to vastly different situations, Arum and his colleagues were able to see that remote, online courses could risk exacerbating inequities. In the early days of the move to remote instruction, students' success in coursework tracked with their reports of stable internet access and quiet places to study. These findings on inequalities in online instruction were consistent with prior research on student success.[44] Interestingly, Arum and his colleagues found that these inequities waned as individual students and the campus adapted to changing circumstances and new instructional modalities. Instructors were encouraged to replace synchronous online lectures with asynchronous interactive coursework and students found creative solutions to their problems as well. By the fall of 2020, six months into remote instruction, students from all backgrounds were achieving success at least at comparable rates to prepandemic in-person instruction. In fact, attrition from the institution had decreased and grade point averages and credit accumulation were up for students from all backgrounds at the diverse, selective research university studied.[45] There are risks in change, but they also need not be disastrous if we are being mindful as we proceed. Over the past twenty years, faculty and administrators in higher education have grown increasingly aware of inequities in the structure of the system, inequities that make the path for first-generation, underserved, and lower-income students more difficult at every point in the process. We have a lot of puzzles to work on to design and implement faculty-driven and student-centered collective approaches to evolving fields of knowledge. I have argued throughout this book that a cloistered, "We must do everything ourselves" resolution will not serve institutions or the sector well. But what the San Jose philosophy professors called "the cruel joke" in which the opportunity to learn about justice (or anything else) is carried out in increasingly unjust and inequitable ways is certainly not the answer. Changing nothing and changing things for the worse are not the only choices we have. They are just the easiest ones.

7

Conclusion

CHOOSING TO CHANGE

While waiting for a few latecomers to a presentation that he was about to make to the presidents of the Associated Colleges of the South in 2001, classics professor and Sunoikisis founder Kenny Morrell decided to conduct an informal focus group. "Do you all generally," he asked, "prefer to collaborate or compete?" A few of the assembled presidents offered responses that consisted of a mix of avoiding the question and boilerplate platitudes. As many of the other presidents looked at their feet or out the window, Morrell thought that the answer was clear.

US higher education has enjoyed more than a hundred years of growth and dominance. But the increasing complexity of the enterprise, the apparently unstoppable progression of increasing costs, and the steady retreat of government subsidies all contribute to a steady change in how institutions set priorities and how society views them. Various strategies aimed at growing revenues become ever more central to the enterprise: fundraising; commercialization of the medical, natural science, and engineering fields; ever-more sophisticated marketing strategies for attracting students who can pay all or most of the sticker price; and graduate programs that may or may not advance students' careers but do strengthen the college or university's bottom line. Growing revenues via new ventures (such as the partnerships with Online Program Managers reviewed on page 17) or fundraising dominates the minds of college and university leaders. And doing so successfully requires differentiating each institution from the others. Presidents, deans, and leaders at every level are selected and promoted on the basis of the degree to which they can compete in a reputation and revenue-generating race without end, a race to that is based on distinguishing that department, school, or institution from its closest competitors.

Warm feelings, empathy for shared struggles, and respect for the innovative ideas of colleagues often abound when deans, other administrators, or colleagues get together via intermediary organizations such as the Associated Colleges of the South, the American Council on Education, or the American Council of Learned Societies. As human beings engaged in a shared and meaningful endeavor, they see themselves as part of a collective effort. Then they return home, where they find full calendars and a set of reward structures that tell them that the only way to thrive is to make their own complicated campus machines run smoother and ever faster. The rules of the market game are not particularly ambiguous. Internal and external market forces whisper in the ears of leaders and those who choose them. Ideas about (and energy for) collaboration fade. Only by winning the race for students, famous faculty, grants, or the like can they see a way forward.

These leaders are not wrong if they believe that approaches focused on reducing costs run the very real risk of demoralizing everyone involved.[1] I have written about what the new intermediaries can do to design and engineer change within today's system. But what must other people and organizations to do to play a part in systemic change? In the world of medical research and drug development, systems thinkers like Michael Milken and Kathy Giusti saw a fragmented landscape of different players with slightly divergent aims. Their efforts to collectively refocus various players on creating cures enabled them to pursue their particular goals. It also allowed capital to flow in a structured and supportive way. At colleges and universities, how can various constituencies feel that they are part of a positive mission for the future of the enterprise?

US higher education, a very loosely associated system that intersects other complex systems (K-12 education, the country's workforce, social and political movements), aims to serve many ends for many and varied people. At the same time, students' voices are fragmented by the wide diversity of results that they are seeking from college. Some are seeking "church" effects (growth, learning, satisfaction), and others are seeking "car dealer" outcomes (material or social advancement). Higher education has not figured out how to support student-centricity. In the meantime, student loans pile up. The promise of "investing in your own human capital" risks overpromising at the same time that it flattens the wide range of reasons for going to college into workforce preparation alone. Believing that they are investing in their personal advancement, students and families solemnly accept the terms of the transaction. But they may not continue to do so. Blake Masters, president of the Thiel Foundation, argues that they shouldn't:

> Of all the bad ideas permeating college campuses, the worst is the self-serving myth that everybody has to go to college, and pay tens or hundreds of thousands of dollars to do it. This is even more obvious when "college" just means wasting time on Zoom.[2]

In an unusual twist on the tradition of philanthropists fostering the ambitions of young people by supporting their college dreams, billionaire Peter Thiel has created a generous fellowship program that pays talented young people *not* to attend college. Just as traditional financial aid programs have signaled "You can do this" to prospective college students, Thiel's program sends the clear signal "You don't have to." An increasing proportion of the population shares Thiel's skepticism regarding US higher education. In a 2013 Gallup poll, 74 percent of people aged 18–29 thought that college was "very important." By 2019, only 41 percent did. In the spring of 2021, college enrollment declined by 3.5 percent (about 600,000 students).[3] In the spring of 2022, college enrollment fell by another 4.7 percent (another 662,000 students).[4]

Underlying the growing skepticism regarding higher education are tuition rates that for decades have been rising faster than inflation. The sticker prices that lead Thiel and other skeptics to argue that college isn't worth the investment have been on an upward trajectory for a long time. The path that we are on is not sustainable, and yet individuals and institutions march along that path with Sisyphean acceptance. In essence, defending the "autonomy at all costs" approach relies on maintaining the current course. Some people might respond to the mission-driven but market-tested collective approaches that I have proposed by calling instead for magical financial subventions to restore the growth of the post–World War II period. At the other end of spectrum are those who view disruption of institutions as a healthy cleansing force that will invent new entities and decimate the old ones. Close to the real work of daily life, thousands of administrators, faculty, and staff recognize the problems that colleges and universities face but see large-scale change as impossible, and hence are resolved to play the local games by the local rules. However, the alternative to playing an active role in systems change is not maintaining the status quo, because the status quo is slipping away. The alternative to supporting models that can preserve institutions and institutional values by collectively containing costs is to watch as powerful forces act on institutions and their treasured autonomy.

The structures that supported the widely admired US higher education system in the twentieth century are eroding. Tenure-track faculty now comprise 55 percent of the teaching force, compared to 80 percent in 1971.[5] Tension in academic departments rises between those who have the security of being on the tenure track and the growing number of their contingently employed colleagues who find out if they have a paying job only when students show up on the first day of class. Even more daunting are the prospects for the scholars emerging from PhD programs, as job markets grow increasingly thin, even for adjuncts. In the fall of 2021, Columbia University graduate students went on strike for ten weeks, demanding a living wage and knowing that their opportunities for faculty positions were shrinking by the day. Professors are confused by the limited prospects for their most promising graduate students. The status quo is not what it used to be. The shrinking of the professoriate is happening, and it will continue to happen in better ways or in worse ways.

At the same time, governments have either led the retreat from supporting higher education or have recognized that there would be little opposition to their doing so. As recently as 2007, the state government of Colorado provided 72.2 percent of the funding for Colorado's flagship public university (Boulder). Today the state provides 4.3 percent of the budget.[6] The cost of college is going up, and no one is coming to the rescue.

For those individuals or institutional philanthropists who care about a particular issue, a synthetic solution could be an opportunity, as it was for Mellon when it wanted to support the teaching of art and cultural history. In 2018, investor Bill Miller donated $75 million to support philosophy at Johns Hopkins University.[7] He knew what he cared about in higher education and was looking for a mechanism to make a significant difference. This scale of financial giving doesn't happen every day, but it might happen more often if venture philanthropists and impact investors see the right players align behind a realistic plan for systems change that will reach across a particular community-wide segment of higher education. Based on what we have learned about the difficulty of myth-rewriting and norm-shifting, the locus for change must be within a circumscribed community, whether an academic field, a discrete segment of student services, or some other part of the enterprise. The National Student Clearinghouse had enough to do in understanding the wants and needs of registrars; imagine how much harder it would have been to be successful if it needed to convince administrators and staff in admissions, career services, international programs, counseling, student activities, disability services, and the library. Phil Ewell's attempt to reframe the intellectual framework of music theory is based on a deep understanding of the traditions, scholarship, and practices within that discipline; imagine the reception if he challenged the religious studies or political science discipline in the same way. Some of the changes required for mutualist models to thrive are more revolutionary, while some are more modest. Still, they will succeed only if they fit in with the life stories and institutional myths that give symbolic context to the mission-driven people who live busy everyday lives within a locally defined and change-resistant context.

The theory of change that I propose boils down to a few simple ideas. Specifically, a proposed synthetic solution must:

- Address both the symbolic and material needs of decision-makers within the mission-driven institution, simultaneously and continuously. Addressing only one of these value systems will not work.
- Hold the promise of significant improvements over what can be done locally, even if those improvements cannot occur immediately.
- Work on all fronts simultaneously. The solution needs to gain the backing of decision-makers from the bottom up and offer an intelligible narrative to those at the top of the institutional resource-allocation pyramid. At the same time, synthesis requires involving the horizontal, cross-cutting, and norm-setting communities that are ultimately needed to promulgate enduring change.

As in the cases of medical research and timber investing, various groups need to be involved and to play a productive role:

- Students and families need to find a collective voice to convey the frustration that they feel. The most power-ful signal they can send is to choose not to go to college, but they also can look to other models for giving voice to collective concerns, in the way that the student-led movement to pressure institutions to divest their endowments from fossil fuels has done.
- Alumni need to target their giving with collective action in mind. Colleges and universities will have to recognize and celebrate donors who target collective solutions rather than local pioneering.

- Faculty must be called upon to think about their field's well-being rather than only about its local instantiation in their department in their college or university. Acting more as a guild than as a disconnected set of individual position-holders could help their field to thrive. Unfortunately, the channels for becoming effective in working beyond one's department or institution are obscure. But as the Sunoikisis effort shows, the idea of collaboration isn't nearly as troubling when there are benefits to forging new collaborative undertakings.
- Opportunities for professional development for staff need to be reimagined, reviewed, and rewarded according to shared institution-wide goals, including cost containment.
- Horizontal communities of all types must consider how they can best contribute to the well-being of the enterprise. They must talk with one another, too. A scholarly society already has the capacity to convene a set of department chairs; might there be a corresponding network of deans or provosts with whom they might strategize? Finding the time to foster the intersecting of intermediaries is in itself more work than anyone has time for. But it is likely to happen only if we share a common purpose and invest in expanding our underdeveloped interinstitutional infrastructure.
- University trustees, administrators, and presidents will always need to distinguish their schools in a competitive marketplace, but they also need to send a signal that controlling costs matters. For example, the various rating organizations might choose to rank schools not on the size of their endowments or their ever-increasing inefficiency (as shown in lower faculty-to-student ratios) but instead on how effectively they control institutional costs. And trustees choosing presidents might consider whether selecting individuals on their capacity to bravely run full speed into an endless arms race really is the best solution.

Finally, recalling the paradox of embedded agency that inhibits change within a human-built system, we need to recognize that the dominant players have no incentive to change. The institutions with endowments big enough to create a bubble around their campus may continue to play the prestige game, and other leading institutions may continue to try to buy their way into that circle. The vast majority of colleges and universities need to resist that trap and focus on a refreshed and renewed norm—valuing affordable approaches to high-quality education over endless creative growth.

The path that balances market-tested values and mission-driven values is not wide. On the extreme of one side is a faith in the creative autonomy of institutional agents that scoffs at the concerns of those who are paying for their pioneering adventures; on the extreme of the other side is a belief system that looks to the market to produce solutions for every societal need. Both of these systems for organizing and incentivizing action have their role to play. Good solutions grow out of competition among innovative campus faculty and staff, and solutions must pass a market test by which they prove themselves worthy of the campus's trust. Only then can collective action nurture these solutions into system-wide savings.

And the complex local context of institutions will always matter. Presidents, faculty, and staff will never be able to get out of bed in the morning, let alone passionately engage with challenges, without local and individual pride at stake. Campuses need a team to cheer for. Twenty years ago, Bill Bowen and I argued that too intense an emphasis on intercollegiate athletics can throw educational values out of alignment, and this misalignment continues to occur in various places across US higher education. But even as we questioned the various costs incurred by schools that compete in up to forty different varsity sports, we also recognized the powerful role of mythology that links college sports to a school's sense of place and identity. The very practical need for schools to differentiate themselves in a crowded higher education market means tapping into the deep psychological needs of alumni/ae, students, and a range of campus and community constituencies. Doing battle in lacrosse, tennis, track, and football seems to be one irresistible means of product differentiation in a market that—to be honest—offers astoundingly similar products. I still believe that the emphasis on and level of investment in college sports is often wasteful and inexplicable. But I grant that it is better to nurture a sense of community around various gophers, badgers, and bulldogs if doing so maintains a campus's identity and distracts constituents from objecting to effective sharing of many other functions.

Despite all of their flaws, institutions matter. "I maintain," writes Johns Hopkins president Ronald Daniels, "that few other social institutions rival the university, at its best, in the sheer breadth of its vaunted contributions to liberal democracy's twin promises of equality and liberty."[8] Daniels also acknowledges the ways in which higher education can better fulfill these promises. But to be their best, colleges and universities need the public's trust and cannot let their costs be seen as a runaway train. The Synthetic University will be different from the college of the 1950s because the world is different now. By seeking the balance that synthesis requires, we'll play a role in our shared fate. The United States has always struggled to balance local concerns with collective needs. Today, it makes sense to Americans that Delaware and Maryland shouldn't have different currencies, but the agreement that we should share a common currency wasn't assured in the early days of the republic. Maybe two hundred years from now, we'll all be celebrating the trade-offs that we designed and built collaboratively in the first half of the 2000s to allow institutions to find a more sustainable balance.

NOTES

Preface

1. Leitch, "Self-Healing, Synthetic Skin Is Grown Directly on a Robotic Finger."
2. Lewens, "From Bricolage to BioBricks™," 641–648.
3. Bowen, "Economic Pressures on the Major Private Universities," 439.
4. Cooke, *Academic and Industrial Efficiency*, 7.
5. "Colleges and Universities are not developed and built up by comparison. There are varying conditions and elements that must be worked out. . . . Men unexpectedly come into the proposition with wise brains and generous gifts and save the little college from the fatal mildew of such unwise and impracticable standardizing as you are attempting." James R. Day, Chancellor of Syracuse University to Henry Pritchett, president of the Carnegie Foundation for the Advancement of Teaching, 1910, cited in Lagemann, *Private Power for the Public Good*, 185.
6. On the accomplishments and contributions of US higher education, see Cole, *The Great American University*.

Chapter 1: The Synthetic Service Provider

1. Kirp, *Shakespeare, Einstein, and the Bottom Line*, 163. Other uncited quotes from Kenny Morrell are from interviews with the author, June 15, 2018, and subsequent email exchanges with the author.
2. Bacow, "The Political Economy of Cost Control on a University Campus."
3. Patterson, *Colleges in Consort*, 124.
4. Times Higher Education, "World University Rankings 2022."
5. Merton, "Manifest and Latent Functions," 94.
6. Dan Boehmer, interview with the author, November 29, 2020.
7. Narayanan et al., "Two-Sided Marketplaces and Engagement."
8. Winston, "Subsidies, Hierarchy, and Peers," 31.
9. C. Anthony Broh, interview with the author, December 3, 2020.
10. Cited in Vaidya, "The Essentiality of Public-Private Partnerships." Also see Renner, "A Few Lessons About Public-Private Partnerships": "Partnerships like these are paramount to the future of higher education. They deliver new services efficiently, meet vital student interests, respond to local urgencies and leverage assets of different types of institutions around a common purpose. In doing so,

they lift up students and prioritize a greater good. They are, in other words, just what success rising out of a pandemic requires."

11. On the tension surrounding the use of Academic Analytics at Rutgers, see Flaherty, "Refusing to be Measured": "The entirely quantitative methods and variables employed by Academic Analytics—a corporation intruding upon academic freedom, peer evaluation, and shared governance—hardly capture the range and quality of scholarly inquiry, while utterly ignoring the teaching, service, and civic engagement that faculty perform," the graduate faculty resolution says. "Taken on their own terms, the measures of books, articles, awards, grants, and citations within the Academic Analytics database frequently undercount, overcount, or otherwise misrepresent the achievements of individual scholars," and those measures "have the potential to influence, redirect, and narrow scholarship as administrators incite faculty and departments to compete for higher scores."

12. The quote is from Wan, "Want to Help Schools Closed by COVID-19?" On what might replace the SAT, see Koenig, "As Colleges Move Away From the SAT, Will Admissions Algorithms Step In?"

13. "Outsourcing at colleges ain't what it used to be. If you hear the term and think 'dining services' or 'bookstore,' you're not wrong." Blumenstyk, "College Leaders Are Getting Serious About Outsourcing." See also P3edu, "About the Event."

14. In response to a question from an audience member at the ASU-GSV conference, May 2017.

15. Wan, "US EdTech Raises $803M in First Half of 2020 as COVID-19 Forces Learning Online," 2020.

16. "U.S. vs. Needy Students." The collusive practices of intercollegiate athletics were, at the same time, deemed entirely acceptable. Price fixing that limited what institutions can offer recruits in terms of scholarship (or bonuses) was exempt from this ruling.

17. Lapovsky, "The Private College Tuition Model Is Broken."

18. Winston, "Subsidies, Hierarchies, and Peers," 31–32.

19. Straumsheim, "A New* System for Student Success Planning"; Pelletier, "Student Success."

20. Laramie County Community College Board of Trustees, *Student Success Technology Recommendation.*

21. Casey, "The Creeping Capitalist Takeover of Higher Education."

22. Casey, "The Creeping Capitalist Takeover of Higher Education."

23. "Postsecondary Data Partnership."

24. Bacchetti and Ehrlich, eds., *Reconnecting Colleges and Foundations*, 257. They observe that many institutions believe that all relevant experience and expertise can be found on their own campuses because their cultures are so inwardly focused.

Chapter 2: Scanning Mona Lisa

1. Shapiro, "Art Historian James Beck Urges the Vatican to Clean Up Its Act, Not Michelangelo's Frescoes."

2. Cotter, "James Beck, 77, Art Scholar and Critic of Conservation, Is Dead."

3. Sinclair, *I, Candidate for Governor*, 109.

4. Email to the author from Lynn Catterson, March 31, 2008.

5. See "The Lexis-Nexis Timeline."

6. Kahneman, *Thinking, Fast and Slow*, 255.

7. Owens, "Hydra's Open Source Approach."

8. Wallach, "Chinese Caves."

9. Northwestern University Center for Scholarly Communication and Digital Curation.

10. Samvera, "Samvera User Profiles."

11. "New Office Will Coordinate Digitization of Yale Resources"; Zuckerman, "Bellinger to Direct Digitizing Office."

12. Email correspondence with the author from Donald Waters, December 2007.

13. Jiang and Wu, "Harvard Pushes Early Retirement."

14. John Harvard's Journal, "The Libraries' Rocky Transition." Also see Kelley, "After Furor, Harvard Library Spokesperson Says 'Inaccurate' That All Staff Will Have to Reapply."

15. Zuckerman, "Bellinger to Direct Digitizing Office."

16. "New Office Will Coordinate Digitization of Yale Resources."

17. Phillipson and Ying, "Next Generation Multimedia Analysis."

18. See Dempsey, "Library Collections in the Life of the User": "Publication is one part of the research workflow, so it is not surprising, for example, to see Elsevier add capacity to support more of the research life cycle (it has acquired SSRN, Mendeley, and Hivebench on the practitioner side, for example, and Pure on the administrative side)." See also Schonfeld, "Strategy & Integration Among Workflow Providers."

19. Dempsey, "Workflow Is the New Content 1."

20. Conversation with the author, Spring 2011.

Chapter 3: The Hard Reality of Observed Practices: Institutional Resistance to Change

1. Cassirer, *Language and Myth*, 32.

2. Clark, "A Note on Pursuing Things That Work," 320.

3. Brest, "The Power of Theories of Change," 48.

4. Nee, "Sources of the New Institutionalism," in Brinton and Nee, *The New Institutionalism in Sociology*, 8.

5. North, *Institutions, Institutional Change, and Economic Performance*, 3.

6. Friedland and Alford, "Bringing Society Back In," 232.

7. Simon, *Administrative Behavior*, 12.

8. Jensen, "Value Maximization, Stakeholder Theory, and the Corporate Objective Function," 236.

9. Jensen, in Agle et al., "Dialogue," 168.

10. Weber, *The Theory of Social and Economic Organization*, 117.

11. Jensen, "Value Maximization, Stakeholder Theory, and the Corporate Objective Function," 242.

12. "Whereas most economists and political scientists focus exclusively on economic or political rules of the game, sociologists find institutions everywhere, from handshakes to marriages to strategic-planning departments. Moreover, sociologists view behaviors as potentially institutionalizable over a wide territorial range, from understandings within a single family to myths of rationality and progress in the world system." DiMaggio and Powell, "Introduction," *The New Institutionalism in Organizational Analysis*, 19.

13. DiMaggio and Powell, "Introduction," *The New Institutionalism in Organizational Analysis*: "The new institutionalism in organization theory and sociology comprises a rejection of rational-actor models, an interest in institutions as independent variables, a turn toward cognitive and cultural explanations, and an interest in properties of supraindividual units of analysis that cannot be reduced to aggregations or direct consequences of individuals' attributes or motives" (18).

14. Friedman and Alford, "Bringing Society Back In," 329.

15. "A nonprofit organization is, in essence, an organization that is barred from distributing its net earnings, if any, to individuals who exercise control over it, such as members, officers, directors, or trustees. By 'net earnings' I mean here pure profits—that is, earnings in excess of the amount needed to pay for services rendered to the organization; in general, a nonprofit is free to pay reasonable compensation to any person for labor or capital that he provides, whether or not that person exercises some control over the organization." Hansmann, "The Role of Nonprofit Enterprise," 838.

16. "The second feature of nonprofit and voluntary organizations sharply differentiates them from business firms, however. While corporations are able to distribute earnings to shareholders, nonprofit and voluntary organizations cannot make such distributions to outside parties. Rather, they must use all residual funds for the advancement of the organization's mission. By retaining residuals rather than passing them on to investors, nonprofit organizations seek to reassure clients and donors that their mission takes precedence over the financial remuneration of any interested parties. The non-distribution constraint has been seen as a tool that nonprofits can use to capitalize on failures in the market. Since there are certain services, such as childcare and healthcare, that some consumers feel uncomfortable receiving if the provider is profit driven, nonprofits are able to step in and meet this demand by promising that no investors will benefit by cutting corners or by delivering unnecessary services." Frumkin, "On Being Nonprofit: The Bigger Picture," 4.

17. Valentinov, "Toward an Economic Interpretation of the Nondistribution Constraint," 60.

18. Glaeser and Schleifer, "Not-For-Profit Entrepreneurs"; and Weisbrod, "Toward a Theory of the Voluntary Nonprofit Sector."

19. AAUP, "Statement on Government of Colleges and Universities."

20. Bowen and Tobin, *Locus of Authority*, 210.

21. Little, "Further Thoughts on Loyalty."

22. "The very occurrence of highly articulated arenas of social construction (such as professional associations) may make change easier to achieve despite

the highly institutionalized setting. The collective structures of professional communities, in other words, might ease change because they enable theorization." Greenwood, Suddaby, and Hinings, "Theorizing Change," 74.

23. DiMaggio and Powell, "The Iron Cage Revisited," 71, citing Perrow, *Organizational Analysis*, 1974. See also Greenwood, Suddaby, and Hinings, "Theorizing Change": "Professional associations are commonly understood as agents of reproduction rather than of change. Through the routines of licensing, training, and professional development and the monitoring and disciplining of behavior, associations supposedly act to underpin existing conventions and values. Prevailing practices become encoded in the associations' organizational routines and, to the extent that routines remain unchanged, encoded institutional logics are reproduced" (73).

24. Greenwood, Suddaby, and Hinings, "Theorizing Change," 59.

25. Greenwood, Suddaby, and Hinings, "Theorizing Change," 60.

26. Jaschik, "Getting (Digital) Respect."

27. Modern Language Association, "Guidelines for Evaluating Work in Digital Humanities and Digital Media."

28. Bowen and Tobin, *Locus of Authority*, 208.

29. Sturm, "The Architecture of Inclusion," 251.

30. Sturm, "The Architecture of Inclusion," 251.

31. Daniel Reid, interview with the author, January 13, 2021.

32. DiMaggio and Powell, "The Iron Cage Revisited," 103.

33. DiMaggio and Powell, "The Iron Cage Revisited," 90. Also Meyer and Rowan, "Institutionalized Organizations": "Institutional isomorphism promotes the success and survival of organizations. Incorporating externally legitimated formal structures increases the commitment of internal participants and external constituents. And the use of external assessment criteria—that is, moving toward the status in society of a subunit rather than an independent system—can enable an organization to remain successful by social definition, buffering it from failure" (349). And "The more uncertain the relationship between means and ends, the greater the extent to which an organization will model itself after organizations it perceives as successful. The mimetic thought process involved in the search for models is characteristic of change in organizations in which key technologies are only poorly understood." DiMaggio and Powell, "The Iron Cage Revisited," 116.

34. DiMaggio and Powell, "The Iron Cage Revisited," 92.

35. DiMaggio and Powell, "The Iron Cage Revisited," 107.

36. Meyer and Rowan, "Institutionalized Organizations," 107.

37. There are overall rankings, but also rankings for bragging rights in particular categories, such as "innovation." See "Agnes Scott College Ranked #1 Most Innovative College."

38. "Opportunity Insights."

39. Jaschik, "Oklahoma Gave False Data for Years to 'U.S. News,' Loses Ranking."

40. Bacow, "The Political Economy of Cost Control on a University Campus," 5–6.

41. Cassirer, *Language and Myth*, 33.

42. McGrath, "A Whole New Ballgame."

43. Malinowski, *Magic, Science, and Religion and Other Essays*, 122.

44. Clark, "The Organizational Saga in Higher Education,"183.

45. Clark Kerr, 1963 Harvard Godkin Lecture, cited in Steven Roberts, "Kerr Says 'Multiversity' Head Must Be 'Mediator,' Not Giant."

46. "Our Mission, Values and Priorities."

47. "Iowa State University Mission Statement."

48. Brooks, *Reading for the Plot*, 6.

49. Brooks, *Reading for the Plot*, 6.

50. DiMaggio, "The New Institutionalisms," 10.

51. Meyer and Rowan, "Institutionalized Organizations," 344. On rational myths, see also Bastedo, "Sociological Frameworks," where he describes them as "symbols of efficiency and effectiveness that actually lack those qualities under closer scrutiny. Organization charts, academic grades, and degree structures all may have these qualities" (306). For Friedland and Alford, "Bringing Society Back In" (343), "They provide individuals with vocabularies of motives and with a sense of self. They generate not only that which is valued, but the rules by which it is calibrated and distributed. Institutions set the limits on the very nature of rationality and, by implication, of individuality. Nonetheless, individuals, groups, and organizations try to use institutional orders to their own advantage."

Chapter 4: Rewriting Myths: Institutional Entrepreneurs

1. John Tormondsen, interview with the author, December 19, 2017.

2. Swensen, *Pioneering Portfolio Management*, 4–5.

3. Ron Liebowitz, interview with the author, January 19, 2017.

4. Data provided from The National Association of College and University Business Officers (NACUBO) in Smith College Board of Trustees memo.

5. Alice Handy, interview with the author, September 12, 2017, and subsequent email exchanges.

6. Von Hippel, *Democratizing Innovation*, 6.

7. Chaplinsky, Harris, and Kelly, *Investure, LLC, and Smith College*, 2.

8. DiMaggio, "Interest and Agency in Institutional Theory," 14.

9. DiMaggio, "The New Institutionalisms," 14–15.

10. Clay Christensen's well-known model for high-growth innovation in a wide range of industries charts how an innovator aims to serve new markets with new approaches rather than responding to the needs of the market leaders: "Disruptive technologies bring to a market a very different value proposition that had been available previously. Generally, disruptive technologies underperform established projects in a mainstream market. But they have other features that a few fringe (and generally new) customers value. Products based on disruptive technologies are typically cheaper, simpler, smaller, and frequently, more convenient to use." Christensen, *The Innovator's Dilemma*, xxiii.

11. Garud, Hardy, and Maguire, "Institutional Entrepreneurship as Embedded Agency," 962.

12. Cornelia Small, interview with the author, October 24, 2017.

13. Thomas Kalaris and Jennifer Reynolds, interview with the author, January 10, 2018.

14. Hjorth and Steyaert, "Introduction," 4.

15. Garud, Jain, and Kumaraswamy, "Institutional Entrepreneurship in the Sponsorship of Common Technological Standards," 196.

16. Garud and Karnøe, "Bricolage versus Breakthrough," 281.

17. Smith College Board of Trustees memo.

18. Thomas Kalaris and Jennifer Reynolds, interview with the author, January 10, 2018.

19. Greenwood, Suddaby, and Hinings, "Theorizing Change," 61.

20. Visual Resources Association (VRA) listserv, 2007.

21. Grossman and Swafford, "Graduate Education Reconsidered."

22. Garud, Hardy, and Maguire, "Institutional Entrepreneurship as Embedded Agency," 961.

23. Henfridsson and Yoo, "The Liminality of Trajectory Shifts in Institutional Entrepreneurship."

24. For a thorough diagnosis of this challenge, see Cassuto and Weisbuch, *The New PhD*.

25. Bourdieu, "Social Space and Field of Power," 34.

26. Garud and Karnøe, "Bricolage versus Breakthrough," 278–279.

27. Garud and Karnøe, "Bricolage versus Breakthrough," 296.

28. Garud and Karnøe, "Bricolage versus Breakthrough," 296.

29. Garud, Jain, and Kumaraswamy, "Institutional Entrepreneurship in the Sponsorship of Common Technological Standards."

30. Suchman, "Managing Legitimacy," 585.

31. "Others have conceptualized entrepreneurs as heroic individuals who are able to prevail by overcoming insurmountable odds. In either case, entrepreneurial agency is located in a few individuals who have the full-blown ability to discover, create, and exploit opportunities that lie beyond the reach of most. Departing from a conceptualization that vests agency with specific individuals, we suggest that technology entrepreneurship is a larger process that builds upon the efforts of many." Garud and Karnøe, "Bricolage versus Breakthrough," 277.

32. Bruce Miller, interview with the author, November 2015.

33. Artstor Board of Trustees materials, June 2007.

34. Artstor Board of Trustees materials, June 2007.

35. "Although research has already moved away from a view of the institutional entrepreneur as hero, it might nevertheless be interesting to question further the issue of agency on several dimensions including the issue of institutional entrepreneurs' intentionality. . . . Future research might usefully be directed at exploring the intentionality and agency of institutional entrepreneurs, the extent to which it affects the institutional change that is eventually achieved, and how

this plays out over time." Leca, Battilana, and Boxenbaum, "Agency and Institutions," 19–20.

36. Digital Scholarship Center: "The DSC also assists faculty and students in methods to incorporate visual literacy into the curriculum. The DSC teaches techniques of image searching and the presentation of images in a classroom environment."

37. Bruce Miller, interview with the author, November 2015.

38. Other measures can be far less accurate; consider the rankings of colleges by publications such as *U.S. News & World Report*, which relies partially on "data" such as asking current college presidents what they think about other peer schools. Good measurement can support a realistic assessment of whether co-creation with an outside provider meets the aims of the organization.

39. David Levy notes the macho values associated with much of the mythology around entrepreneurs: "Though the emotive, mythical character of the entrepreneur might well be critical to a project of institutional transformation, we need to remain alert to the discursive power and strategic implications of the term 'entrepreneurship.' . . . 'Entrepreneurship' conjures masculine images of heroic individuals amassing wealth rather than collective action toward more democratic, egalitarian goals." Levy and Scully, "The Institutional Entrepreneur as Modern Prince," 16.

Chapter 5: The Incomplete Financing System for Mission- and Market-Compatible Ventures

1. Bannick and Goldman, *Priming the Pump*, 5.
2. Milken, "Prostate Cancer: New Hope for Patients."
3. Kornbluth, *Highly Confident*, 367.
4. Stein, *A License to Steal*, 187.
5. Milken, "Prostate Cancer: New Hope for Patients."
6. Milken, "Prostate Cancer: New Hope for Patients."
7. Moore, *A Call to Action*, 10–11.
8. Milken, "The Democratization of Capital."
9. "FasterCures."
10. Christensen et al., *Disrupting College*, 3–4.
11. National Center for Education Statistics, "Undergraduate Graduation Rates."
12. Chen, "The Catch-22 of Community College Graduation Rates."
13. "Badges."
14. "Credly Raises Seed Financing."
15. See Mintz, "Partners or Predators?": "Some foundations, which doubt the ability of many individual campuses to develop, deliver, and sustain services in essential areas, are investing in third parties. For example, the Lumina Foundation has made strategic investments in Acadeum, an online course-sharing marketplace; Civitas Learning, which offers tools to optimize retention and completion; Credly, a platform for verifying, sharing, and managing digital badges and credentials; Mentor Collective, which matches students with peer, alumni, and

career mentors; and BridgeEdU, a provider of intervention services to at-risk first-year college students."

16. Wan, "What 'Impact Investing' Means in Education."

17. Mintz, "Partners or Predators?": "Strategic partnerships hold out the prospect of providing guidance and increasing institutional capacity, efficiency, and effectiveness at an affordable cost. The third parties can provide proven expertise, tested technologies, and start-up funding. But the downsides to reliance on third-party providers are obvious."

18. In January 2022, Credly was acquired by Pearson. "Pearson Acquires Digital Credentialing Leader Credly."

19. "University Innovation Alliance."

20. Goldrick-Rab, *Paying the Price*, 234.

21. Saul, "At N.Y.U., Students Were Failing Organic Chemistry."

22. Thorp, "Stop Passing the Buck on Intro Science."

23. Brown, "Most Americans Say Higher Ed Is Heading in Wrong Direction."

24. Fleishman, *The Foundation*, 249–250.

25. Cited in Shelterforce, "What Is Philanthropic Equity?"

26. "Only five one hundredths of one percent of US foundation capital deployed went to equity PRIs, which represents the type of capital necessary to help fund innovators." Bannick, *Priming the Pump*, 14.

27. Fleishman, *The Foundation*, 9.

28. Letts, Ryan, and Grossman, "Virtuous Capital."

29. New Profit, "Our Story."

30. New Profit, "Venture Philanthropy."

31. Zurcher, "Foundations," 16."

32. Miller, "Capital, Equity, and Looking at Nonprofits as Enterprises." See also Levere et al., *Blueprint for Enterprise Capital.*

33. Miller, "Capital, Equity, and Looking at Nonprofits as Enterprises."

34. "We partner with investors to pool their philanthropic resources and invest more effectively and efficiently than any of us could alone. This model unlocks the flow of large sums of capital aimed at boosting economic mobility—we make strategic, long-term investments, which can be as much as $100 million in each initiative—and investors share the costs, risks, and successes." Blue Meridian Partners, "Our Approach."

35. Brady, "Health & Science."

36. Brady, "Health & Science."

37. In some interesting cases the "impact investor" only provides the promise of a backstop—a promise of providing capital if a risky but socially desirable effort is undertaken. See, for example, the example of The Gates Foundation's promise to underwrite Bayer's risk if they changed the pricing of a low-volume, high-cost birth control implant so that it could be made widely available in the developing world. Bill & Melinda Gates Foundation, "Innovative Partnership Reduces Cost of Bayer's Long-Acting Reversible Contraceptive Implant By More Than 50 Percent," and Bank, "Guaranteed Impact."

38. Global Impact Investing Network, "Impact Investing."

39. "Though his Grameen Bank was neither the first nor the largest of the modern microfinance lenders, Yunus [microfinance pioneer Muhammad Yunus, winner of the Nobel Peace Prize in 2006] served as the international face of this new brand-building agenda, quietly charismatic as he tirelessly gave speeches and sat for interviews, often in traditional Bangladeshi dress. A 1989 profile of Grameen on the US news show *60 Minutes* ushered in a new era of heightened attention to microfinance strategies as an effective tool in addressing poverty." Bugg-Levine and Emerson, *Impact Investing*, 42.

40. Bugg-Levine and Emerson, *Impact Investing*: "Microfinance could have ended up as another in a long list of development innovations that seemed promising to some but ultimately never reached substantial scale or impact. But as word spread about the success these organizations were having, similar initiatives rose across the developing world, and some of the early pioneers grew substantially. Over succeeding years, nonprofit and government-run microfinance operations proliferated. Eventually donor funding allowed pioneers to refine the operating model enough that some microfinance institutions could not only lend sustainably but also make substantial profits. Over the past ten years, these lucrative microfinance businesses began to attract commercial attention and investment capital" (41).

41. Geczy et al., "Contracts with Benefits," 2–3.

42. Global Impact Investing Network, "What You Need to Know About Impact Investing."

43. Bugg-Levine and Emerson, *Impact Investing*, 47.

44. Baxter et al., *Two Case Studies on the Financing of Forest Conservation*, 30.

45. "Renaissance Acquires Schoolzilla to Make Insights Actionable for Education Leaders Worldwide."

46. Baker, "California Benefit Corporations."

47. Baker, "California Benefit Corporations."

48. Petersen and Poulson, "New Approaches to Ed-Tech Funding," 45: "Schoolzilla has opted not to raise any funding from traditional venture capital firms. Instead, it has raised capital from an array of impact investors and foundations. To date, the company has raised $8.5 million, and that money has come from impact-oriented organizations—including the Charles and Helen Schwab Foundation, the Impact America Fund, Kapor Capital, NSVF, Reach Capital, and Serious Change LP—and from individual angel investors. (Aspire retains a 15 percent stake.)"

49. Lynzi Ziegenhagen, interview with the author, February 26, 2021.

50. "Renaissance Acquires Schoolzilla to Make Insights Actionable for Education Leaders Worldwide." Quotation is from Lynzi Ziegenhagen interview with the author, February 26, 2021.

51. Brest and Born, "Unpacking the Impact in Impact Investing," 14.

52. Others have recognized this need for systemic work as well. "Efficient intermediation alone cannot accelerate impact investing, given the challenges constraining the industry and the risk that impact investing may become too hard or too easy. Basic infrastructure must also be built to enable metrics for impact,

develop a common language, integrate social and environmental factors into economic theory, and to make visible the demonstrated successes of impact investing." Monitor Institute, *Investing for Social and Environmental Impact*, 66.

53. Giusti and Hamermesh, "How Nonprofit Foundations Can Sustainably Fund Disease Research."

54. Etzel, Bannick, and Collins, "Opinion: Maverick 'Impact-First' Investing Sits between Philanthropy and Market-rate Returns."

55. "When the science for a disease is far enough along, efforts to find cures can tap investment funds that were created to earn market-rate returns." Giusti and Hamermesh, "How Nonprofit Foundations Can Sustainably Fund Disease Research."

56. Bannick and Goldman, *Priming the Pump*, 4.

57. Smith, "Reed Alumni Pay to Help Current Students, Recent Grads."

58. Brandel et al., "Zebras Fix What Unicorns Break."

59. Adeniji, "Ensembles of Change." See also Kirsch et al., "Why Social Ventures Need Systems Thinking."

60. Brandel et al., "Zebras Fix What Unicorns Break."

61. Brandel et al., "Zebras Fix What Unicorns Break."

62. Voinea, "Top 100 Co-operatives."

63. Valentinov, "Toward an Economic Interpretation of the Nondistribution Constraint": "On the other hand, the outputs generated by cooperatives ordinarily promote some monetary motivations of the members. Hansmann (1980, 889) suggests that 'cooperatives often appear to be established to limit the price charged to the consumer.' Additionally, although cooperatives as legal entities are not themselves entitled to accumulate profits, they may distribute their net earnings to members rather than reinvest them in the operation."

64. Heller, "Is Venture Capital Worth the Risk?"; Griffith, "More Start-Ups Have an Unfamiliar Message for Venture Capitalists."

65. Cha, "Sean Parker, Silicon Valley's Bad Boy Genius."

66. Leuty, "Sean Parker's Cancer-Fighting Institute Aims 1st Trial at Tough Target."

67. New Profit, "Ecosystem Building."

68. Knight Foundation Fund, *Lessons from the Early Years of Mission-Related Investing at Knight Foundation*, 15.

69. Bannick and Goodman, *Priming the Pump*, 10.

70. Baxter et al., *Two Case Studies on the Financing of Forest Conservation*, 2.

71. Baxter et al., *Two Case Studies on the Financing of Forest Conservation*, 7.

72. Baxter et al., *Two Case Studies on the Financing of Forest Conservation*, 15.

73. Baxter et al., *Two Case Studies on the Financing of Forest Conservation*, 12.

74. Baxter et al., *Two Case Studies on the Financing of Forest Conservation*, 8.

75. Bennet, "The Innovator Connecting Impact Investing to the Creative Economy."

76. Moellenbrock, Gafarou, and Callanan, *Hiding in Plain Sight*.

77. Sullivan, "A Push to Invest in the Arts Grows Stronger."

78. Sullivan, "A Push to Invest in the Arts Grows Stronger."

Chapter 6: The Possibilities of the Collective Curriculum

1. Sandel, "Michael Sandel Responds."

2. Harris, "SJSU/edX Adds More Campuses, Courses"; Rivard, "San Jose State University Faculty Pushes Back."

3. At the time of its creation, Harvard president Drew Faust had praised both the experimental aspect of the effort and its potential for democratizing education: "EdX gives Harvard and MIT an unprecedented opportunity to dramatically extend our collective reach by conducting groundbreaking research into effective education and by extending online access to quality higher education." MIT News Office, "MIT and Harvard Announce EdX."

4. Harris, "SJSU/EdX Adds More Campuses, Courses."

5. San Jose State University, "Enrollment by Demographics."

6. "Traditionally, higher education institutions had to continually increase tuition to maintain top-notch programs, but what if there was a better way? Updating your on-site dining experience can add value to your school and help with the recruitment and retention of on-campus students. Partnering with Aramark for meal plan optimization gives your campus the opportunity to increase sales while satisfying the needs of students." Aramark, "Optimizing Meal Plan Sales on Today's Higher Ed Campuses."

7. Friedman, "Revolution Hits the Universities." See the critique in Warner, "An Ad Hominem Attack against Thomas Friedman."

8. Scott, *Knowledge, Power, and Academic Freedom*, 102.

9. "Free Speech and Academic Freedom."

10. Menand, "The Limits of Academic Freedom," 8.

11. Menand, "The Limits of Academic Freedom," 18.

12. Bureau of Labor Statistics, "Postsecondary Teachers, Occupational Outlook Handbook.

13. Greenwood, Suddaby, and Hinings, "Theorizing Change," 59–60.

14. Alvi et al., "4 Lessons from Online Learning That Should Stick after the Pandemic"; Nworie, "Beyond COVID-19"; June, "Did the Scramble to Remote Learning Work?"

15. Fox et al., "Time for Class COVID-19 Edition Part 2."

16. Bigman and Mitchell, "Teaching Online in 2020."

17. McKay, "Thoughts on the Transcript of the Future." Also see fuller exposition in Koester et al., "Building a Transcript of the Future."

18. Mitchell, "Interview."

19. Seltzer, "Many Trustees See Faculty as Barrier to Change."

20. Kirp, *Shakespeare, Einstein, and the Bottom Line*, 151.

21. See also Morrell, quoted in Kirp, *Shakespeare, Einstein, and the Bottom Line*: "The only way we can grow as a discipline—the only way we can survive—is by creating demand for our product. . . . The only way that we are going to survive is to get students in our classroom. The only way that we can create an stimulating and inviting and provocative world of study for the students is collectively" (152).

22. Email correspondence with Kenny Morrell, June 29, 2018.

23. Ewell, "Music Theory and the White Racial Frame."

24. Botstein, "Schenker the Regressive," 239.

25. Ewell, "Music Theory and the White Racial Frame," 5.

26. Ishida, "5 Questions to Philip Ewell."

27. Hayes, "How Should Textbook Authorship Count in Evaluating Scholarly Merit, or Should It Count at All?"

28. See Senack, *Fixing the Broken Textbook Market*, 11: "Not only are students choosing not to purchase the materials they are assigned by their professor, but they are *knowingly* accepting the risk of a lower grade to avoid paying for the textbook. . . . Publishers use a set of tactics to drive prices skyward, including releasing new editions every three to four years or selling the books as loose-leaf sheets to avoid their being re-sold." Responding to the complaints of students, families, and instructors regarding the high price of textbooks, the textbook industry seems to have found models that lessen the amount of cost frustration directed their way. By renting digital or print versions for limited time periods at lower prices, publishers are spreading their cost-recovery and profit-seeking out over longer periods rather than trying to recapture all of their revenue in a one-term sale.

29. David G. Myers, interview with the author, June 23, 2021.

30. Macmillan Learning, Instructor Catalog.

31. Adams, "MasterClass Just Raised $100 Million to Produce More Celebrity Edutainment."

32. Rees, *MOOCs*. See also Fain, "Takedown of Online Education," and Orbey, "How Harvard's Star Computer Science Professor Built a Distance-Learning Empire." Orbey tells how Harvard professor David Malan's introduction to computer science (CS50) is used by students around the world, including students at Harvard's arch-rival Yale. But this act of being efficient and effective across the college system wasn't universally celebrated, as noted by the article's author: "In 2015, when CS50 launched its partnership with Yale, many students and professors there voiced skepticism, fearing that importing Malan's course would undermine Yale's own computer-science department. . . . The growth catalyzed by CS50, one professor told me, might have been achieved by developing an introductory course of comparable quality within the institution."

33. Ishida, "5 Questions to Philip Ewell."

34. Robb Manzer, interview with the author, July 7, 2021.

35. Lieberman, "Sharing Courses Far and Wide."

36. Grossman, correspondence with the author, July 22, 2022.

37. Davoren, "How Are Labor Unions and Guilds Similar?"

38. Herpich, "Harvard and MIT-led Nonprofit to Tackle Longstanding inequities in Education."

39. Mintz, "edX: A Look Backward."

40. Feldstein, "The edX Aftermath."

41. Feldstein, "The edX Aftermath."

42. Conversation with the author, January 12, 2022.

43. Swaak, "An Overseas Ed-Tech Firm Wants to Buy 2U."

44. Xu and Jaggars, "Performance Gaps between Online and Face-to-Face Courses."

45. Correspondence with Richard Arum, August 2022.

Chapter 7: Conclusion: Choosing to Change

1. As Bill Bowen predicted when articulating the cost disease in 1968, retrenchment is no fun: "Institutional morale is a delicate thing and depends at least as much on the direction in which events are moving as on the state of affairs at any point in time. In the face of the kinds of decisions which would have to accompany any process of retrenchment, it would be very difficult to retain key administrative and faculty personnel and maintain general morale" (Bowen, "Economic Pressures on the Major Private Universities," 439).

2. "Thiel Foundation Announces 2020 Thiel Fellows."

3. June, "Spring Enrollment's Final Count Is In."

4. National Student Clearinghouse Research Center, "Current Term Enrollment Estimates."

5. Caron, Dever, and Justice, "The Future of Tenure": "In 1993–94, more than half (56.2 percent) of faculty members at institutions with a tenure system had tenure. By 2018–19, that number had fallen to 45.1 percent. These declines are driven in part by declines in the percentage of full-time faculty across the university. In 1970–71, almost 80 percent of faculty members were full-time. By 2018–19, that number was under 55 percent."

6. St. Amour, "CU Boulder, Colorado Follow National Trend in Higher Ed's Reliance on Tuition Revenue," and Associated Press, "Colorado Isn't Funding Higher Ed Like It Used To."

7. Schuessler, "A Wall Street Giant Makes a $75 Million Bet on Academic Philosophy."

8. Daniels, *What Universities Owe Democracy*, 20.

BIBLIOGRAPHY

Adams, Susan. "MasterClass Just Raised $100 Million to Produce More Celebrity Edutainment." *Forbes.com*, May 20, 2020. https://www.forbes.com/sites/susanadams/2020/05/20/masterclass-just-raised-100-million-to-produce-more-celebrity-edutainment/?sh=75b1bd503428.

Adeniji, Ade. "Ensembles of Change: A Wall Street Winner Champions 'Systems Entrepreneurs.'" *Inside Philanthropy*, February 1, 2017.

Agle, Bradley R., Thomas Donaldson, R. Edward Freeman, Michael C. Jensen, Ronald K. Mitchell, and Donna J. Wood. "Dialogue: Toward Superior Stakeholder Theory." *Business Ethics Quarterly* 18, no. 2 (2008): 153–190.

Agnes Scott College. "Agnes Scott College Ranked #1 Most Innovative College for the Fifth Consecutive Year." September 12, 2022. https://news.agnesscott.org/the-latest-headlines/faculty/agnes-scott-college-ranked-1-most-innovative-for-the-fifth-consecutive-year/.

Alvi, F. Haider, Deborah Hurst, Janice Thomas, and Martha Cleveland-Innes. "4 Lessons from Online Learning That Should Stick After the Pandemic." The Conversation, May 1, 2022. https://theconversation.com/4-lessons-from-online-learning-that-should-stick-after-the-pandemic-179631.

Anderson, Wayne, and Suzanne Bonefas. "Technology Partnerships for Faculty: Case Studies and Lesson Learned." *New Directions for Higher Education*. Hoboken: Wiley Periodicals, Inc., 2002.

ARAMARK. "Optimizing Meal Plan Sales on Today's Higher Ed Campuses." Accessed January 16, 2023, from https://www.aramark.com/content/dam/aramark/en/industries/education/higher-education/thought-leadership/insights-content/higherEdInsights_guide_optimizingMealPlanSales.pdf.

Associated Colleges of the South. *Assessment of the ACS Classics and Archaeology Program ("Sunoikisis"): A Proposal to the Andrew W. Mellon Foundation from the Associated Colleges of the South*. Atlanta, GA: Associated Colleges of the South, 2001.

———. *A Proposal for the ACS Archaeology Program and the Virtual Department of Classical Studies ("Sunoikisis")*. Atlanta, GA: Associated Colleges of the South, 2001.

———. *A Proposal to the Andrew W. Mellon Foundation: Preparing Faculty for the Next Millennium*. Atlanta, GA: Associated Colleges of the South, 1998.

———. *Summary of Sunoikisis Program Evaluation and Program Design: A Grant from the Andrew W. Mellon Foundation to the Associated Colleges of the South.* Atlanta, GA: Associated Colleges of the South, 2005.

Bacchetti, Ray, and Thomas Ehrlich, eds., *Reconnecting Colleges and Foundations: Turning Good Intentions into Educational Capital.* New York: Wiley, 2006.

Bacow, Lawrence S. "The Political Economy of Cost Control on a University Campus." Lecture, Clark Kerr Lecture Series from University of California–Berkeley, Berkeley, CA, April 20, 2017. https://www.harvard.edu/president/speeches/2017/the-political-economy-of-cost-control-on-a-university-campus/.

Badelt, Christoph. "Entrepreneurship Theories of the Non-profit Sector." *Voluntas: International Journal of Voluntary and Nonprofit Organizations* 8, no. 2 (1997): 162–178.

"Badges." Credly. Accessed January 15, 2023, from https://www.credly.com/organizations/credly/badges.

Baker, Michelle. "California Benefit Corporations." *Nonprofit Law Blog by NEO Law Group* (2013). Accessed January 15, 2023, from https://nonprofitlawblog.com/california-benefit-corporations/.

Bank, David. "Guaranteed Impact." *Making Markets Work for the Poor—Stanford Social Innovation Review* (Summer 2016 supplement): 16–18.

Bannick, Matt, and Eric Hallstein. "Learning from Silicon Valley." *Stanford Social Innovation Review* 10, no. 3 (2012): A8–A11.

Bannick, Matt, and Paula Goldman. "Gaps in the Impact Investing Capital Curve." *Stanford Social Innovation Review*, 2012. https://doi.org/10.48558/1KQX-VV35.

———. *Priming the Pump: The Case for a Sector Based Approach to Impact Investing.* Redwood City, CA: Omidyar Network, 2008.

Bannick, Matt, Paula Goldman, Michael Kubzansky, and Yasemin Saltuk. *Across the Returns Continuum.* Redwood City, CA: Omidyar Network, 2016.

Barber, Brad M., Adair Morse, and Ayako Yasuda. "Impact Investing." *Journal of Financial Economics* 139, no. 1 (2021): 162–185.

Bastedo, Michael. "Sociological Frameworks for Higher Education Policy Research." In *Sociology of Higher Education: Contributions and their Contexts*, edited by Patricia J. Gumport, 295–318. Baltimore: Johns Hopkins University Press, 2007.

Battilana, Julie. "Agency and Institutions: The Enabling Role of Individuals' Social Position." *Organization* 13, no. 5 (2006): 653–676.

Battilana, Julie, and Silvia Dorado. "Building Sustainable Hybrid Organizations: The Case of Commercial Microfinance Organizations." *Academy of Management Journal* 53, no. 6 (2010): 1419–1440.

Baum, Sandy, and Kim Rueben. "Understanding State and Local Higher Education Resources." White paper prepared for the National Commission on Financing 21st Century Higher Education. University of Virginia Miller Center, Charlottesville, VA, 2016. https://s3.amazonaws.com/web.web1-misc/commissions/higher-ed/Rueben_No6.pdf.

Baxter, Andrew, Connor Cash, Josh Lerner, and Ratnika Prasad. *Two Case Studies on the Financing of Forest Conservation*. Cambridge, MA: Harvard Business School, 2020.

Bennett, Amy. "The Innovator Connecting Impact Investing to the Creative Economy." RealLeaders, November 30, 2018. https://real-leaders.com/the-innovator-connecting-impact-investing-to-the-creative-economy/.

Bigman, Maxwell, and John C. Mitchell. "Teaching Online in 2020: Experiments, Empathy, Discovery." *2020 IEEE Learning with MOOCs (LWMOOCs)*, (2020), 156–161.

Bill & Melinda Gates Foundation. "Innovative Partnership Reduces Cost of Bayer's Long-Acting Reversible Contraceptive Implant by More Than 50 Percent." *Bill & Melinda Gates Foundation—Strategic Investment Fund*. February 27, 2013.

Blumenstyk, Goldie. "College Leaders Are Getting Serious about Outsourcing. They Still Have Plenty of Concerns, Too." *Chronicle of Higher Education*, March 26, 2019.

Born, Kelly, and Paul Brest. "Unpacking the Impact in Impact Investing." *Stanford Social Innovation Review*, 2013. https://doi.org/10.48558/7X1Y-MF25.

Botstein, Leon. "Schenker the Regressive: Observations on the Historical Schenker." *The Musical Quarterly* 86, no. 2 (2002): 239–247.

Boumgarden, Peter, and John Branch. "Collective Impact or Coordinated Blindness?" *Stanford Social Innovation Review*, 2013. https://doi.org/10.48558/VBZR-ZA80.

Bourdieu, Pierre. "Social Space and Field of Power." In *Practical Reason*, 31–34. Stanford, CA: Stanford University Press, 1998.

Bowen, William G. "Economic Pressures on the Major Private Universities." In *The Economics and Financing of Higher Education in the United States: A Compendium of Papers Submitted to the Joint Economic Committee, Congress of the United States*, 399–439. Government Printing Office, 1969.

Bowen, William G., and Eugene M. Tobin. *Locus of Authority: The Evolution of Faculty Roles in the Governance of Higher Education*. The William G. Bowen Series, 83. Princeton, NJ: Princeton University Press, 2015.

Brady, Dennis. "Health & Science: Are Risks Worth the Rewards When Nonprofits Act Like Venture Capitalists?" *Washington Post*, July 2, 2015. https://www.washingtonpost.com/national/health-science/in-hunt-for-new-treatments-nonprofits-are-acting-like-venture-capitalists/2015/07/02/c6094578-19b8-11e5-93b7-5eddc056ad8a_story.html.

Brandel, Jennifer, Mara Zepeda, Astrid Scholz, and Aniyia Williams. "Zebras Fix What Unicorns Break." *Medium.com*, March 8, 2017. https://medium.com/zebras-unite/zebrasfix-c467e55f9d96.

Brest, Paul. "The Power of Theories of Change." *Stanford Social Innovation Review* 8, no. 2 (2010): 47–51.

Bridges Ventures and Wharton Social Impact Initiative. *MIINT 2015–2016 Syllabus*. Philadelphia, PA: Wharton School of Business, University of Pennsylvania, 2015.

Brinton, Mary C., and Victor Nee. *The New Institutionalism in Sociology*. New York: Russell Sage Foundation, 1998.

Brooks, Peter. *Reading for the Plot: Design and Intention in Narrative*. Boston: Harvard University Press, 1992.

Brown, Anna. "Most Americans Say Higher Ed Is Heading in Wrong Direction, but Partisans Disagree on Why." Pew Research Center, July 26, 2018. https://www.pewresearch.org/fact-tank/2018/07/26/most-americans-say-higher-ed-is-heading-in-wrong-direction-but-partisans-disagree-on-why/.

Brown, Jessie, and Deanna Marcum. *CIC Consortium for Online Humanities Instruction: Evaluation Report for Second Course Iteration Treatment*. New York: ITHAKA S+R, 2016.

Bugg-Levine, Antony, and Jed Emerson. *Impact Investing: Transforming How We Make Money While Making a Difference*. Hoboken, NJ: Jossey-Bass, 2011.

Burnham, Kristin. "The Impact Learning Analytics Is Having on Higher Education." *Northeastern University Graduate Programs Blog* (April 17, 2018).

Caron, Paul L., Carolyn Dever, and George Justice. "The Future of Tenure: Rethinking a Beleaguered Institution." *The Chronicle of Higher Education Review*, April 7, 2021. https://www.chronicle.com/article/the-future-of-tenure.

Cassirer, Ernst. *Language and Myth*. Translated by Susan Langer. New York: Dover, 1946.

Cassuto, Leonard, and Robert Weisbuch. *The New PhD*. Baltimore: Johns Hopkins University Press, 2021.

Cha, Ariana Eunjung. "Sean Parker, Silicon Valley's Bad Boy Genius, Wants to Kick the *!$% Out of Cancer." *Washington Post*, April 15, 2016.

Chaplinsky, Susan, Robert S. Harris, and Dorothy C. Kelly. *Investure, LLC, and Smith College*. Charlottesville, VA: Darden Business Publishing, 2007.

Chen, Grace. "The Catch-22 of Community College Graduation Rates." *Community College Review*, updated June 15, 2020. https://www.communitycollegereview.com/blog/the-catch-22-of-community-college-graduation-rates.

Christensen, Clayton M. *The Innovator's Dilemma: When New Technologies Cause Great Firms to Fail*. Boston: Harvard Business Review Press, 2015.

Christensen, Clayton M., Michael B. Horn, Louis Caldera, and Louis Soares. *Disrupting College: How Disruptive Innovation Can Deliver Quality and Affordability to Postsecondary Education*. Washington, DC: Center for American Progress & Innosight Institute, 2011.

Clark, Burton. "A Note on Pursuing Things That Work." In *Sociology of Higher Education: Contributions and their Contexts*, edited by Patricia J. Gumport, 319–324. Baltimore: Johns Hopkins University Press, 2007.

———. "The Organizational Saga in Higher Education." *Administrative Science Quarterly* 17, no. 2 (June 1972): 178–184.

Cole, Jonathan. *The Great American University: Its Rise to Preeminence, Its Indispensable National Role, Why It Must Be Protected*. New York: Public Affairs, 2010.

Colomy, Paul. "Neofunctionalism and Neoinstitutionalism: Human Agency and Interest in Institutional Change." *Sociological Forum* 13, no. 2 (1998): 265–300.

"Colorado Isn't Funding Higher Ed Like It Used To, So Students Make Up the Difference." Associated Press, May 24, 2018. https://www.cpr.org/2018/05/24/colorado-isnt-funding-higher-ed-like-it-used-to-so-students-make-up-the-difference/.

Committee on Information Technology. *Guidelines for Evaluating Work in Digital Humanities and Digital Media*. New York: Modern Language Association, 2012.

Cooke, Morris Llewellyn. *Academic and Industrial Efficiency*. New York: Carnegie Foundation for the Advancement of Teaching, 1910.

Cotter, Holland. "James Beck, 77, Art Scholar and Critic of Conservation, Is Dead." *New York Times*. May 29, 2007.

"Credly Raises Seed Financing to Build on Its Leadership in Digital Credentials." *The Credly Blog*, April 24, 2019. https://learn.credly.com/blog/credly-raises-seed-financing-to-build-on-its-leadership-in-digital-credentials.

"Current Term Enrollment Estimates." National Student Clearinghouse Research Center. May 26, 2022. https://nscresearchcenter.org/current-term-enrollment-estimates.

Cusher, Taylor, Anna DeGarmo, and Cynthia Grossman. *Patient-Centric Initiatives: Focusing for Impact*. New York: Milken Institute, 2020.

Daniels, Ronald (with Grant Shreve and Phillip Spector). *What Universities Owe Democracy*. Baltimore: Johns Hopkins University Press, 2021.

Davoren, Julie. "How Are Labor Unions and Guilds Similar?" *Chron*, April 18, 2018. https://smallbusiness.chron.com/labor-unions-guilds-similar-60488.html.

Dempsey, Lorcan. "Library Collections in the Life of the User: Two Directions." *Liber Quarterly*, October 2016. https://doi.org/10.18352/lq.10170.

———. "Workflow Is the New Content 1: Looking at Research Support and Engagement." LorcanDempsey.net, February 21, 2011. https://www.lorcandempsey.net/p/b5b00a6c-3e62-462f-8d2e-994f5404417b.

Digital Scholarship Center, University of Massachusetts, Amherst. Accessed January 15, 2023, from https://www.umass.edu/arthistory/digital-scholarship-center.

DiMaggio, Paul. "Conclusion: The Futures of Business Organization and Paradoxes of Change." In *The Twenty-First-Century Firm*, 211–243. Princeton, NJ: Princeton University Press, 2001.

———. "Culture and Cognition." *Annual Review of Sociology* 23 (1997): 263–287.

———. "Interest and Agency in Institutional Theory." In *Research on Institutional Patterns: Environment and Culture*, edited by L. G. Zucker, 3–21. Cambridge, MA: Ballinger Publishing Co., 1998.

———. "The New Institutionalisms: Avenues of Collaboration." *Journal of Institutional and Theoretical Economics* 154, no. 4 (1998): 696–705.

———. "Nonprofit Organizations and the Intersectoral Division of Labor in the Arts." In *The Nonprofit Sector: A Research Handbook*, 2nd ed., edited by Walter W. Powell and Richard Steinberg, 432–461. New Haven, CT: Yale University Press, 2006.

DiMaggio, Paul J., and Walter W. Powell. "Introduction." In *The New Institutionalism in Organizational Analysis*, 7–60. Chicago: University of Chicago Press, 1991.

———. "The Iron Cage Revisited: Institutional Isomorphism and Collective Rationality in Organizational Fields." In *The New Institutionalism in Organizational Analysis*, 97–125. Chicago: University of Chicago Press, 1991.

Dorado, Silvia. "Institutional Entrepreneurship, Partaking, and Convening." *Organization Studies* 26, no. 3 (2005): 385–414.

Dorsa, Daniel, Anastasia Samoylova, Anurag Banerjee, Yves Bachmann, and Kate Warren. "Worthy Investment." *The Monocle Forecast*. January 2019: 84–87.

"Ecosystem Building." New Profit. Accessed December 20, 2022, from https://www.newprofit.org/approach/ecosystem-building/.

Eisenstadt, S. N. "Cultural Orientations, Institutional Entrepreneurs, and Social Change: Comparative Analysis of Traditional Civilizations." *American Journal of Sociology* 85, no. 4 (1980): 840–869.

Etzel, Michael, Matt Bannick, and Mariah Collins. "Opinion: Maverick 'Impact-First' Investing Sits between Philanthropy and Market-rate Returns." MarketWatch, May 8, 2021. https://www.marketwatch.com/story/maverick-impact-first-investing-sits-between-philanthropy-and-market-rate-returns-11619560034.

Ewell, Philip A. "Music Theory and the White Racial Frame." *Music Theory Online* 26, no. 2 (2020).

Fain, Paul. "Takedown of Online Education." *Inside Higher Ed*. January 26, 2019.

Farrington, Camille, David W. Johnson, Elaine Allensworth, Jenny Nagaoka, Melissa Roderick, Nicole Williams Beechum, and Tasha Seneca Keyes. "Readiness for College: The Role of Noncognitive Factors and Context." *Voices in Urban Education*, no. 38 (2013). https://consortium.uchicago.edu/publications/readiness-college-role-noncognitive-factors-and-context.

"FasterCures." Milken Institute. Accessed January 15, 2023, from https://milkeninstitute.org/centers/fastercures.

Feldstein, Michael. "The edX Aftermath." Eliterate Blog, September 7, 2021. https://eliterate.us/the-edx-aftermath.

Field, Anne. "New Structures for Protecting Impact Companies' Missions." *Forbes.com*, October 28, 2019. https://www.forbes.com/sites/annefield/2019/10/28/new-structures-for-protecting-impact-companies-missions/?sh=251175a6b372.

Flaherty, Colleen. "Refusing to Be Measured," *Inside Higher Ed*, May 11, 2016.

———. "Whose Music Theory?" *Inside Higher Ed*, August 7, 2020.

Fleishman, Joel L. *The Foundation: A Great American Secret; How Private Wealth Is Changing the World*. New York: Public Affairs, 2009.

Fligstein, Neil. "Reviewed Works: *Institutional Patterns and Organizations: Culture and Environment* by Lynne G. Zucker." *Administrative Science Quarterly* 34, no. 3 (1989): 501–503.

———. "Social Skill and the Theory of Fields." *Sociological Theory* 19, no. 2 (2001): 105–125.

Fligstein, Neil, and Doug McAdam. "Toward a General Theory of Strategic Action Fields." *Sociological Theory* 29, no. 1 (2011): 1–26.

Ford Foundation. *Transformative Capital: How Mission-Related Investing Can Deepen Foundations' Impact.* New York: The Ford Foundation, 2019.

Foster, William. "Money to Grow On." *Stanford Social Innovation Review* 6, no. 4 (2008): 50–55.

Fox, Kristen, Nandini Khedkar, Nicole Lin, Anh Nguyen, and Gates Bryant. "Time for Class COVID-19 Edition Part 2." Tyton Partners, October 5, 2020. https://tytonpartners.com/time-for-class-covid-19-edition-part-2.

"Free Speech and Academic Freedom: Academic Freedom Is Not a First Amendment Right for University Employees, Cautioned Yale Law School Dean Robert Post, in a Speech at Columbia Law School." Columbia Law School, March 7, 2016. https://www.law.columbia.edu/news/archive/free-speech-and-academic-freedom.

Friedland, Roger, and Robert Alford. "Bringing Society Back In: Symbols, Practices, and Institutional Contradictions." *The New Institutionalism in Organizational Analysis* (1991): 232–266.

Friedman, Thomas L. "Revolution Hits the Universities." *New York Times*, January 13, 2013.

Frumkin, Peter. "On Being Nonprofit: The Bigger Picture." *Harvard Business Review*. September 9, 2002.

Garud, Raghu, and Antonio Paco Giuliani. "A Narrative Perspective on Entrepreneurial Opportunities." *Academy of Management Review* 38, no. 1 (2013): 157–160.

Garud, Raghu, Cynthia Hardy, and Steve Maguire. "Institutional Entrepreneurship as Embedded Agency: An Introduction to the Special Issue." *Organization Studies* 28, no. 7 (2007): 957–969.

Garud, Raghu, Sanjay Jain, and Arun Kumaraswamy. "Institutional Entrepreneurship in the Sponsorship of Common Technological Standards: The Case of Sun Microsystems and Java." *Academy of Management Journal* 45, no. 1 (2002): 196–214.

Garud, Raghu, and Peter Karnøe. "Bricolage versus Breakthrough: Distributed and Embedded Agency in Technology Entrepreneurship." *Research Policy* 32 (2003): 277–300.

Garud, Raghu, Henri A. Schildt, and Theresa K. Lant. "Entrepreneurial Storytelling, Future Expectations, and the Paradox of Legitimacy." *Organization Science* 25, no. 5 (2014): 1479–1492.

Geczy, Christopher, Jessica S. Jeffers, David K. Musto, and Anne M. Tucker. "Contracts with Benefits: The Implementation of Impact Investing." *Journal of Financial Economics*, European Corporate Governance Institute–Finance Working Paper No. 674/2020, and Jacobs Levy Equity Management Center for Quantitative Financial Research Paper, June 12, 2020. http://dx.doi.org/10.2139/ssrn.3159731.

Gewin, Virginia. "Can Mission-Driven Food Companies Scale Up without Selling Out?" *Civil Eats*, December 19, 2019. https://civileats.com/2019/12/19/can-mission-driven-food-companies-scale-up-without-selling-out/.

Gioia, Dennis A., and Kumar Chittipeddi. "Sensemaking and Sensegiving in Strategic Change Initiation." *Strategic Management Journal* 12, no. 6 (1991): 433–448.

Giusti, Kathy, and Richard G. Hamermesh. "How Medical Nonprofits Set Winning Strategy." *Harvard Business Review*, March 6, 2020. https://hbr.org/2020/03/how-medical-nonprofits-set-winning-strategy.

———. "How Nonprofit Foundations Can Sustainably Fund Disease Research." *Harvard Business Review*, September 30, 2020. https://hbr.org/2020/09/how-nonprofit-foundations-can-sustainably-fund-disease-research.

Glaeser, Edward L., and Andrei Shleifer. "Not-For-Profit Entrepreneurs." NBER Working Papers 6810, National Bureau of Economic Research, 1998.

Goldrick-Rab, Sara. *Paying the Price: College Costs, Financial Aid, and the Betrayal of the American Dream.* Chicago: University of Chicago Press, 2016.

Greenwood, Royston, and C. R. Hinings. "Understanding Radical Organizational Change: Bringing Together the Old and the New Institutionalism." *Academy of Management Review* 21, no. 4 (1996): 1022–1054.

Greenwood, Royston, and Roy Suddaby. "Institutional Entrepreneurship in Mature Fields: The Big Five Accounting Firms." *Academy of Management Journal* 49, no. 1 (2006): 27–48.

Greenwood, Royston, Roy Suddaby, and C. R. Hinings. "Theorizing Change: The Role of Professional Associations in the Transformation of Institutionalized Fields." *Academy of Management Journal* 45, no. 1 (2002): 58–80.

Griffith, Erin. "More Start-Ups Have an Unfamiliar Message for Venture Capitalists: Get Lost." *New York Times*, January 13, 2019.

Grossman, James, and Emily Swafford, "Graduate Education Reconsidered." *Perspectives on History: The Newsmagazine of the American Historical Association*, April 12, 2016.

Gumport, Patricia J. *Sociology of Higher Education: Contributions and their Contexts.* Baltimore: Johns Hopkins University Press, 2007.

Hanleybrown, Fay, Jennifer Splansky Juster, and John Kania. "Essential Mindset Shifts for Collective Impact." *Stanford Social Innovation Review* 12, no. 4 (2014): A2–A5.

Hansmann, Henry B. "The Role of Nonprofit Enterprise." *Yale Law Journal* 89, no. 5 (1980): 835–902.

Harris, Pat Lopes. "EdX Adds More Campuses, Courses." SJSU NewsCenter Blog, April 10, 2013. https://blogs.sjsu.edu/newsroom/2013/sjsuedx-expansion/.

Hart, Oliver. "Thinking about the Firm: A Review of Daniel Spulber's *The Theory of the Firm.*" *Journal of Economic Literature* 49, no. 1 (2011): 101–113.

Hayes, Nicky, and Robert J. Sternberg. "How Should Textbook Authorship Count in Evaluating Scholarly Merit, or Should It Count at All?" AAUP. September–October 2017. https://www.aaup.org/article/how-should-textbook-authorship-count-evaluating-scholarly-merit-or-should-it-count-all#.YtqZP73MI2w.

Heller, Nathan. "Is Venture Capital Worth the Risk?" *The New Yorker*, January 20, 2020. https://www.newyorker.com/magazine/2020/01/27/is-venture-capital-worth-the-risk.

Henfridsson, Ola, and Youngjin Yoo. "The Liminality of Trajectory Shifts in Institutional Entrepreneurship." *Organization Science* 25, no. 3 (2014): 932–950.

Henke, Nicolaus, Jacques Bughin, Michael Chui, James Manyika, Tamim Saleh, Bill Wiseman, and Guru Sethupathy. "The Age of Analytics: Competing in a Data-Driven World." Brussels, London, and Shanghai: McKinsey Global Institute (McKinsey & Company), December 7, 2016.

Herpich, Nate. "Harvard and MIT-led Nonprofit to Tackle Longstanding Inequities in Education." *Harvard Gazette*. June 29, 2021.

Hjorth, Daniel, and Chris Steyaert. "Introduction." In *Narrative and Discursive Approaches in Entrepreneurship: A Second Movements in Entrepreneurship Book*, 1–7. Cheltenham: Edward Elgar Publishing, 2004.

"Home Page." Upstart Co-Lab. Accessed January 15, 2023, from https://upstartco-lab.org/.

"Impact Investing." Global Impact Investing Network. Accessed December 20, 2022, from https://thegiin.org/impact-investing/.

"Iowa State University Mission Statement." Accessed August 8, 2021, from https://www.president.iastate.edu/projects/mission.

Ishida, Lauren. "5 Questions to Philip Ewell." *I Care If You Listen*, July 23, 2020. https://icareifyoulisten.com/2020/07/5-questions-philip-ewell-author-music-theory-white-racial-frame/.

James, William. *Pragmatism*. Philosophical Classics. Garden City, NY: Dover, [1907] 1995.

Jaschik, Scott. "Getting (Digital) Respect." *Inside Higher Ed*. April 30, 2012.

———. "Oklahoma Gave False Data for Years to 'U.S. News,' Loses Ranking." *Inside Higher Ed*. May 28, 2019.

Jensen, Michael C. "Value Maximization, Stakeholder Theory, and the Corporate Objective Function." *Business Ethics Quarterly* 12, no. 2 (2002): 235–256.

Jiang, Athena Y., and June Q. Wu. "Harvard Pushes Early Retirement." *The Harvard Crimson*, February 11, 2009.

John Harvard's Journal. "The Libraries' Rocky Transition." *Harvard Magazine* (May 2012).

Joo, Jenna, Deanna Marcum, and Daniel Rossman. *CIC Consortium for Online Humanities Instruction II: Evaluation Report for First Course Iteration*. New York: ITHAKA S+R, 2017.

———. *CIC Consortium for Online Humanities Instruction II: Evaluation Report for the Second Course Iteration*. New York: ITHAKA S+R, 2018.

Joo, Jenna, Jeffrey J. Selingo, and Rayane Alamuddin. *Unlocking the Power of Collaboration: How to Develop a Successful Collaborative Network in and around Higher Education*. New York: ITHAKA S+R, 2019.

Joo, Jenna, and Richard R. Spies. *Aligning Many Campuses and Instructors around a Common Adaptive Learning Courseware in Introductory Statistics (Lessons from a Multi-Year Pilot in Maryland)*. New York: ITHAKA S+R, 2019.

June, Audrey Williams. "Did the Scramble to Remote Learning Work? Here's What Higher Ed Thinks." *Chronicle of Higher Education*, June 8, 2020. https://www

.chronicle.com/article/did-the-scramble-to-remote-learning-work-heres-what
-higher-ed-thinks.

June, Audrey Williams. "Spring Enrollment's Final Count Is In. Colleges Lost 600,000 Students." *Chronicle of Higher Education.* June 10, 2021.

Kahneman, Daniel. *Thinking, Fast and Slow.* New York: Farrar, Straus and Giroux, 2011.

Kelley, Michael. "After Furor, Harvard Library Spokesperson Says 'Inaccurate' That All Staff Will Have to Reapply." *Library Journal,* January 20, 2012.

Kelly, Andrew P. "New Directions in Private Financing." White paper prepared for the National Commission on Financing 21st Century Higher Education. University of Virginia Miller Center, Charlottesville, VA, 2016. https://s3 .amazonaws.com/web.web1-misc/commissions/higher-ed/Kelly_No7.pdf.

Kirp, David L. *Shakespeare, Einstein, and the Bottom Line: The Marketing of Higher Education.* Cambridge, MA: Harvard University Press, 2004.

Kirsch, Vanessa, Jim Bildner, and Jeffrey Walker. "Why Social Ventures Need Systems Thinking." *Harvard Business Review,* July 25, 2016.

Knight Foundation Fund. *Lessons from the Early Years of Mission-Related Investing at Knight Foundation.* Miami: Knight Foundation, 2019.

Koenig, Rebecca. "As Colleges Move Away From the SAT, Will Admissions Algorithms Step In?" *Edsurge,* July 10, 2020.

Koester, Benjamin P., James Fogel, William Murdock, Galina Grom, and Timothy A. McKay. "Building a Transcript of the Future." In *Proceedings of the Seventh International Learning Analytics & Knowledge Conference,* 299–308. New York: Association for Computing Machinery, 2017.

Kornbluth, Jesse. *Highly Confident: The Crime and Punishment of Michael Milken.* New York: Morrow, 1992.

Kovner, Anna, and Josh Lerner. "Doing Well by Doing Good? Community Development Venture Capital." *Journal of Economics & Management Strategy* 24, no. 3 (2015): 643–663.

Lagemann, Ellen. *Private Power for the Public Good: A History of the Carnegie Foundation for the Advancement of Teaching.* New York: Harper & Row, 1983.

Lapovsky, Lucie. "The Private College Tuition Model Is Broken: Tuition Up, Enrollment and Net Revenue Down." *Forbes,* May 28, 2021. https://www.forbes .com/sites/lucielapovsky/2021/05/28/the-private-college-tuition-model-is -broken-tuition-up-enrollment-and-net-revenue-down/?sh=6bd448974226.

Laramie County Community College Board of Trustees. "Student Success Technology Recommendation." Laramie County Community College, Cheyenne, WY, 2018. http://lccc.wy.edu/Documents/About/Board/Agendas/2018/December _5/Student%20Success%20Technology%20-%20Case%20Study%20-%20 Final%2012-3-18.pdf; http://lccc.wy.edu/about/index.aspx.

Lawrence, Thomas B., and Roy Suddaby. "Institutions and Institutional Work." In *Sage Handbook of Organization Studies,* edited by Stewart R. Clegg, Cynthia Hardy, Thomas B. Lawrence, and Walter R. Nord, 215–254. London: Sage Publications, 2006.

Leca, Bernard, Julie Battilana, and Eva Boxenbaum. "Agency and Institutions: A Review of Institutional Entrepreneurship." *Academy of Management Annals* (2008): 1–51.

Leitch, Carmen. "Self-Healing, Synthetic Skin Is Grown Directly on a Robotic Finger." Labroots, June 12, 2022. https://www.labroots.com/trending/cell-and-molecular-biology/22965/self-healing-synthetic-skin-grown-directly-robotic-finger.

Lemann, Nicholas. *The Big Test: The Secret History of the American Meritocracy.* New York: Farrar, Straus and Giroux, 1999.

Letts, Christine W., William P. Ryan, and Allen S. Grossman. "Virtuous Capital: What Foundations Can Learn from Venture Capitalists." *Harvard Business Review* (March–April 1997).

Leuty, Ron. "Sean Parker's Cancer-Fighting Institute Aims 1st Trial at Tough Target." *San Francisco Business Times*, September 20, 2017. https://www.bizjournals.com/sanfrancisco/news/2017/09/20/sean-parker-pancreatic-cancer-apexigen-bmy.html.

Levere, Andrea, Corey Baron, Elizabeth Davidson, Bryan Fike, Alexandra Sing, and Vicky Zhang. *Blueprint for Enterprise Capital: A Strategy for Aligning Capital and Capacity to Magnify Nonprofit Impact.* New Haven, CT: Yale School of Management, 2020.

Levy, Andrea. "The Soul of the Research University." *Chronicle of Higher Education.* April 28, 2014.

Levy, David, and Maureen Scully. "The Institutional Entrepreneur as Modern Prince: The Strategic Face of Power in Contested Fields." *Organization Studies* 28, no. 7 (2007): 1–22.

Lewens, Tim. "From Bricolage to BioBricks™: Synthetic Biology and Rational Design." *Studies in History and Philosophy of Science Part C: Studies in History and Philosophy of Biological and Biomedical Sciences* 44, no. 4, Part B (2013): 641–648.

"The Lexis-Nexis Timeline." Lexix-Nexis. Accessed January 15, 2023, from http://www.lexisnexis.com/anniversary/30th_timeline_fulltxt.pdf.

Lieberman, Mark. "Sharing Courses Far and Wide." *Inside Higher Ed*, March 6, 2019.

Little, Ann M. "Further Thoughts on Loyalty." Historiann, June 17, 2010. https://historiann.com/2010/06/17/further-thoughts-on-loyalty.

Lounsbury, Michael, and Mary Ann Glynn. "Cultural Entrepreneurship: Stories, Legitimacy, and the Acquisition of Resources." *Strategic Management Journal (Special Issue: Strategic Entrepreneurship: Entrepreneurial Strategies for Wealth Creation)* 22, no. 6/7 (2001): 545–564.

Macmillan Learning, Instructor Catalog. Accessed January 15, 2023, from https://www.macmillanlearning.com/college/us/product/Psychology/p/1319132103.

Making Caring Common. *Turning the Tide: Inspiring Concern for Others and the Common Good through College Admissions.* Boston: Harvard Graduate School of Education, 2016.

Malinowski, Bronisław. *Magic, Science, and Religion and Other Essays.* Boston: Beacon Press, 1948.

Marcum, Deanna, and Clara Samayoa. "Leveraging Technology in the Liberal Arts." Case study for the Council of Independent Colleges Consortium for Online Humanities Instruction. ITHAKA S+R, New York, 2015. https://doi .org/10.18665/sr.275024.

McGrath, Charles. "A Whole New Ballgame." *New York Times.* September 15, 2002.

McKay, Tim. "Thoughts on the Transcript of the Future." 21stCenturyHigherEd, December 11, 2016. https://21stcenturyhighered.com/2016/12/11/thoughts-on -the-transcript-of-the-future/.

Menand, Louis. "The Limits of Academic Freedom." In *The Future of Academic Freedom,* edited by Louis Menand, 3–20. Chicago: University of Chicago Press, 1996.

Merton, Robert K. "Bureaucratic Structure and Personality." *Social Forces* 18, no. 4 (1940): 560–568.

———. "Manifest and Latent Functions." In *Social Theory and Social Structure,* 73–138. New York: Free Press, 1968.

Meyer, John W., and Brian Rowan. "Institutionalized Organizations: Formal Structure as Myth and Ceremony." *American Journal of Sociology* 83, no. 2 (1977): 340–363.

Milken, Michael. "The Democratization of Capital." *California Lawyer,* July 2000.

———. "Prostate Cancer: New Hope for Patients." Excerpt from *Prostate Cancer: Signaling Networks, Genetics, and New Treatment Strategies.* Accessed January 15, 2023, from https://www.mikemilken.com/articles.taf?page=28.

———. "Where's Sputnik?" *NCI Cancer Bulletin,* April–June 2011.

Miller, Clara. "Capital, Equity, and Looking at Nonprofits as Enterprises." *New Gatekeepers of Philanthropy* 20, no. 2 (2013): 32–37.

Mintz, Steven. "edX: A Look Backward." LinkedIn, June 30, 2021. https://www .linkedin.com/pulse/edx-look-backward-steven-mintz.

———. "Partners or Predators?" *Inside Higher Ed,* May 11, 2020.

MIT News Office. "MIT and Harvard Announce edX; Joint Partnership Builds on *MITx* and Harvard Distance Learning; Aims to Benefit Campus-based Education and Beyond." Cambridge, MA: MIT, May 2, 2012.

Mitchell, John. "Interview with Monica Campbell." *The World,* 2021.

Mochari, Ilan. "16 Startups Poised to Disrupt the Education Market." *Inc.com,* April 14, 2015. https://www.inc.com/ilan-mochari/16-startups-that-will -disrupt-the-education-market.html.

Moellenbrock, Bonny, Julien Gafarou, and Laura Callanan. *Hiding in Plain Sight: Impact Investing in the Creative Economy.* Upstart Co-Lab, October 2018. https://www.upstartco-lab.org/wp-content/uploads/2018/10/Hiding-in-Plain -Sight-Imp-Inv-in-the-Creative-Economy-.pdf.

Monitor Institute. *Investing for Social and Environmental Impact: A Design for Catalyzing an Emerging Industry,* 2009.

Moore, Geoffrey E. *A Call to Action.* Santa Monica, CA: Prostate Cancer Foundation, 2004.

Morrell, Kenneth Scott. "Sunoikisis: Computer-Mediated Communication in the Creation of a Virtual Department." *CALICO Journal* 18, no. 2 (2001): 223–233.

Narayanan, Chandra, Allison Tielking, and Hem Wadhar. "Two-Sided Marketplaces and Engagement." *Sequoia Capital Publication*, December 14, 2018. https://medium.com/sequoia-capital/two-sided-marketplaces-and-engagement-ded7d5dcfe71.

National Commission of Financing 21st Century Higher Education. *Investing in the Future: Sharing Responsibility for Higher Education Attainment.* Charlottesville, VA: University of Virginia Miller Center, 2016.

"New Office Will Coordinate Digitization of Yale Resources." Yale News, September 26, 2008. https://news.yale.edu/2008/09/26/new-office-will-coordinate-digitization-yale-resources.

North, Douglas. *Institutions, Institutional Change, and Economic Performance.* Cambridge: Cambridge University Press, 1990.

Northwestern University Center for Scholarly Communication and Digital Curation. Accessed August 28, 2020, from http://cscdc.northwestern.edu/.

Nworie, John. "Beyond COVID-19: What's Next for Online Teaching and Learning in Higher Education?" Educause, May 19, 2021. https://er.educause.edu/articles/2021/5/beyond-covid-19-whats-next-for-online-teaching-and-learning-in-higher-education.

Opportunity Insights. Accessed January 15, 2023, from https://opportunityinsights.org/.

Orbey, Eren. "How Harvard's Star Computer-Science Professor Built a Distance-Learning Empire." *The New Yorker*, July 21, 2020. https://www.newyorker.com/news/our-local-correspondents/how-harvards-star-computer-science-professor-built-a-distance-learning-empire.

"Our Approach." Blue Meridian Partners. Accessed December 20, 2022, from https://www.bluemeridian.org/our-approach.

"Our Mission, Values and Priorities." Northwestern University. Accessed January 25, 2023, from https://www.northwestern.edu/about/.

"Our Story." New Profit. Accessed December 20, 2022, from https://www.newprofit.org/our-story/.

Owens, Trevor. "Hydra's Open Source Approach: An Interview with Tom Cramer." The Signal, 2013. https://blogs.loc.gov/thesignal/2013/05/hydras-open-source-approach-an-interview-with-tom-cramer/.

P3edu. Accessed January 25, 2023, from https://www.p3edu.com.

Parsons, Talcott. "Prolegomena to a Theory of Social Institutions." *American Sociological Review* 55, no. 3 (1990): 319–333.

Patterson, Franklin. *College in Consort: Institutional Cooperation Through Consortia.* Hoboken, NJ: Jossey-Bass, 1974.

"Pearson Acquires Digital Credentialing Leader Credly." Pearson, January 31, 2022. https://plc.pearson.com/en-US/news/pearson-acquires-digital-credentialing-leader-credly.

Pelletier, Kathe. "Student Success: 3 Big Questions." *Educause Review*. October 14, 2019.

Perrow, Charles. *Organizational Analysis: A Sociological View*. London: Tavistock: 1974.

Petersen, Julie, and Shauntel Poulson. "New Approaches to Ed-Tech Funding." *Stanford Social Innovation Review* 14, no. 2 (2016): 41–47.

Phillips, Nelson, and Paul Tracey. "Opportunity Recognition, Entrepreneurial Capabilities, and Bricolage: Connecting Institutional Theory and Entrepreneurship in Strategic Organization." *Strategic Organization* 5, no. 3 (2007): 313–320.

Phillipson, Marc, and William Ying. "Next Generation Multimedia Analysis: Introducing MediaThread." Coalition for Networked Information, last updated September 3, 2011. https://www.cni.org/topics/user-services/next-generation -multimedia-analysis.

"Postsecondary Data Partnership." National Student Clearinghouse. Accessed January 15, 2023. https://www.studentclearinghouse.org/colleges/pdp/.

"Postsecondary Teachers, Occupational Outlook Handbook." Bureau of Labor Statistics, last updated October 4, 2022. https://www.bls.gov/ooh/education -training-and-library/postsecondary-teachers.htm.

"Provost's Postdoctoral Fellows." University of Chicago. Accessed December 19, 2022, from https://provostpostdoc.uchicago.edu/.

Purpose Foundation and RSF Social Finance. "State of Alternative Ownership in the US: Emerging Trends in Steward-ownership and Alternative Financing." *Learning Journey Report*. Hamburg, Germany and San Francisco, CA: Purpose Foundation and RSF Social Finance, 2019.

Rao, Hayagreeva. "Caveat Emptor: The Construction of Nonprofit Consumer Watchdog Organizations." *American Journal of Sociology* 103, no. 4 (1998): 912–961.

Rao, Hayagreeva, Calvin Morrill, and Mayer N. Zald. "Power Plays: How Social Movements and Collective Action Create New Organizational Forms." *Research in Organizational Behaviour* 22 (2000): 237–281.

Rees, Jonathan. *MOOCs: A Postmortem*. Jonathan Rees blog, February 9, 2017. http://moreorlessbunk.net/technology/moocs/moocs-a-postmortem/.

Reisman, Jane, Anne Gienapp, Kasey Langley, and Sarah Stachowiak. *Theory of Change: A Practical Tool for Action, Results, and Learning*. Seattle, WA: Organizational Research Services, 2004. 1–49.

"Renaissance Acquires Schoolzilla to Make Insights Actionable for Education Leaders Worldwide." Renaissance, October 29, 2019. https://www.renaissance .com/2019/10/29/news-renaissance-acquires-schoolzilla/.

Rivard, Ry. "San Jose State University Faculty Pushes Back Against edX." *Inside Higher Ed*, May 3, 2013. https://www.insidehighered.com/quicktakes/2013/05 /03/san-jose-state-university-faculty-pushes-back-against-edx.

Renner, Charles. "A Few Lessons About Public-Private Partnerships." *Inside Higher Ed*, January 28, 2019.

Roberts, Steven. "Kerr Says 'Multiversity' Head Must Be 'Mediator,' Not Giant." *The Harvard Crimson*, April 24, 1963.

Rockefeller Philanthropy Advisors. "Impact Investing: An Introduction." *Rockefeller Philanthropy Advisors' Philanthropy Roadmap Series*. New York: Rockefeller Philanthropy Advisors, 2012.

"Samvera User Profiles." Samvera. Accessed December 19, 2022, from https://samvera.org/samvera-partners/samvera-user-profiles/#05.

Sandel, Michael. "Michael Sandel Responds." *The Chronicle of Higher Education*, May 2, 2013. https://www.chronicle.com/article/michael-sandel-responds/.

San Jose State University. "Enrollment by Demographics." Accessed January 16, 2023, from https://analytics.sjsu.edu/t/IRPublic/views/enroll_by_demographics_live/EnrollmentByDemographicsDashboard?%3Aembed_code_version=3&%3Aembed=y&%3AloadOrderID=0&%3Adisplay_spinner=no&%3AshowAppBanner=false&%3Adisplay_count=n&%3AshowVizHome=n&%3Aorigin=viz_share_link

Saul, Stephanie. "At N.Y.U., Students Were Failing Organic Chemistry. Who Was to Blame?" *New York Times*, October 3, 2022.

Schmidt, Vivien A. "Discursive Institutionalism: The Explanatory Power of Ideas and Discourse." *Annual Review of Political Science* 11 (2008): 303–326.

Schonfeld, Roger C. "Strategy & Integration among Workflow Providers." The Scholarly Kitchen, November 7, 2017. https://scholarlykitchen.sspnet.org/2017/11/07/strategy-integration-workflow-providers

Scott, Joan. *Knowledge, Power, and Academic Freedom*. New York: Columbia University Press, 2019.

Scott, John C. "The Mission of the University: Medieval to Postmodern Transformations." *Journal of Higher Education* 77, no. 1 (2006): 1–39.

Schuessler, Jennifer. "A Wall Street Giant Makes a $75 Million Bet on Academic Philosophy." *New York Times*, January 16, 2018. https://www.nytimes.com/2018/01/16/arts/bill-miller-75-million-gift-philosophy-johns-hopkins.html

Selingo, Jeffrey J. "Transformations Affecting Postsecondary Education." White paper prepared for the National Commission on Financing 21st Century Higher Education. University of Virginia Miller Center, Charlottesville, VA, 2016. https://s3.amazonaws.com/web.web1-misc/commissions/higher-ed/Selingo.pdf.

Seltzer, Rick. "Many Trustees See Faculty as Barrier to Change." *Inside Higher Ed*, November 15, 2017

Senack, Ethan. *Fixing the Broken Textbook Market: How Students Respond to High Textbook Costs and Demand Alternatives*. Washington, DC: Center for Public Interest Research, 2014.

Shapiro, Harriet. "Art Historian James Beck Urges the Vatican to Clean Up Its Act, Not Michelangelo's Frescoes." *People Magazine*, March 30, 1987.

Shelterforce Staff. "What Is Philanthropic Equity? A Roundtable Discussion." Shelterforce, March 26, 2014. https://shelterforce.org/2014/03/26/what_is_philanthropic_equity_a_roundtable_discussion/

Sherer, Todd. "A To-Do List for Parkinson's Researchers." *Scientific American*, September 25, 2013.

Shulman, James L., and William G. Bowen. *The Game of Life: College Sports and Educational Values*. Princeton, NJ: Princeton University Press, 2001.

Simon, Herbert A. *Administrative Behavior*. London: Free Press, 2013.

Sinclair, Upton. *I, Candidate for Governor: And How I Got Licked*. Berkeley: University of California Press, 1934.

Smets, Michael, Tim Morris, and Royston Greenwood. "From Practice to Field: A Multilevel Model of Practice-Driven Institutional Change." *Academy of Management Journal* 55, no. 4 (2012): 877–904.

Smith, Mitch. "Reed Alumni Pay to Help Current Students, Recent Grads." *Inside Higher Ed*, March 14, 2012.

St. Amour, Madeline. "CU Boulder, Colorado Follow National Trend in Higher Ed's Reliance on Tuition Revenue." *Denver Post*, April 9, 2019.

Starr, Kevin. "We're Beating Systems Change to Death." *Stanford Social Innovation Review*, 2021. https://doi.org/10.48558/DBP6-0H46.

"Statement on Government of Colleges and Universities." American Association of University Professors. Accessed December 19, 2022, from https://www.aaup .org/report/statement-government-colleges-and-universities##4.

Stein, Benjamin. *A License to Steal*. New York: Simon & Schuster, 1992.

Straumsheim, Carl. "A New* System for Student Success Planning." *Inside Higher Ed*, July 5, 2017.

Sturm, Susan. "The Architecture of Inclusion: Advancing Workplace Equity in Higher Education." *Harvard Journal of Law & Gender* 29 (2006): 247–334.

Suchman, Mark C. "Managing Legitimacy: Strategic and Institutional Approaches." *Academy of Management Review* 20, no. 3 (1995): 571–610.

Sullivan, Paul. "A Push to Invest in the Arts Grows Stronger." *New York Times*, October 19, 2018.

Swaak, Taylor. "An Overseas Ed-Tech Firm Wants to Buy 2U. What Could That Mean for Colleges?" *Chronicle of Higher Education*, July 21, 2022.

Swensen, David F. *Pioneering Portfolio Management: An Unconventional Approach to Institutional Investment*. Revised ed. New York: Free Press, 2009.

Taplin, Dana H., and Helene Clark. *Theory of Change Basics: A Primer on Theory of Change*. New York: ActKnowledge, 2012.

"Thiel Foundation Announces 2020 Thiel Fellows: New Class Includes 24 Entrepreneurs in Software, Healthcare, Blockchain and More." Business Wire, December 30, 2020. https://www.businesswire.com/news/home/20201230005363 /en/Thiel-Foundation-Announces-2020-Thiel-Fellows#.

Thorp, Holden. "Stop Passing the Buck on Intro Science." *Science*, 378 (6616). https://doi.org/10.1126/science.adf2231.

Townley, Barbara. "The Role of Competing Rationalities in Institutional Change." *Academy of Management Journal* 45, no. 1 (2002): 163–179.

"Undergraduate Graduation Rates." National Center for Education Statistics. Accessed December 19, 2022, from https://nces.ed.gov/fastfacts/display.asp ?id=40.

University Innovation Alliance. Accessed January 15, 2023, from https://theuia .org/.

US Impact Investing Alliance. *Private Capital Public Good: Leveraging Impact Investing to Support a Just & Equitable Recovery.* New York: US Impact Investing Alliance, December 2020.

"U.S. vs. Needy Students." Editorial. *New York Times,* May 3, 1992. https://www.nytimes.com/1992/05/03/opinion/us-vs-needy-students.html.

Vaidya, Ashish. "The Essentiality of Public-Private Partnerships." *Inside Higher Ed,* July 9, 2020.

Valentinov, Vladislav. "Toward an Economic Interpretation of the Nondistribution Constraint." *International Journal of Not-for-Profit Law* 9, no. 1 (2006): 60–71.

"Venture Philanthropy." New Profit. Accessed December 20, 2022, from https://www.newprofit.org/approach/venture-philanthropy/.

Voinea, Anca. "Top 100 Co-operatives in the US Have Revenues of $228.2bn." *COOP News,* October 22, 2020.

von Hippel, Eric. *Democratizing Innovation.* Cambridge, MA: MIT Press, 2005. https://doi.org/10.7551/mitpress/2333.001.0001.

———. *The Sources of Innovation.* New York: Oxford University Press, 1988.

Walker, Jeffrey C. "Solving the World's Biggest Problems: Better Philanthropy through Systems Change." *Stanford Social Innovation Review,* 2017. https://doi.org/10.48558/743S-NV97.

Wallach, Harlan. "Chinese Caves." National Geographic, June 2010. https://mti.it.northwestern.edu/2010/05/national-geographic-dunhuang-feature.

Wallis, John Joseph. *What Institutions Are: The Difference between Social Facts, Norms, and Institutions and Their Associated Rules and Enforcement.* College Park, MD: University of Maryland, 2017.

Wan, Tony. "US EdTech Raises $803M in First Half of 2020 as COVID-19 Forces Learning Online." *EdSurge,* July 29, 2020.

———. "Want to Help Schools Closed by COVID-19? Don't Pitch Them Right Now." *EdSurge,* March 16, 2020.

———. "What 'Impact Investing' Means in Education." *EdSurge* podcast, July 9, 2019. https://www.edsurge.com/news/2019-07-09-impact-investing-not-whitewashing-how-lumina-s-venture-arm-works.

Warner, John. "An Ad Hominem Attack against Thomas Friedman." *Inside Higher Ed,* March 6, 2013.

Weber, Max, A. M. Henderson, and Talcott Parsons. *The Theory of Social and Economic Organization.* Eastford, CT: Martino Fine Books, [1947] 2012.

Weisbaum, Herb. "College Textbook Costs More Outrageous Than Ever." *CNBC,* January 28, 2014.

Weisbrod, Burton. "Toward a Theory of the Voluntary Nonprofit Sector in a Three-Sector Economy." In *The Voluntary Nonprofit Sector,* edited by Burton Weisbrod. Lexington, MA: DC Heath, 1977.

"What You Need to Know About Impact Investing." Global Impact Investing Network. Accessed December 20, 2022, from https://thegiin.org/impact-investing/need-to-know.

Winston, Gordon C. "Subsidies, Hierarchy, and Peers: The Awkward Economics of Higher Education." *Journal of Economic Perspectives* 13, no. 1 (1999): 13–36.

———. *Why Can't a College Be More Like a Firm?* Williamstown, MA: Williams College, 1997.

"World University Rankings 2022." Times Higher Education. Accessed December 19, 2022, from https://www.timeshighereducation.com/world-university-rankings/2022/world-ranking#!/page/0/length/25/sort_by/rank/sort_order/asc/cols/stats.

Xu, Di, and Shanna Jaggars. "Performance Gaps between Online and Face-to-Face Courses: Differences across Types of Students and Academic Subject Areas." *Journal of Higher Education* 85, no. 5 (2014).

Young, Dennis R., and Mary Clark Grinsfelder. "Social Entrepreneurship and the Financing of Third Sector Organizations." *Journal of Public Affairs Education* 17, no. 4 (2011): 543–567.

Zemsky, Robert, and William F. Massy. *Thwarted Innovation: What Happened to e-learning and Why*. Philadelphia: The Learning Alliance at the University of Pennsylvania, 2004.

Zilber, Tammar B. "The Work of the Symbolic in Institutional Processes: Translations of Rational Myths in Israeli High Tech." *Academy of Management Journal* 49, no. 2 (2006): 281–303.

Zuckerman, Esther. "Bellinger to Direct Digitizing Office." *Yale Daily News*, September 24, 2008.

Zurcher, Arnold J. "Foundations: How They Operate as Society's Risk Capital." *Challenge* 4, no. 1 (October 1955): 16–19.

INDEX

A NOTE ON THE TYPE

This book has been composed in Adobe Text and Gotham. Adobe Text, designed by Robert Slimbach for Adobe, bridges the gap between fifteenth- and sixteenth-century calligraphic and eighteenth-century Modern styles. Gotham, inspired by New York street signs, was designed by Tobias Frere-Jones for Hoefler & Co.